BETWEEN LIFE AND THOUGHT

Existential Anthropology and the Study of Religion

Edited by Don Seeman and Devaka Premawardhana

Existential anthropology is an approach inspired by existential and phenomenological thought to further our understanding of the human condition. Its ethnographic methodology emphasizes embodied experience and focuses on what is at stake for people amid the contingencies, struggles, and uncertainties of everyday life. While anthropological research on religion abounds, there has been little systematic attention to the ways anthropology and religious studies might benefit from better consideration of one another or from the adoption of a shared existential perspective.

Between Life and Thought gathers leading anthropologists and religion scholars, including some of existential anthropology's most recognized advocates and thoughtful critics. The collection opens with a comprehensive introduction to phenomenology and existentialism in anthropology and religious studies and concludes with an analysis of how existential anthropology might address the long-standing problem of constructivism and perennialism in religious studies. The chapters altogether present existential anthropology as an especially generative paradigm with which to rethink and remake both anthropology and the academic study of religion.

A timely and significant intervention across multiple areas of research, *Between Life and Thought* is an invaluable source for critically exploring the prospects, as well as the limits, of an anthropological approach to religion grounded in experiential ethnography and existential thought.

DON SEEMAN is an associate professor in the Department of Religion and the Tam Institute for Jewish Studies at Emory University.

DEVAKA PREMAWARDHANA is an associate professor in the Department of Religion and current occupant of a Winship Distinguished Research chair at Emory University.

Between Life and Thought

Existential Anthropology and the Study of Religion

EDITED BY DON SEEMAN AND
DEVAKA PREMAWARDHANA

UNIVERSITY OF TORONTO PRESS
Toronto Buffalo London

© University of Toronto Press 2024
Toronto Buffalo London
utorontopress.com
Printed and bound by CPI Group (UK) Ltd, Croydon, CR0 4YY

ISBN 978-1-4875-5258-9 (cloth)   ISBN 978-1-4875-5872-7 (EPUB)
ISBN 978-1-4875-5475-0 (paper)   ISBN 978-1-4875-5626-6 (PDF)

Library and Archives Canada Cataloguing in Publication

Title: Between life and thought : existential anthropology and the study
   of religion / edited by Don Seeman and Devaka Premawardhana.
Names: Seeman, Don, 1968– editor. | Premawardhana, Devaka, editor.
Description: Includes bibliographical references and index.
Identifiers: Canadiana (print) 20230573355 | Canadiana (ebook) 2023057338X |
   ISBN 9781487554750 (paper) | ISBN 9781487552589 (cloth) |
   ISBN 9781487558727 (EPUB) | ISBN 9781487556266 (PDF)
Subjects: LCSH: Anthropology – Philosophy. |
   LCSH: Phenomenological anthropology. | LCSH: Anthropology of religion.
Classification: LCC BD450 .B48 2024 | DDC 128 – dc23

Cover design: Will Brown
Cover image: Casey Horner/Unsplash

We wish to acknowledge the land on which the University of Toronto Press
operates. This land is the traditional territory of the Wendat, the Anishnaabeg,
the Haudenosaunee, the Métis, and the Mississaugas of the Credit First Nation.

Support for this book was provided by Emory University Faculty Research
Funds and the Judith London Evans Director's Fund of the Tam Institute for
Jewish Studies.

University of Toronto Press acknowledges the financial support of the
Government of Canada, the Canada Council for the Arts, and the Ontario Arts
Council, an agency of the Government of Ontario, for its publishing activities.

  Canada Council   Conseil des Arts
     for the Arts   du Canada

Contents

Introduction: Religion, Phenomenological Anthropology, and the Existential Turn 1
DEVAKA PREMAWARDHANA

1 Existential Anthropology and Religious Studies: A Personal Account 35
MICHAEL JACKSON

2 Eye and Mind Revisited: The Work of Art in Ethnography 55
PAUL STOLLER

3 Blood, Flesh, and Emotions: An Anthropologist and Her Fieldwork in Meat-Packing Plants 73
KRISTY NABHAN-WARREN

4 Recesses of the Ordinary: Michael Jackson's Reinvention of Philosophical Anthropology 95
TYLER ROBERTS

5 *Ruta Graveolens*: Open and Closed Bodies in a Bahian Town 113
MATTIJS VAN DE PORT

6 Destiny as a Relationship and a Theory 133
SAMULI SCHIELKE

7 Worlds Colliding? Transnational Religion in Phenomenological Perspective 155
KIM E. KNIBBE

8 The Plain Sense of Things: Time, History, and the Dream 179
ADITYA MALIK

vi   Contents

9 Boundary Situations: An Existential Account of Wounded
   Healing   197
   SÓNIA SILVA

10 Sartre's Jews and Jackson's Witches: What (Who) Is Real in
   Existential Anthropology?   217
   DON SEEMAN

Afterword: "Not Ethnology but Ethnosophy!"   247
   MICHAEL LAMBEK

Contributors   261

Index   265

Introduction:
Religion, Phenomenological Anthropology, and the Existential Turn

DEVAKA PREMAWARDHANA

In recent decades, the academic study of religion has definitively reached beyond its traditional domain of texts and philosophies, myths and worldviews. Increasingly among religious studies scholars one sees anthropological and other ethnographic research cited, taught, and conducted. Also in recent decades, the discipline of anthropology has spawned an array of new subfields with which to approach its longstanding concern with religion. While between the two there has always been some shared ground, ethnographically oriented religious studies scholars and religion-focused anthropologists have, for the most part, proceeded on parallel tracks.[1] The aim of this volume is to introduce existential anthropology – along with phenomenological anthropology, from which it derives – as a space of convergence. It is a particularly promising one because of its grounding in philosophical and literary, rather than social-scientific, sensibilities. As such, existential anthropology furnishes a bridge not only between anthropology and religious studies, but also between anthropology and the humanities at large (Jackson and Piette 2015b, 2).

Examples of this interdisciplinarity are not hard to find. Prominent religious studies theorist Robert Orsi, for one, has made ample use of existential and phenomenological approaches to anthropology and credited them with "[restoring] the common and recognizable humanity of religious practitioners" (Orsi 2012, 154–5). In 2005, Orsi successfully recruited Michael Jackson, one of phenomenological anthropology's foundational theorists, to Harvard Divinity School (HDS, see Jackson, this volume), and it was soon thereafter that Jackson recast his approach as existential anthropology. Jackson's move to HDS exposed, for the first time, large numbers of religion students and scholars to Jackson's ideas while it also put Jackson in the company of theologians, philosophers, and historians of religion. This seems to have been generative: since joining HDS, Jackson has been publishing on average more than one academic book per year, making him, in one recent assessment, "without a doubt, the most prolific writer in contemporary anthropology" (Pandian 2019, 56). Jackson's own take on his institutional affiliation suggests a reason for this productivity: "There's no doubt that religious studies programs and divinity schools today are perhaps the last locations in the academy where one can read widely in the humanistic tradition. I'm an anthropologist, but I'm much more comfortable intellectually in a divinity school than I would be in an anthropology department, because anthropologists are less concerned with humanity in the most general sense of the word."[2]

In what follows, I offer an introduction to and genealogy of existential anthropology, doing so by way of its connections to this broad humanistic tradition and to religious studies as a particular humanistic field. I take as my organizing motif the notion of "between" that is featured also in this volume's title – existential anthropology not only as a bridge *between* anthropology and the humanities, but also as a paradigm that inhabits the between, that honours indeterminacy, that refuses end points and absolutisms. It is no coincidence that one of Orsi's most celebrated books is titled *Between Heaven and Earth* (2005), and that Paul Stoller, also known for integrating phenomenological anthropology and religion, counts *The Power of the Between* (2009) among his publications. Both works elevate the potential of the liminal and the relational to convey the ambiguities of life as lived.

In Jackson's writings, the theme of between-ness manifests nowhere more than in his most explicit treatment of religion, *The Palm at the End of the Mind: Relatedness, Religiosity, and the Real* (2009). Jackson begins this book by paying homage to a Harvard predecessor – the psychologist and philosopher William James, who also, it so happens, figures prominently in the history of religious studies theory. James's ideas deeply inform the scholarship of Jackson, most pointedly in his early book on the ethnographic implications of James's philosophy of radical empiricism (Jackson 1989). Jackson commends this intellectual program for refusing the reifications and abstractions that have mattered dearly to academics as much in James's time as in ours, and for giving space instead to the fluid and transitory qualities of lived experience.

Yet the phenomenology of liminality by which Jackson describes *The Palm at the End of the Mind* (2009, 6n5), and which could well describe both radical empiricism and existential anthropology generally, rests on shaky ground. This is one reason James is so readily written off as naïve and passé, perhaps nowhere more strenuously than in certain sectors of religious studies. For post-phenomenological (if not anti-phenomenological) constructivists, James is a prime example of bygone generations' lack of scholarly precision and rigour.[3] This should not be surprising, given that rationalist claims of certainty are, as Jackson put it, "more conducive to asserting and establishing one's authority than a provisional, sceptical, ironic, or relativist worldview" such as that underpinning radical empiricism. As such, Jackson admits, one may legitimately wonder whether any academy – or, for that matter, any academic field – could stay afloat if it actually embraced this intellectual tradition (Jackson 2016, 80). So long as standards of academic rigour remain wedded to rationalism, logical order, and system-thinking, a degree of marginality and a measure of misfit are bound to accompany the likes of Jackson, James, and others whose work is premised on the limits of knowledge.

Jackson of course does enjoy a significant reputation, as a leader in phenomenological anthropology and as the founder of its more recent existential variant – also, beyond the realm of theory, as an ethnographer, memoirist, and poet. Yet his standing within his home discipline of social or cultural anthropology has never been entirely secure, except among humanistic and narrative ethnographers who themselves tend to occupy the margins of mainstream anthropology. As the references throughout this introduction and the chapters throughout this volume attest, it seems to be from religious studies scholars, including ethnographers of religion, that Jackson has received his warmest reception. Yet, it is also out of religious studies that phenomenology in general has in recent decades been roundly challenged if not altogether dismissed. Even among religion scholars sympathetic to Jackson's project, existential anthropology and phenomenological anthropology have been critiqued – constructively so, I will suggest – which itself says something of their relevance to the field.

What, then, is the relationship between existential anthropology and the study of religion? I explore this question in what follows by describing key themes in the wide range of Jackson's work – from his classic expressions of phenomenological anthropology to his more recent existential turn – and how those themes bear on religions, religious lives, and religious studies. Along the way, I highlight exemplary studies of religion that apply Jackson's ideas and build on his example. These include works that turn existential and phenomenological anthropology against earlier idealist expressions of phenomenology in religious studies, but also against the extreme constructivist reaction that the phenomenology of religion incited. There is a striking resonance between phenomenological anthropology and recent theoretical turns in religious studies – towards embodiment, practice, and materiality, for

4   Devaka Premawardhana

example – as well as between existential anthropology and the existential dimensions of religion itself. In these resonances lies the potential of Jackson's philosophical anthropology to invigorate the academic study of religion.

At the same time, however, there are aspects of religion, attended to by many religious studies scholars, which Jackson mostly downplays. The argument with which I conclude is that, while existential anthropology helps to enhance the project of religious studies, religious studies can in turn be made to enhance the project of existential anthropology. It would do so by preserving analytical space for what has been mostly neglected in foregoing formulations of existential anthropology: institutions and traditions, ideas and worldviews, and intellectual traditions beyond the canon of Western philosophy. What this chapter ultimately calls for is a dialectical approach that draws on the best of *both* religious studies *and* existential anthropology. This approach could well be described as liminal or relational. It dwells in the space of the between. As such, even as it points to certain flaws in existential anthropology, it attests to what is best in it.

From the Phenomenology of Religion to Phenomenological Anthropology

With his edited 1996 volume *Things as They Are*, and especially with his masterful introduction to it, Michael Jackson sealed his status as pioneer and prime theorist of phenomenological anthropology (Jackson 1996). As high an achievement as this was, however, it presented an immediate obstacle to the reception of his work in the academic study of religion, which over the past decades has taken shape largely as a revolt against phenomenology. To many contemporary scholars of religion, the phenomenology of religion – associated with the likes of Rudolf Otto and Mircea Eliade – represents a false start for religious studies, if not its original sin (McCutcheon 1997, Fitzgerald 2000). Early phenomenologists of religion argued for understanding religion on the basis of empathy, for a diminishing of the distance between religion scholars and religious practitioners. Yet it was not only an entering into experience, but also a securing of foundations that phenomenologists sought. Eliade located those foundations in such metaphysical structures and a priori categories as the numinous, the sacred, and his idealized construct of the *homo religiosus* (Eliade 1954). With this, the phenomenology of religion turned ontological and ahistorical.

Phenomenological anthropology should not be conflated with the phenomenology of religion. They of course share common ground in

Edmund Husserl's critique of rationalism and reductionism, and in his positive appraisal of intuitive, pre-reflective experience. Yet what distinguishes the phenomenology of religion and phenomenological anthropology is enough to make them antithetical. According to Kim Knibbe and Els van Houtert, "in phenomenological anthropology the aim is not to come to an insight into the real nature or essence of things," as it is in the phenomenology of religion, "but rather to understand and evoke in writing and art how the embodied being in the world of different peoples takes place" (Knibbe and van Houtert 2018, 7). It is in this emphasis on the concrete and the sensory that the contrast with Eliade's disembodied *homo religiosus* could not be clearer.

Only once does Jackson bother to clarify the relationship between his anthropological version of phenomenology and the phenomenology that once dominated religious studies. "I eschew a phenomenology that defines religion in terms of an allegedly sui generis modality of experience or existence," he writes, "since what is important, in my view, is the unstable *relationship* … *between* our experience of immediate and nonimmediate fields of experience – a mutually constituting and fluid relationship that lacks any essence that can be tagged with one particular label" (Jackson 2009, 6n5). In other words, it is not the extrahuman objects of enquiry – the sacred, the numinous, or any other version of what Husserl called the "things themselves" – that interest Jackson, but rather the ever-shifting domains of alterity *within* human experience, within the realm of the ordinary (see Roberts, this volume). This is closer to another of Husserl's key concepts – the lifeworld (*Lebenswelt*), glossed by Jackson as the "domain of everyday, immediate social existence and practical activity" that, as such, precedes and exceeds intellectual reflection (Jackson 1996, 7–8; see Husserl 1970).

Most of his oppositional energies Jackson directs towards his disciplinary home of anthropology. Sociocultural anthropology, in particular, traffics in an array of disembodied abstractions and theoretical constructs, Jackson contends, reifying such categories as society, culture, and history, and thereby distancing itself from the lived experiences of ordinary men and women. Anthropology tends to dehumanize – ironically, given the word's etymology – by presupposing "an isomorphic relation between words and world, or between experience and episteme" and by privileging the logocentric pole of those binaries (Jackson 2013a, 7).[4] Felt experience is embodied experience, and it is precisely the theme of embodiment, derived for Jackson and fellow phenomenological anthropologists from the work of Maurice Merleau-Ponty, that distinguishes phenomenological anthropology from anthropological approaches governed by cognitive, linguistic, and idealist models of meaning. To be sure, with the rise of poststructuralism and practice theory, the body has received significant attention in both anthropology and religious studies. Yet much of this literature takes the body to be a relatively blank slate inscribed by the symbol systems and objective structures of a given culture or society. By contrast, phenomenological anthropologists consider the body to be what Thomas Csordas calls "the existential ground of culture and self," the null point from which one's experience of the world is arrayed (Csordas 1994; see also Desjarlais 1992, Jackson 1983, and Stoller 1997). At play here is a rejection of persistent Cartesian dualisms and hierarchies that regard the body as significant but ultimately secondary to its discursive construction, political formation, or cultural meaning.[5] To treat the body as a text to be interpreted or an object that is moulded is to miss the practical and pre-reflective dimensions of knowledge that are irreducible and indeterminate, and with which most humans operate most of the time.

It would be wrong to regard the weight phenomenological anthropologists place on lived immediacy and embodied experience as an individualizing move. The human, for Jackson, is not simply an individual, but an individual-in-relation. Intersubjectivity is the basis upon which humans experience the world. It is, in turn, the basis upon which researchers glean some understanding of human experience. Ethnography in general is nothing if not relational and embodied. It is as distant as could be from the text-centeredness of phenomenologists of religion and of religious studies scholarship generally. But phenomenological anthropologists take special pains to accentuate the experiential and participatory aspects of research. Their modality is what Paul Stoller calls "sensuous scholarship" (Stoller 1997) or, in this volume, "artful ethnography." Here the researcher operates less as a detached expert than as an involved novice who learns through immersive engagement and practical activity – by doing things rather than by uncovering the foundations of things. The output of ethnographic research, consequently, is less theory building than storytelling (Knibbe and van Houtert 2018, 6), less systematic analysis than evocative description – of, for example, the stench and clamour of an industrial meatpacking plant (see Nabhan-Warren, this volume). Such is the open-ended disposition embraced by phenomenological anthropologists: a willingness to dwell in the mundane messiness of lived experience without jumping too swiftly to the sturdier realms of explanatory models, hidden structures, and theoretical constructs. This is far from the surety of transcendental universals and metaphysical essences that interested phenomenologists of religion. It is far even from the typical scholarly impulse towards coherence, closure, and conclusiveness. The priority of phenomenological anthropologists, instead, finds expression in John Keats' notion of negative capability – "being in uncertainties, mysteries, doubts, without any irritable reaching after fact or reason" (as quoted in Jackson 1989, 16, and Stoller 1998, 254).

Phenomenological Anthropology in Research on Religion

Phenomenological anthropology poses radical challenges to conventional research paradigms in the study of religion. Jackson's own attention to such topics as ritual, divination, and healing already indicates the potential for significant interplay between phenomenological anthropology and religious studies. Here I foreground the work of others: scholars who have explicitly drawn from or built on phenomenological anthropology in their own research on religion and in their own critiques of established approaches. Their work clusters around four interrelated themes: embodiment, experience, epistemic openness, and intellectual humility.

As phenomenological anthropology helped correct for anthropology's longstanding neglect of the lived body, it likewise has done so for religious studies. The intervention here is arguably even more needed due to religious studies' traditional orientation towards the question of meaning and the study of texts. Even when religious studies scholars opened up to anthropology, this took the hermeneutic or semiotic form associated with Clifford Geertz, an anthropology that regards cultures and religions primarily in terms of their belief systems and worldviews. To the extent the body comes into play here, it does so as a text to be read and interpreted. As such this version of anthropology has provided scholars of religion a social-scientific language with which to remain in the realm of meaning and discourse (Vasquez 2011, 212). The toolkit expanded, but the paradigm endured.

A shift in the paradigm is signalled by religion scholars' increasing invocation of phenomenological anthropologists such as Jackson, Stoller, and Csordas. In his elaboration of a materialist approach to the study of religion, Manuel Vasquez discusses all three at length, underscoring how their phenomenology of embodiment contrasts with and corrects for the idealism and essentialism of early phenomenologists of religion (Vasquez 2011, 87–122). Kevin Schilbrack also draws on phenomenological philosophers and anthropologists in his proposal for a reconfigured philosophy of religion, one that considers religious practices and pre-reflective experience, and not just doctrines and texts, worthy of philosophical attention (2014, 35). In an article notably subtitled "The Case for Phenomenologically Oriented Religious Studies

Ethnographies," Kristy Nabhan-Warren argues for the need to overcome religious studies' Protestant-derived logocentrism – its privileging of sacred scriptures over ritual practices, beliefs over behaviours, and minds over bodies. Traditional approaches fail especially to account for the devotional practices she observed at immigrant Catholic shrines, where "[r]eligion was tasted, smelled, seen, heard and touched" (Nabhan-Warren 2011, 380). Because her research subjects engage the world primarily through their flesh and bones, so too, Nabhan-Warren holds, must she as an ethnographer. This embodied methodology furnishes a foundation for interpersonal and intercultural understanding: "When we eat, drink, dance, and pray alongside our interlocutors in the field, we gain an understanding of religion as it is lived that would not be possible if we viewed our bodies as detached and irrelevant to what we research and write" (Nabhan-Warren 2011, 382).

If ethnography offers a method for overcoming the limits of textualism, it is not any kind of ethnography, but rather ethnography that is "experience-near" rather than "experience-distant" (Wikan 1991). The concern for experience – not so much religious experience in a mystical, otherworldly sense, but rather the experiential dimension of religious practice as well as the everydayness of lived experience – joins embodiment as another major motif among religion scholars oriented towards phenomenological anthropology. Don Seeman, for example, makes "the plenitude of situated human experiences" (Seeman 2018, 337) grounds for his research on religion and argues that the first obligation of experience-near ethnography is to "the thick and detailed description not of culture but of what is at stake for real people in local setting" (Seeman 2009, 6). Methodologically, this entails a refusal to limit ethnographic research to question-and-answer interviews removed from the context of everyday life. Meredith McGuire elaborates this point in her phenomenological critique of the sociology of religion. There is a "subtle violence," she writes, in quantitative studies, those deriving prestige from their massive data sets, large-scale surveys, and reproducible comparisons. Such research tools license scholars to reach conclusions without actually interacting with anyone. McGuire's call instead is for research predicated on the immediacy of embodied existence (McGuire 2002).

This commitment to experience has important epistemological implications. It entails a withholding of judgment, a bracketing, as to the nature or even the existence of an experienced object. Worldviews and cosmologies are evaluated not for their origins or their ontological status. Rather, "they are understood as *experiences* of reality that arise out of the daily life and practical concerns of people, without reducing

Introduction 9

them to socio-economic conditions or principles external to the situation itself" (Knibbe and Versteeg 2008, 49). This non-reductive principle is worth underscoring given that so much research in religious studies presumes religion scholars know better than religious practitioners what is really going on. Quoting Kim Knibbe and Peter Versteeg again, "[a]ccording to phenomenological anthropology, we have forgotten to look at what is, so to speak, *revealed* to us, right in front of our eyes, and instead we look beyond and behind the things for their meaning" (Knibbe and Versteeg 2008, 51). To dwell on the phenomena themselves is to eschew the need to uncover the *real* sources of religious experiences, practices, and discourses. Science and religion are but two ways to apprehend reality. Perspectives should be evaluated not along such binaries as true/false, real/illusory, rational/irrational, but rather pragmatically – in terms of their experiential entailments and effects, how they operate as sensible and workable truths.[6]

The upshot is a thoroughgoing epistemic pluralism, and it is here that phenomenological anthropology makes its most radical critique of religious studies – not only of the phenomenology of religion's idealism but also of the extreme constructivist reaction to it. That reaction is associated with an influential set of contemporary scholars who aim to model religious studies on the natural sciences, who see the task of the scholar primarily as historicizing, contextualizing, theorizing, and explaining religion in terms that are secular and rational.[7] A political charge attends to this constructivist approach, which, as Knibbe and Versteeg describe it, unmasks reality "to the extent that everything seems a lie, strategically used for political gain or to oppress others" (Knibbe and Versteeg 2008, 50). Constructivism has the virtue of highlighting the human dimensions of purportedly metaphysical phenomena, and also of augmenting religious studies' respectability within a university system that prizes the sciences over the humanities. It fails, however, to reckon with the elusiveness of religion. Against the reductionism of constructivist approaches, numerous scholars of religion have voiced opposition – not in a bid to revive Eliade's onto-theology but in recognition of how so many of Eliade's recent critics traffic in ontological claims and foundational certainties of their own.

Historian Mary Dunn, for example, proposes as an alternative to constructivism the radical empiricism outlined by James and advanced by Jackson. Referring to their common effort to make space for uncertainty, ambiguity, and excess, Dunn writes, "Experience is always *more than* – more than nature, more than culture, more than practice, more than theory" (Dunn 2016, 889). In this, Dunn is echoing philosopher Tyler Robert's extended argument that the rich complexity of human experience, and especially of religious experience, eludes grasp and articulation (Roberts 2013), and Orsi's view that narratives of divine encounter "are shot through with 'unknowingness,' studded with 'opacities'" (Orsi 2016, 61). One of the most compelling applications of this sensibility to the study of religion is Mattijs van de Port's ethnography of Brazilian Candomblé. Van de Port's central thesis is that the path to knowledge in Candomblé, a religion of spirit possession, visions, and lengthy initiations, is both embodied and implicit. As a religion whose "very essence" is "inarticulability," Candomblé demands that researchers relinquish the will to authorship of their or others' worlds (van de Port 2011, 14).[8] It invites scholars to reckon with mystery, excess, and incompletion, to make space for "the-rest-of what-is" (van de Port 2011, 18–19). As such, Candomblé, and any approach to scholarship that would be true to it, undercuts fundamental premises of the social sciences – above all, their relentless quest for certainty. The call here is for an epistemic openness, akin to what van de Port in this volume describes as an embodied openness, which permits multiple approaches and admits multiple realities. It refuses to concede absolute authority to scientific rationality, however hegemonic it may be.

The call is thus also for humility, for the kind of intellectual humility that comes uneasily to those who stake their professional if not also their personal identities on academic credentials and claims to expertise. Echoing Orsi's call for scholars to embrace doubt and ambiguity, Dunn writes that the value in bringing multiple narratives and approaches into one's scholarship is precisely the possibility of a misfit with one's self-understanding, the outcome of which is confusion and agitation (Dunn 2016, 896–7). Likewise, Roberts urges "a willingness to be disturbed and unsettled in one's identity with respect to a particular vision of the world or way of life that is different yet somehow compelling" (Roberts 2013, 141). Francis X. Clooney has operationalized this approach through the method of comparative theology, which entails departing from one's home tradition, immersing oneself in another, and allowing oneself to be changed as a result of those multiple dwellings. In a chapter framing this approach to theology in terms of Jackson's approach to anthropology, Clooney argues that the fundamental requirement is risk and vulnerability: an openness to rethinking and even dislodging, in light of new experiences, what one earlier took for granted (Clooney 2018). At the core of these projects is a drive less to know the other than to be changed by the other. Jackson uses religious terminology to describe this aspect of research: *metanoia* or conversion – an ongoing series of transformations that "involves physical upheaval, psychological turmoil, and moral confusion" (Jackson 2013a, 11).

Introduction 11

Painful and rupturing though conversion may be, it is indispensable for understanding.

The Existential Turn

Exemplifying this disposition to change, Michael Jackson in recent decades has undergone his own intellectual shift – not an abandonment of phenomenological anthropology, but rather a turn towards existential anthropology.[9] As evident in the term's frequent appearance in recent book titles (Jackson 2005, 2013a; Jackson and Piette 2015a), this is Jackson's preferred new framing for his scholarship. It is a pivot with precedence in continental philosophy. Whereas Edmund Husserl and Martin Heidegger are associated with phenomenology, the uptake of their ideas by Jean-Paul Sartre, Maurice Merleau-Ponty, and others more often goes by the name existential phenomenology or, simply, existentialism.[10] Similarities between phenomenology and existentialism abound: a concern with describing human existence without the distortion of scientific presuppositions, a recognition of the non-rational dimensions of experience, an acknowledgment of the limits of concepts and categories. Existential philosophy adds attention to anxiety in the face of death, responsibility for the exercise of freedom, and the absurdity of everyday life (Wrathall and Dreyfus 2009). Importantly, however, existential anthropology is not wedded to these well-known motifs. In their introduction to *What is Existential Anthropology?*, Jackson and Albert Piette make precisely this point by warning against "popular conflations of existentialism with postwar Left Bank preoccupations with alienation" (Jackson and Piette 2015b, 3). Here, instead, is Jackson's own take on his existential turn:

> In reconsidering the way in which I understood the phenomenological project twenty years ago, I think that I failed to emphasize the complementarity of phenomenology and existentialism. In defining phenomenology *against* positivism or objectivism I inadvertently committed the very error I was attributing to science, and failed to take my own advocacy of relationality and intersubjectivity as seriously as it merited. Rather than draw hard and fast distinctions between competing epistemologies – fact and fiction, subjectivity and objectivity, science and religion – I would now argue that such terms are best seen as rough and ready ways in which human beings apprehend oscillations in consciousness that reflect changing life situations and practical interests, and should not be assumed to denote mutually exclusive states of mind, let alone different personalities, ethnicities or ontologies. (Jackson 2015, 293–4)

The limitation Jackson has come to identify in phenomenology is its reliance on a static conception of human existence, albeit one that, as discussed above, does much to contest the reductionism of rationalism. Jackson's existential turn – emphasizing people's ever-shifting engagements with the panoply of experiences and epistemologies at hand – can be described as a radicalizing of his commitment to the irreducibility of lived experience.

Michael Lambek, author of this volume's afterword, offers further clarity in his previously published assessment of existential anthropology. Noting that existential anthropology already resonates with the large corpus of anti-essentialist anthropological literature, much of it derived from Foucault, Lambek credits existential anthropology with adding a pro-existentialist stance, much of this derived from Sartre (Lambek 2015, 59). Existential anthropology does not stop at deconstructing essences; it goes on to reconstruct a positive rendering of human existence. In the words of Jackson and Piette, it is *both* a refusal *and* an exploration: "a refusal to reduce lived reality to culturally or socially constructed representations, and a determination to explore the variability, mutability, and indeterminacy of that lived reality as it makes its appearance in real time, in specific moments, in actual situations" (Jackson and Piette 2015b, 3–4). The positive pole – the exploration called for here – entails four overlapping foci: ordinary individuals, critical events, freedom, and existential mobility.

The starting point for existential anthropology, as for existentialism at large, is the concrete human in her or his irreducible singularity, "the first-person point of orientation of each and any biographical human being" (Wardle 2023, 37). This figure is all too often written out of scholarly accounts. As Jackson and Piette observe, "one can move from one academic treatise to another without encountering a living soul. Individuals are cited, to be sure, but they are usually other academics" (Jackson and Piette 2015b, 4). Ordinary individuals often serve as ciphers or stand-ins for this or that culture, this or that group, this or that theoretical point. Subjectivity disappears behind the objectivity of system-thinking (Denizeau 2015, 217). Existential anthropology seeks to restore and re-centre the voices of anonymous if not invisible individuals, to describe them in depth and detail, in terms of their projects, practices, dreams, and desires. This person-centred approach does not deny that human beings are always and inevitably situated. To privilege the existing individual in all her or his concreteness is not to discount the force of structures, cultures, and histories. It is to offer the modest reminder that vitality and agency abide not only in such transpersonal realms, but also in persons themselves (Jackson and Piette 2015b, 4).

Introduction   13

In fact, however, existential anthropology's concern has never been with the individual in isolation but rather with the individual in situations (Jackson 2005). What matters about human existence is "the micropolitics of interpersonal relations in everyday life" (Jackson and Piette 2015b, 13), the manner in which lives unfold and transform in quotidian interactions, circumstances, and events. This makes the existing individual rarely identical with, and often irreducible to, a priori categories of the social, the cultural, the political, and the historical. Yet the pull towards conceptual reductionism is strong in academic institutions governed by theoretical reason. Against a post-Enlightenment rationality that threatens to eclipse the variety of ways of being human, Jackson emphasizes how all modalities, even and sometimes especially those written off as irrational, figure in the human struggle for well-being (Jackson 2005, xxix). Scholars therefore ought not only discover hidden causes, motives, and meanings but also bear witness to the idiosyncrasies of human experience, and thus avoid "reducing lifeworlds to worldviews and life to language" (Jackson 2013a, 22).

Succinctly, "Existential anthropology is … a reminder that life is irreducible to the terms with which we seek to grasp it" (Jackson and Piette 2015b, 9). There is always an excess beyond the reach of reason: the space of paradox, contingency, and contradiction. Neglected though it tends to be in much scholarly writing, that space – of events and situations as opposed to typologies and classifications – concerns existential anthropologists, even though such concern comes at the cost of certitude and comprehension. It is precisely the forms of life marked by elusiveness and ambiguity "that are existentially most imperative to us, and are at stake in the critical moments that define our lives" (Jackson 2005, xxix).

Freedom is another pillar in this analytic of indeterminacy – a freedom that, as Tyler Roberts well puts it, can only be defined negatively. "To invoke freedom," he writes, "is not really to explain something – an action or an idea – but to say that explanation has run its course, that something new has happened" (Roberts 2013, 94). For existential anthropologists, freedom is the very real portal to novelty and surprise. Existential anthropologists appreciate that no experience of freedom is entirely unconstrained or wholly unbound (Jackson 2011). But even within limits, humans rely on at least a sense of such freedom to be able to act as if they have a hand in determining their destiny, as if they are not ruled by impersonal and implacable forces.

To a degree usually underreported in conventional accounts, human thought and behaviour are messy. What interests existential anthropologists is precisely the mess: the ways individuals in everyday situations

14   Devaka Premawardhana

at times live up to and at other times depart from their conditioning. Whereas the social sciences generally aim at identifying the causes and determinants of human action, existential anthropology stresses the misalignments and the slippages, the new and the emergent – how people, without merely replicating their conditioning, make something of what they are made (Sartre 1969, 45). To create the sense that life is worth living, humans convert facticity into choice and orient themselves towards possible futures, becoming thus creators and not mere creatures of their circumstances (Jackson 2013a, 19).

Resulting from all this is the most pronounced motif of Jackson's recent existential turn – the critique of identity thinking and its replacement with what might be called mobility thinking (Jackson 2019). Jackson's preferred term is existential mobility, which posits the human subject as several rather than singular, as shifting rather than settled. While awareness of the manifold nature of human subjectivity has been commonplace among literary artists and contrarian philosophers for centuries (Jackson 2013b, 201–8), much anthropological scholarship continues to assume the consistency of the self. The problem with identity thinking is that, in the act of labelling people, categorizing and classifying them, we stand to miss the dynamic, experimental, and oscillatory nature of everyday existence, the "malleability and multiplicity of the human subject" (Jackson and Piette 2015b, 6). In Jackson's words, we are "not stable or set pieces, with established and immutable essences, destinies, or identities; we are constantly changing, formed and reformed, in the course of our relationships with others and our struggle for whatever helps us sustain and find fulfillment in life" (Jackson 2013a, 5). Existentially, we are all unsettled – mobile and mutable, eclectic and experimental. So universalizing a claim may be read as essentialist. If it is, it is ironically so: the only quality we "essentially" possess is our irreducibility to the conceptual essences with which we are customarily identified.

Religion and Existential Anthropology 1: Agency and Subjectivity

Compared to phenomenological anthropology, the uptake of existential anthropology among scholars of religion has been muted.[11] While explicit engagements are few, however, implicit engagements abound – mainly among scholars pursuing existentialist themes present in Jackson's work prior to his existential turn. First among those themes is the concrete individual as analytical starting point, a focus already announced in Jackson's 1996 introduction to phenomenological anthropology: "Our task is clear: to revalidate the everyday life of

Introduction 15

ordinary people, to tell their stories in their own words, to recover their names" (Jackson 1996, 36).[12] Phenomenological anthropologist Robert Desjarlais offers a compelling Buddhist-studies application of this person-centred approach in his book *Sensory Biographies: Lives and Deaths among Nepal's Yolmo Buddhists* (Desjarlais 2003). Exploring questions of selfhood and sensation, Desjarlais focuses the entire book on no more than two Tibetan Buddhist individuals, garnering from their singular stories insights into larger historical and cultural processes. Existential anthropologist Albert Piette also attends to the religious lives of particular individuals. It is out of his research on French Catholics that Piette develops his "existential theory of ordinary religion," premised on "detailed observations of separate individuals" (Piette 2015, 203, 179). This attention to singularity allows Piette to observe shifts in religious commitments – the alternation of moments of believing with moments of scepticism or distraction. Historian Robert Orsi invokes Sartrean existentialism and phenomenological anthropology to elaborate what is, in comparison to Piette, a far more intersubjective understanding of lived Catholicism, yet one that also recounts the stories and records the names of actually existing individuals (Orsi 2005, 234n.3). This is needed, Orsi argues, to ground religious studies empirically, in lived experience.

As for Orsi, so too for Jackson – the focus is not individual existents but individuals in the relations and situations of their everyday lives.[13] In *The Palm at the End of the Mind*, Jackson explores religiosity specifically through border situations and critical junctures, those moments "where we come up against the limits of language, the limits of our strength, the limits of our knowledge" (Jackson 2009, xi–xii). These are situations into which we feel thrown, and yet situations that, "paradoxically, may throw us open to new possibilities and new connections, lying beyond the horizons we have hitherto known" (Jackson 2009, 37). This space beyond goes by many labels – the real, for example, or the religious – but for Jackson the name is less germane than the experience, and what practically follows from it. Echoing here William James's pragmatist outlook, Jackson holds that what matters is not the ontological status of the object of belief, nor the name we give it, but rather how and to what end we relate with the wider fields of being experienced as extensions of ourselves (Jackson 2009, 5–6).

Not only is the precise term insignificant. Precision itself is beside the point. Ambiguity is of the essence, for the space of the religious is penumbral. In their resistance to codification or certification, liminal spaces and religious experiences allow humans to venture beyond the reach of reason (Jackson 2009, 5). Here we arrive at existential anthropology's most direct, though necessarily capacious, definition of religion: "what we call religion is a set of ideas and practices for getting in touch with an 'elsewhere,' an 'otherness,' or a 'wider self' that lies beyond the horizons of one's immediate lifeworld" (Jackson and Piette 2015b, 12). Such extensions – for example, into the realm of dreams and destiny (see Malik, this volume, and Schielke, this volume), into transnational religious spaces (see Knibbe, this volume), or into novel experiences of the everyday (see Jackson, this volume) – are life-giving reservoirs of well-being. But they are also unstable and dangerous, a duality exemplified best in one of the most recurring images in Jackson's writing: the bush-town dialectic (see, e.g., Jackson 2013a, 14–18). In much West African thought, the town is the settled, ordered space, while the bush is home to djinn, ancestors, and wild energies. Crossing from town to bush is never casually done; it always entails risk. Yet it is only by perennially opening ourselves to new connections and new possibilities – to an elsewhere and otherwise – that revitalization ensues.

Agency, or at least the experience of oneself as an actor rather than as one acted upon, is crucial for existential anthropology's approach to ritual action. Jackson's ethnographic studies of Kuranko divination and shapeshifting well illustrate the ramifications of religious practice on subjectivity: the possibility of changing if not a given situation then at least how one experiences that situation (Jackson 2013a, 31–50, 93–114). Thus, Jackson contends, it is not edifying to judge magic or play as rational or irrational, true or false. It matters more that we understand the biographical particulars of the people we study and place their ritual engagements in the context of the troubles and confusions of life, the threats all of us at some time face to our social worth and sense of self-mastery. Ritual is especially well suited to restore hope and replenish strength because of how it relies on a simulacrum of the problem at hand, a scaled-down version that allows a person to exert influence and thereby attain a sense of adequacy, amplitude, and control (Jackson 2005, 75–110). These subjective transformations may then be transferred beyond the ritual setting to productively influence everyday life, making ritual more a supplement than a substitute for mundane, technical action.[14]

A younger generation of ethnographers trained by Jackson, working in an array of ethnographic contexts, has done much to advance this existential approach to ritual and religion. Sónia Silva writes of basket divination as a means for wartime refugees in Central Africa to cope with adversity and redress feelings of uncertainty and diminution (Silva 2011). Among Transylvanian Catholics, Marc Loustau describes

Introduction   17

storytelling as a mode of improvisation used to experiment and adapt, and thus to generate possibilities and potentialities (Loustau 2016). Kate DeConinck, in her research on September 11th memorialization, documents how bereaved families make use of material objects, physical sites, and embodied practices to foster a sense of agency and stability (DeConinck 2019). In my own work I have explored how financial tithing by impoverished Pentecostals refashions their sense of self – from beneficiary to benefactor – and thereby offers one of the few mechanisms of empowerment available to them (Premawardhana 2012). Finally, Hans Lucht, in his study of West Africans' high-risk escapes to Europe, argues for an existential outlook that sees them not solely as economic refugees, but as agents imaginatively drawing the world into their own domain of influence so as to counter threats of uncertainty and negation (Lucht 2012).

Lucht's work also introduces a needed caveat: loss and violence also sometimes factor into projects of existential realization, as in the case of the Ghanaian mother in his study who concedes the death of her migrant son so as better to cope with it (Lucht 2012, 216–58). Ritual action carries the potential simultaneously to sustain and to deprive a person. Agency is not always about heroic resistance and active striving; it is also sometimes about giving up and letting go (Jackson 2005, 182). Self-effacement – as one finds, for example, in rituals of spirit possession, in practices of renunciation, in submitting to a higher power, and, as Silva shows in this volume, in the wounds of the healer – can itself be self-affirming, a recovery of the sense that one has a hand in one's destiny.

Religion and Existential Anthropology 2: Beyond Religious Identities

Another sustained application of existential anthropology to the study of religion appears in the paradigm of "everyday religion," elaborated by Samuli Schielke and Liza Debevec as an approach conjoining daily practices and grand schemes, lived experiences and normative doctrines (Schielke and Debevec 2012b). This holism is grounded in what they call "an existential, phenomenological perspective that grants primacy to the complexity and openness of practices and experiences" and exposes the "essentially unsystematic nature of religion as lived practice" (Schielke and Debevec 2012b, 3). Issued here is a radical challenge to what Jackson and Piette call a monothetic approach to religion, in which "we accept the reified categories of Christianity, Judaism, Buddhism, and Islam, and frame our research in these terms from the outset" (Jackson and Piette 2015b, 13). Similar critiques are found among researchers of "lived religion," some of whose proponents – Meredith McGuire and Robert Orsi, for example – tie their own work to phenomenological if not explicitly existential thought. In the anthropology of religion, Don Seeman's research on Ethiopian Jews makes the case for thinking beyond statist and culturalist classifications that reduce belonging and relatedness "to the spare sociological and bureaucratic language of 'identity' conceived as relatively fixed and self-explanatory categories" (Seeman 2009, 32).

Such insights have become especially pertinent in recent decades with the rise of anthropological research programs premised on the presumed coherence of one or another religious tradition. While there surely is heuristic and pedagogical value in the anthropology of Islam and the anthropology of Christianity, for example, in that they make possible the cross-cultural examination of a shared set of questions, these frameworks also introduce a problem endemic to much research in religious studies, one varyingly critiqued as the "religious congruence fallacy" (Chaves 2010) and "methodological religionism" (Hausner and Gellner 2012, 975). Underlying this problem is the assumption that religious ideas, identities, and institutions hang together seamlessly. As Schielke writes in his challenge to the anthropology of Islam, piety and ethical perfection are not the only pursuits that drive Muslims; subjective experience is far more ambivalent, contradictory, and complex. The construction of Islam as a discursive tradition allows for comparison with other idealized traditions, but at the cost of overlooking how Islam matters in the lives of everyday Muslims. Building on Jackson and Orsi, among others, Schielke presents what he calls his "more existential approach" (Schielke 2010, 3) as a "farewell to the project of an anthropology of Islam" (Schielke 2010, 14).

I have likewise disputed on existential grounds the viability of the anthropology of Christianity, questioning specifically its tendency to conflate the usually exclusivist and perfectionist discourse of church leaders with the practices of everyday Christians whose association with the tradition is mostly ambivalent (Premawardhana 2018). This is not to suggest a weak or halfhearted engagement on the part of my interlocutors, and it is certainly not to disparage any of them for "falling short"; such would be the judgment of those who hold uncompromising commitment to be the ideal. Rather, it is to suggest a multiplicity of commitments pursued pragmatically, a state of religious fluidity that undermines totalizing accounts of religious identity.[15]

The most noted problem with anthropological research framed by a single religious tradition is the barrier it erects between the religious

Introduction   19

and the secular in individuals' lives. Writing of how Islam commingles with cultures of commercial media, romantic love, and global capitalism, Schielke writes: "these are not different worlds. They are constituents, parts, of people's lifeworlds – lifeworlds that can never be explained by any single principle but that must be understood in their complexity and openness" (Schielke 2015, 12). The phenomenological category of the lifeworld – antithetical as it is to the drive towards consistency, clarity, and closure – similarly leads DeConinck to highlight how "human responses to tragedy are situated in webs of reciprocal relationships … that are continually shifting and often ambiguous," and how this demands a rethinking of memorial sites beyond the sacred/secular binary (DeConinck 2019, 132–3n8). Likewise, George González elaborates what he calls an existential archaeology to elucidate the "spirituality" of late modern capitalism – the coexistence of seemingly disparate domains that one can only appreciate when human praxis is taken as the point of departure (González 2016).

Yet the pull towards reductionism is strong, especially given that many religious traditions themselves demand total allegiance. This often leads scholars to presume an isomorphic relation between identity and behaviour, to treat religious affiliations as master categories that preordain an individual's entire faith and practice (McGuire 2008, 186). Existential anthropologists emphasize that while religious traditions certainly shape life, they rarely if ever determine it. To capture this indeterminacy, it helps to turn with Jackson in his most recent writings from the essentialist analytic of identity to the existentialist analytic of mobility. Despite the totalizing nature of many religions – their tendency to "put themselves out there as all-encompassing life programs" (van de Port 2017, 125) – existential mobility is perhaps nowhere more evident than in people's religious lives. These generally prioritize neither rationality and logic nor consistency and coherence, but rather emotion, faith, and the pragmatic pursuit of well-being. Even the most rigid forms of religion can scarcely contain the ambiguities of everyday practice, especially in situations of crisis and duress. In such situations, according to Orsi, people appropriate "religious idioms [plural] as they need them" (Orsi 1997, 8).

Mattijs van de Port's term for this is "fluctuating intensities of religious identifications," the logical outcome of the insufficiently acknowledged fact that "religion as lived is not the same as religion as talked about" (van de Port 2017, 124–5). Michael Lambek describes a both/and logic operative among those he has researched in Mayotte and Madagascar. This contrasts with the either/or thinking that undergirds fundamentalist and rationalist systems. People juggle and

20   Devaka Premawardhana

improvise around multiple religious registers, switching directions and altering commitments as circumstances demand. Citing Jackson and Piette's dictum that life is irreducible to any one set of terms, Lambek credits existential anthropology with reminding anthropologists of religion "that no one system is every fully complete or fully consistent; there is always something that escapes even the most elegant models" (Lambek 2015, 60). Indeed, life's irreducibility to models and ideals is a central theme of existential anthropology. Applied to the study of religion, this requires shifting focus from religious identities to religious mobilities, from the fixity of categories to the fluidity of life.

Conclusion: Critical Takes and Paths Forward

Long after phenomenology rose and subsequently receded within the academic study of religion, a revival of sorts has been gathering momentum. It takes the form of existential anthropology or, as I have sketched it here, phenomenological anthropology along with its existential turn. Yet while this paradigm preserves earlier phenomenologists' challenge to rationalism and reductionism, it otherwise has no truck with the phenomenology of religion. It entails neither disembodied enquiry into inner experience nor ahistorical constructions of *homo religiosus*. The phenomenology argued for in this chapter is far more empirical, embodied, and existential than that which came before.

It also has the virtue of resonating with significant existentialist strands of religious traditions themselves. It is well established that theistically committed thinkers – Søren Kierkegaard and Fyodor Dostoevsky, for example – shaped what came to be known as existential philosophy. Despite the commonplace association of existentialism with atheism, there is a striking consonance between existentialism's concerns with purpose, particularity, and the limits of human reason, and concerns arising within the Judeo-Christian tradition (Dreyfus 2009, Premawardhana 2020, 2023). In non-Abrahamic religions as well, existentialist considerations frequently surface (see, e.g., Malik 2016, Patel 2023). There are, as such, ample grounds for admitting existentialist thought into religious studies, whether on its own or mediated through existential anthropology.

Those grounds are in fact already well laid in the work of two influential religion scholars of the mid-twentieth century. One is the historian Wilfred Cantwell Smith, well known for challenging the scholarly tendency to focus on religious systems at the expense of religious persons, and on beliefs at the expense of commitments (W.C. Smith 1963, 1977). The other is anthropologist Godfrey Lienhardt, who argues against

Introduction 21

understanding cosmologies in terms of "theoretical 'beings' whose existence is posited, as it were, before the human experience to which they correspond" (1961, 169). Existence precedes essence, in short. Relations outrank reifications. Even if not naming existentialism as their orientation, Smith and Lienhardt demonstrate that the approach to religion argued for in this chapter is neither out of place nor altogether novel.

Yet for existential anthropology to gain traction within religious studies, some challenges must be answered. These challenges differ little from those already levelled against phenomenological anthropology in general.[16] The argument I wish to make in these concluding pages is that the field of religious studies has within it resources for helping existential-phenomenological anthropology deal with the critiques made of it, to reckon with and even redress its lingering blind spots.

The overarching problem is that of methodological individualism – of subjectivism, solipsism, and the privatizing of experience. There are multiple layers to the issue. First is the contingency of the category of experience itself, its romantic associations with inwardness, introspection, and individualism (Desjarlais 1997, 17–19), a critique that Jackson has conceded and taken as an opportunity to clarify that all human experience is socially and historically determined, though simultaneously never entirely reducible to such pre-givens (Jackson 2005, xxii, n17; Jackson 2015, 293–4). Second is the downplaying of political contexts and socio-economic constraints. Of course, nothing about attending to individuals' lives necessitates disregard for larger forces and dynamics. Nevertheless, some existential and phenomenological anthropologists have responded to this issue by recasting the project as a "critical phenomenology" to emphasize how particular modes of being-in-the-world are configured socio-politically, though here again without letting macro-scale dynamics overshadow individual struggles to make life viable (Desjarlais 1997, 24–7; Willen 2019). Others re-envision structure not as that which grants objectivity to a social field, but rather as an emergent property contingent upon individuals' worldmaking gestures (Wardle 2023). However one strikes a balance between the personal and the structural, it would be wrong to judge phenomenological anthropology or its existential variant as wholly apolitical insofar as its concern with lived experience and embodied knowledge centres the realities and epistemologies of marginalized people (Jackson 1996, 36–8).

Existential-phenomenological anthropology's person-centred analyses may also be seen as minimizing the networks in which such persons are inevitably enmeshed – from histories and heritages to collectivities and cosmologies. Significantly for this volume, prominent ethnographers of religion Joel Robbins (2009) and Robert Orsi have each, on their own, raised this concern – Orsi especially pointedly when he decries "the archetypal existential man of phenomenological anthropology" as "an avatar of the modernist fantasy of the unencumbered and radically individual self" (Orsi 2012, 151). Direct rejoinders have emphasized that the full scope of existential phenomenology is not individualist but intersubjective. It is less about perception and consciousness than about the multifarious relationships that constitute one's being-in-the-world (Zigon 2009; Jackson and Piette 2015b, 11, 26n13). Any analytical treatment of individuals as individuals would have to be deemed inadmissible. So too, however, would the far more common treatment of individuals as mere manifestations of pre-existing conditions.

A stronger case can be made that existential perspectives fail to account sufficiently for the governing force of cultures, traditions, and – of importance to this volume – religions. These, along with the institutions and authorities that sustain them, have generally little place in the work of existential anthropologists. Yet they matter. There is a thickness to social and cultural formations, to discursive and religious traditions, that gives them weight and influence despite the irreducibility of lived experience to any one of them.

An existential anthropology informed by and engaged with religious studies would be well equipped to recognize this. It would steer a middle course *between* (to evoke this chapter's keyword) the hypostasizing and the minimizing of religious cultures. Anthropologist Thomas Csordas models this path in his promotion of an existentially grounded cultural phenomenology that conjoins "the immediacy of embodied experience with the multiplicity of cultural meaning in which we are always and inevitably immersed" (Csordas 1999, 143). His concern is with documenting how people learn context-specific ways of attending to the world through the inculcation of culturally meaningful embodied dispositions (see also Desjarlais 1992).

How to give proper due to religious structures and religious cultures without once again erasing the intricacies of individuals' lived experiences is a persisting and perhaps irresolvable conundrum.[17] It is, however, worth noting, as I have in my own attempt at a synthesis (Premawardhana 2018, 19–21), that certain traditions – and perhaps most traditions, when viewed existentially – contain within them catalysts for thinking beyond them.[18] As Orsi has put it, there is a power in inherited idioms "both to shape and discipline thought and as well to give rise to religious creativity and improvisation" (Orsi 1997, 16). Thus, as Schielke and Debevec argue, religious practice "is embedded in traditions, relations of power and social dynamics, but is not determined by them" (Schielke and Debevec 2012b, 8).

Introduction   23

But this embeddedness sometimes receives short shrift in existential anthropology, which, in its strenuous critique of cultural reductionism, risks succumbing to what Seeman in this volume terms "existential reductionism." Incidentally, the solution to this could come by correcting for a subsidiary problem in Jackson's articulation of existential anthropology. This is the problem of referencing exclusively Euro-American philosophers, with little attention paid to intellectual lineages beyond the West. To be sure, Jackson's ethnographic work is fundamentally a challenge to what he rightly terms the "incorrigibly Eurocentric" assumptions of dominant philosophies, including the assumption that knowledge production takes only discursive form (Jackson 2016, 11). Yet it is worth mentioning that Eurocentrism has been and can be challenged through studied attention not only to ethnographic particulars, but also to philosophical – and religious – traditions originating from and speaking to experiences beyond the West.[19] Were existential anthropologists to engage non-Western religions as carefully as religious studies scholars do, they may find a means of affirming existential freedom beyond the paradigm of liberal subjectivity, not unlike how global perspectives on feminism have disclosed the Euro-American fallacy of locating agency exclusively against or outside the bounds of tradition (Mahmood 2009). Existentialism outside the Euro-American West (e.g., Gordon 2000 and Kalmanson 2020) can make clear how self-realization and creativity manifest sometimes within traditional structures – including within religions – and not merely in transcending them.

Perhaps the point of greatest tension between existential anthropology and the study of religion concerns the relationship between practices and ideas, between life and thought. Jackson does not altogether dismiss the relevance of beliefs and worldviews, concepts and theories. Yet their status is clearly secondary to the imperatives of existence: "Conceptualization, reflection, and representation tend to follow *from* our actions; they are seldom scripts or scores that precede it" (Jackson 2013a, 25). Ideas and beliefs interest Jackson only in their service as tools for coping with unsettling situations in an unstable world.

As I have argued above, this prioritizing of lifeworlds over worldviews is a salutary intervention, a rare challenge from within the academy to academia's inveterate intellectualism. Yet can it be denied that ideas and ideologies, once set in motion, sometimes exert a force experienced by individuals as coming at them from without, as having a life of their own? Even on experiential grounds, ideas matter enough to be taken seriously and granted, at least sometimes, analytical priority. This goes for theological ideas as well, despite Jackson expressly minimizing them (e.g., Jackson 2009, 12). Yet the question whether ideas

24 Devaka Premawardhana

generate experiences or experiences generate ideas may be better left open and decided on empirical grounds, grounds that – existential anthropologists rightly insist – rarely if ever permit of single and settled solutions.[20]

This, in fact, seems to be where William James would come down. Jackson draws most on James to buttress existential anthropology's challenge to abstract reason. Yet one of his most repeated references to James, on the oscillations of human consciousness, emphasizes "relations as well as relata – flights and perchings, rivers and embankments, verbs and substantives, conjunctions and disjunctions" (Jackson 2009, 5, paraphrasing James 1950, 243). While Jackson's and James's point here is commonly to urge that the flux of relations be taken seriously, James importantly calls for nevertheless retaining a place for the solidity of relata. Flights matter but so too do perchings; connections matter but so too do the points connected. By extension, emotional and embodied registers demand our attention, but so too do idealist and even institutional registers.[21]

Within religious studies there is a common view that only James's psychology of religious experience matters for his theory of religion. Read holistically, however, alongside his philosophies of pluralism and radical empiricism, James's project precludes reduction to any singularity (Carrette and Lamberth 2017). As such, it allows a more nuanced take on the interplay of psyche and society, thought and practice, worldviews and lifeworlds. Jackson is not ignorant of this interplay. He insists that discursive constructs are not inherently flawed; the flaw enters only with their reification and fetishization. Yet against criticisms that existential anthropology fails sufficiently to deal with ideas and values, institutions and structures, it is worth stressing, as I am trying to do here, that Jackson's fundamentally relational anthropology, like James's fundamentally pluralist philosophy, has within itself resources for mounting a defence.

Those resources are latent, but they could easily be sparked by pairing existential anthropology with unrelated scholarly programs. The dialogue realized by this volume – between existential anthropology and religious studies – is just one example.[22] Yet rather than interdisciplinary dialogue, it might be better construed as interdisciplinary fieldwork, as an ethnographic engagement of the type Jackson exemplarily models and persuasively promotes. This kind of ethnography requires immersion and entails risk. One's customary roles and routines may be disturbed, as may one's very identity.

In his own critique of Jackson's work, philosopher James K.A. Smith proposes just this kind of interdisciplinary fieldwork, inviting Jackson

Introduction 25

to submit to the norms of the philosophical discipline and the authority of its texts as openly, attentively, and humbly as he does to the demands of his foreign field sites (J. Smith 2017). What if existential anthropologists approached religious studies – or, for that matter, religious traditions – this way, by fully immersing in it, by submitting to its norms and demands? This could be a means towards coming to see intellectual and religious traditions, worldviews, and theologies – along with the institutions that authorize them – not only as derivative but also as generative of human action. Such an approach would be premised on the complementarity of life and thought, individuals and institutions, transitives and substantives.

The opening to such an approach – to an existential anthropology that reaches beyond existential anthropology – can be found within existential anthropology itself, in its fundamentally relational ethos that not only permits but in fact impels engagement with alterity and openness to self-critique. If existential anthropology is concerned with "interleaving a multiplicity of particular points of view in a way that calls into question *all* claims for privileged understanding" (Jackson 2005, 49), then no single approach can suffice to address existential concerns, not even that of existential anthropology.

The burden of this chapter, in opening this volume, has been to show how much the field of religious studies can learn and profit from existential anthropology – from, for example, its principle of epistemic pluralism, its phenomenology of embodiment, its person-centred narratives, and its embrace of ambiguity. But appropriately, for a project so predicated on liminality and mobility, the benefits of such bridge-building could in fact flow both ways. Just as religious studies stands to gain by opening itself to existential anthropology, so too does existential anthropology stand to gain by opening itself to religious studies.

NOTES

1 For religious studies scholars, those tracks include, among others, lived religion, performance studies, practice theory, race and ethnic studies, feminist and womanist theory, and ethnographic theology. For anthropologists of religion, they include the anthropology of a single religion (Islam, Christianity, etc.), the anthropology of ethics and morality, the ontological turn, medical and psychological anthropology, and theologically engaged anthropology. The occasional points of overlap include interpretive or symbolic anthropology and, more recently, the turn towards material religion and everyday religious practice.

2 Interview with Claire Laine entitled "The Politics of Storytelling." https://hds.harvard.edu/news/2017/10/13/michael-d-jackson-politics -storytelling#.

3 For a discussion of radical empiricism (James's as well as Jackson's) in relation to religion, with extensive coverage of the criticisms James has drawn from contemporary religion scholars, see Dunn 2016. For another overview and rebuttal to James's critics, see Carrette and Lamberth 2017.

4 As another phenomenological anthropologist, Robert Desjarlais, has put it, the problem with conventional anthropology is its stress on "representation over presentation, or discourse over felt experience" (Desjarlais 1992, 249). See also see also Desjarlais and Throop (2011, 91–2) and Knibbe and van Houtert (2018, 6).

5 Yet, as Kalpana Ram and Christopher Houston make clear in their introduction to a volume on phenomenology in anthropology, there is no real opposition between a phenomenology of experience and post-structural accounts of power "if we recognize, instead, the ways in which phenomenology contains within itself many of the 'decentering' moves we associate with post-structuralism, but without giving up on 'experience'" (Ram and Houston 2015, 6).

6 Jackson draws heavily on the American pragmatist tradition – William James but also John Dewey and Richard Rorty – to advance this anti-foundationalist critique of scientific rationality (see, e.g., Jackson 2012, 22–32).

7 For overviews and critical rejoinders to this approach, see Roberts (2013) and Dunn (2016).

8 Philip Francis, in his argument for why and how religious enchantment and disenchantment occur beneath the level of discourse and intellect, similarly writes with reference to James and Jackson, among others, of what may be gained by relinquishing the need for intellectual dominance (Francis 2017, 103–5).

9 In referring to this shift as an existential turn, I of course invite comparison to the much discussed "ontological turn" in contemporary anthropology. There are commonalities in the two paradigms' attention to embodiment, uncertainty, and ways of being-in-the-world. But there is a significant difference, namely in the tendency of at least certain strands of the ontological turn to prioritize collective representations, cosmological systems, and extra-human subjectivities. It is important to distinguish between studies at the level of ontology and studies at the level of existence. The latter help keep in view empirical particularity and individual variability. For a full elaboration of existential anthropology's critique of the ontological turn, see Jackson and Piette (2015b, 19–25).

10 However, prior to even the earliest phenomenologists, thinkers prefiguring and later associated with existentialism were already at work:

Søren Kierkegaard, Fyodor Dostoevsky, and Friedrich Nietzsche, most prominently.

11 This volume, of course, aims to change that.

12 For a series of chapters that applies especially this essay of Jackson's to the study of "everyday religion" – in every case focused on the stories of individual religious practitioners – see chapters in Schielke and Debevec's *Ordinary Lives and Grand Schemes* (2012a), especially Graw 2012, Debevec 2012, Bacchiddu 2012, and Peterson 2012.

13 For an assessment of what differentiates Jackson's intersubjective existential anthropology from Piette's more subject-centred *anthropologie existentielle*, see Denizeau 2015.

14 On the difference between substitutes and supplements, see Lienhardt (1961, 283), on whom Jackson draws in his theorization of ritual (e.g., Jackson 2005, 95).

15 For additional critiques of the anthropology of Christianity on similarly existential anthropological grounds, see Seeman (2015) and Fesenmyer (2020).

16 In their respective reviews of phenomenological anthropology, Desjarlais and Throop (2011) and Knibbe and Versteeg (2008) have enumerated these succinctly.

17 From within the tradition of existential-phenomenological anthropology, see George González's reckoning with this tension in his work on institutional practices that undergird biographically particular expressions of spirituality (González 2016). For other valuable attempts to conjoin religious experience with such extra-subjective domains as authorized/ authorizing structures and cultural theories of mind, see the works of anthropologists of religion Birgit Meyer (2008) and Tanya Luhrmann (2020).

18 Consider, for example, Pierre Hadot's in-depth treatment of ancient philosophical schools such as Stoicism and Epicureanism. In his examination of the existential attitude with which these were approached, and in his argument that the abstract theories generated were intended to justify the existential attitude, he shows that the pedagogical contexts for these philosophies are not thereby any less worthy of analysis in all their particularities (Hadot 2002).

19 Here, in addition, religious studies' postcolonial turn can complement Jackson's existential turn through the attention it gives to the imperial politics of "religion" among other epistemic categories (e.g., Asad 1993, Chidester 1996, Masuzawa 2005).

20 In this I echo my co-editor's friendly challenge to existential anthropology's theological blind spot (Seeman 2018). See also Michael Lambek's and Samuli Schielke's respective calls for a better balance between lived experience and conceptual thought (Lambek 2015, 64; Schielke 2015, 16) and a

recent multidisciplinary attempt at a theologically engaged anthropology (Lemons 2018). It is worth noting that the balance I am pushing for here is not far from Max Weber's own ultimately dialectical posture. Although often seen as the theorist of religion who grants primacy to ideas – theologies as the motor of human action and historical change – his is ultimately a heuristic exercise meant to highlight the power of beliefs to change the course of history at given junctures, not to deny the dense tangle of causes that undergird human action. See Weber (1958, 183).

21 This point can be summarized with the image James, in his appreciative critique of Henri Bergson, gives of time as flowing like water, but also of time occasionally coming in drops – this, too, like water (James 1909, 232).

22 Indeed, it is not the only one. As noted by Desjarlais and Throop, phenomenological approaches to anthropology often "work in tandem with other approaches, such as cultural analyses; semiotic and linguistic perspectives; psychological, neuroscientific, and psychodynamic theories; or considerations of political economy" (Desjarlais and Throop 2011, 95).

WORKS CITED

Asad, Talal. 1993. *Genealogies of Religion: Discipline and Reasons of Power in Christianity and Islam*. Baltimore: Johns Hopkins University Press.

Bacchiddu, Giovanna. 2012. "'Doing Things Properly': Religious Aspects in Everyday Sociality in Apiao, Chilé." In *Ordinary Lives and Grand Schemes: An Anthropology of Everyday Religion*, edited by Samuli Schielke and Liza Debevec, 1–16. New York: Berghahn.

Carrette, Jeremy, and David Lamberth. 2017. "William James and the Study of Religion: A Critical Reading." In *Religion, Theory, Critique: Classic and Contemporary Approaches and Methodologies*, edited by Richard King, 203–12. New York: Columbia University Press.

Chaves, Mark. 2010. "Rain Dance in the Dry Season: Overcoming the Religious Congruence Fallacy." *Journal for the Scientific Study of Religion* 49, no. 1: 1–14. https://doi.org/10.1111/j.1468-5906.2009.01489.x.

Chidester, David. 1996. *Savage Systems: Colonialism and Comparative Religion in Southern Africa*. Charlottesville: University Press of Virginia.

Clooney, Francis X. 2018. "Comparative Theology: Writing between Worlds of Meaning." In *Theologically Engaged Anthropology*, edited by J. Derrick Lemons, 280–95. Oxford: Oxford University Press.

Csordas, Thomas J. 1994. "Introduction: The Body as Representation and Being-in-the-World." In *Embodiment and Experience: The Existential Ground of Culture and Self*, edited by Thomas J. Csordas, 1–24. Cambridge: Cambridge University Press.

–. 1999. "Embodiment and Cultural Phenomenology." In *Perspectives on Embodiment: The Intersections of Nature and Culture*, edited by Gail Weiss and Honi Fern Haber, 143–62. New York: Routledge.

Debevec, Liza. 2012. "Postponing Piety in Urban Burkina Faso: Discussing Ideas on When to Start Acting as a Pious Muslim." In *Ordinary Lives and Grand Schemes: An Anthropology of Everyday Religion*, edited by Samuli Schielke and Liza Debevec, 33–47. New York: Berghahn.

DeConinck, Kate Yanina. 2019. "Rebuilding, Remembrance, and Commerce: Perspectives on the Economic Revitalization of Lower Manhattan." *Journeys* 20, no. 1: 53–74. https://doi.org/10.3167/jys.2019.200104.

Denizeau, Laurent. 2015. "Considering Human Existence: An Existential Reading of Michael Jackson and Albert Piette." In *What Is Existential Anthropology?*, edited by Michael Jackson and Albert Piette, 214–36. New York: Berghahn.

Desjarlais, Robert. 1992. *Body and Emotion: The Aesthetics of Illness and Healing in the Nepal Himalayas*. Philadelphia: University of Pennsylvania Press.

–. 1997. *Shelter Blues: Sanity and Selfhood among the Homeless*. Philadelphia: University of Pennsylvania Press.

–. 2003. *Sensory Biographies: Lives and Deaths among Nepal's Yolmo Buddhists*. Berkeley: University of California Press.

Desjarlais, Robert, and C. Jason Throop. 2011. "Phenomenological Approaches in Anthropology." *Annual Review of Anthropology* 40: 87–102. https://doi.org/10.1146/annurev-anthro-092010-153345.

Dreyfus, Hubert L. 2009. "The Roots of Existentialism." In *A Companion to Phenomenology and Existentialism*, edited by Hubert L. Dreyfus and Mark A. Wrathall, 135–61. Oxford: Wiley-Blackwell.

Dunn, Mary. 2016. "What Really Happened: Radical Empiricism and the Historian of Religion." *Journal of the American Academy of Religion* 84, no. 4: 881–902. https://doi.org/10.1093/jaarel/lfw011.

Eliade, Mircea. 1954. *The Myth of the Eternal Return: Or, Cosmos and History*. Princeton, NJ: Princeton University Press.

Fesenmyer, Leslie. 2020. "'Living as Londoners Do': Born-Again Christians in Convivial East London." *Social Anthropology / Anthropologie Sociale* 28, no. 2: 402–17. https://doi.org/10.1111/1469-8676.12770.

Fitzgerald, Timothy. 2000. *The Ideology of Religious Studies*. New York: Oxford University Press.

Francis, Philip. 2017. *When Art Disrupts Religion: Aesthetic Experience and the Evangelical Mind*. New York: Oxford University Press.

González, George. 2016. "Towards an Existential Archeology of Capitalist Spirituality." *Religions* 7, no. 7: 85. https://doi.org/10.3390/rel7070085.

Gordon, Lewis. 2000. *Existentia Africana: Understanding Africana Existentialist Thought*. New York: Routledge.

Graw, Kent. 2012. "Divination and Islam: Existential Perspectives in the Study of Ritual and Religious Praxis in Senegal and Gambia." In *Ordinary Lives and Grand Schemes: An Anthropology of Everyday Religion*, edited by Samuli Schielke and Liza Debevec, 17–32. New York: Berghahn.

Hadot, Pierre. 2002. *What is Ancient Philosophy?* Translated by Michael Chase. Cambridge, MA: Belknap Press of Harvard University Press.

Hausner, Sondra L., and David N. Gellner. 2012. "Category and Practice as Two Aspects of Religion: The Case of Nepalis in Britain. *Journal of the American Academy of Religion* 80, no. 4: 971–97. https://doi.org/10.1093/jaarel/lfs083.

Husserl, Edmund. 1970. *The Crisis of European Sciences and Transcendental Phenomenology: An Introduction to Phenomenological Philosophy*. Evanston: Northwestern University Press.

Jackson. Michael. 1983. "Thinking through the Body: An Essay on Understanding Metaphor." *Social Analysis: The International Journal of Anthropology* 14: 127–49. https://www.jstor.org/stable/23170418.

–. 1989. *Paths toward a Clearing: Radical Empiricism and Ethnographic Inquiry*. Bloomington: Indiana University Press.

–. 1996. "Introduction: Phenomenology, Radical Empiricism, and Anthropological Critique." In *Things as They Are: New Directions in Phenomenological Anthropology*, edited by Michael Jackson, 1–50. Bloomington: Indiana University Press.

–. 2005. *Existential Anthropology: Events, Exigencies and Effects*. New York: Berghahn.

–. 2009. *The Palm at the End of the Mind: Relatedness, Religiosity, and the Real*. Durham: Duke University Press.

–. 2011. *Life within Limits: Well-Being in a World of Want*. Durham: Duke University Press.

–. 2012. *Between One and One Another*. Berkeley: University of California Press.

–. 2013a. *Lifeworlds: Essays in Existential Anthropology*. Chicago: The University of Chicago Press.

–. 2013b. *The Wherewithal of Life: Ethics, Migration, and the Question of Well-Being*. Berkeley: University of California Press.

–. 2015. "Afterword." In *Phenomenology in Anthropology: A Sense of Perspective*, edited by Kalpana Ram and Christopher Houston, 293–304. Bloomington: Indiana University Press.

–. 2016. *As Wide as the World Is Wise: Reinventing Philosophical Anthropology*. New York: Columbia University Press.

–. 2017. "The Politics of Storytelling." Interview by Claire Laine. Harvard Divinity School News Archive, October 13. https://hds.harvard.edu/news/2017/10/13/michael-d-jackson-politics-storytelling#.

–. 2019. *Critique of Identity Thinking*. New York: Berghahn.

Jackson, Michael, and Albert Piette, eds. 2015a. *What is Existential Anthropology?* New York: Berghahn.

Jackson, Michael, and Albert Piette. 2015b. "Anthropology and the Existential Turn." In *What Is Existential Anthropology?* edited by Michael Jackson and Albert Piette, 1–29. New York: Berghahn.

James, William. 1909. *A Pluralistic Universe.* New York: Longmans, Green.

–. 1950. *The Principles of Psychology.* Vol. 1. New York: Dover.

Kalmanson, Leah. 2020. *Cross-Cultural Existentialism: On the Meaning of Life in Asian and Western Thought.* London: Bloomsbury Academic.

Knibbe, Kim, and Peter Versteeg. 2008. "Assessing Phenomenology in Anthropology: Lessons from the Study of Religion and Experience." *Critique of Anthropology* 28, no. 1: 47–62. https://doi.org/10.1177/0308275X07086557.

Knibbe, Kim, and Els van Houtert. 2018. "Religious Experience and Phenomenology." In *The International Encyclopedia of Anthropology*, edited by Hillary Callan, 1–10. Hokoken, NJ: Wiley Blackwell.

Lambek, Michael. 2015. "Both/And." In *What Is Existential Anthropology?*, edited by Michael Jackson and Albert Piette, 58–83. New York: Berghahn.

Lemons, J. Derrick, ed. 2018. *Theologically Engaged Anthropology.* Oxford: Oxford University Press.

Lienhardt, Godfrey. 1961. *Divinity and Experience: The Religion of the Dinka.* Oxford: Oxford University Press.

Loustau, Marc Roscoe. 2016. "Risking a Miracle: Transcendentally Oriented Improvisation and Catholic Charismatics' Involvement in a Transylvanian Canonization." *Journal of Contemporary Religion* 31, no. 3: 335–50. https://doi.org/10.1080/13537903.2016.1206229.

Lucht, Hans. 2012. *Darkness before Daybreak: African Migrants Living on the Margins in Southern Italy Today.* Berkeley: University of California Press.

Luhrmann, T.M. 2020. "Mind and Spirit: A Comparative Theory about Representation of Mind and the Experience of Spirit." *Journal of the Royal Anthropological Institute* 26, no. S1: 9–27. https://doi.org/10.1111/1467-9655.13238.

Mahmood, Saba. 2009. "Agency, Performativity, and the Feminist Subject." *Pieties and Gender* 9: 11–45. https://doi.org/10.1163/ej.9789004178267.i-236.5.

Malik, Aditya. 2016. *Tales of Justice and Rituals of Divine Embodiment: Oral Narratives from the Central Himalayas.* New York: Oxford University Press.

Masuzawa, Tomoko. 2005. *The Invention of World Religions: Or, How European Universalism Was Preserved in the Language of Pluralism.* Chicago: University of Chicago Press.

McCutcheon, Russell T. 1997. *Manufacturing Religion: The Discourse on Sui Generis Religion and the Politics of Nostalgia.* New York: Oxford University Press.

McGuire, Meredith. 2002. "New-Old Directions in the Social Scientific Study of Religion: Ethnography, Phenomenology, and the Human Body." In

Personal Knowledge and Beyond: Reshaping the Ethnography of Religion, edited by James V. Spickard, J. Shawn Landres, and Meredith B. McGuire, 195–211. New York: New York University Press.

–. 2008. *Lived Religion: Faith and Practice in Everyday Life*. Oxford: Oxford University Press.

Meyer, Birgit. 2008. "Religious Sensations: Why Media, Aesthetics and Power Matter in the Study of Contemporary Religion." In *Religion: Beyond a Concept*, edited by H. de Vries, 704–23. New York: Fordham University Press.

Nabhan-Warren, Kristy. 2011. "Embodied Research and Writing: A Case for Phenomenologically Oriented Religious Studies Ethnographies." *Journal of the American Academy of Religion* 79, no. 2: 378–407. https://doi.org/10.1093/jaarel/lfq079.

Orsi, Robert. 1997. "Everyday Miracles: The Study of Lived Religion." In *Lived Religion in America: Toward a History of Practice*, edited by David D. Hall, 3–21. Princeton: Princeton University Press.

–. 2005. *Between Heaven and Earth: The Religious Worlds People Make and the Scholars Who Study Them*. Princeton: Princeton University Press.

–. 2012. "Afterword: Everyday Religion and the Contemporary World: The Un-Modern, or What Was Supposed to Have Disappeared but Did Not." In *Ordinary Lives and Grand Schemes: An Anthropology of Everyday Religion*, edited by Samuli Schielke and Liza Debevec, 146–61. New York: Berghahn.

–. 2016. *History and Presence*. Cambridge: The Belknap Press of Harvard University Press.

Pandian, Anand. 2019. *A Possible Anthropology: Methods for Uneasy Times*. Durham: Duke University Press.

Patel, Roshni. 2023. "Existential Finitude in Indian Buddhist Philosophy." In *The Routledge International Handbook of Existential Human Science*, edited by Huon Wardle, Nigel Rapport, and Albert Piette, 212–22. London: Routledge.

Peterson, Jennifer. 2012. "Going to the Mulid: Street-Smart Spirituality in Egypt." In *Ordinary Lives and Grand Schemes: An Anthropology of Everyday Religion*, edited by Samuli Schielke and Liza Debevec, 113–30. New York: Berghahn.

Piette, Albert. 2015. "Existence, Minimality, and Believing." In *What Is Existential Anthropology?*, edited by Michael Jackson and Albert Piette, 178–213. New York: Berghahn.

Premawardhana, Devaka. 2012. "Transformational Tithing: Sacrifice and Reciprocity in a Neo-Pentecostal Church." *Nova Religio* 15, no. 4: 85–109. https://doi.org/10.1525/nr.2012.15.4.85.

–. 2018. *Faith in Flux: Pentecostalism and Mobility in Rural Mozambique*. Philadelphia: University of Pennsylvania Press.

–. 2020. "In Praise of Ambiguity: Everyday Christianity through the Lens of Existential Anthropology." *Journal of World Christianity* 10, no. 1: 39–43. https://doi.org/10.5325/jworlchri.10.1.0039.

–. 2023 "Faith and the Existential." In *The Routledge International Handbook of Existential Human Science*, edited by Huon Wardle, Nigel Rapport, and Albert Piette, 183–93. London: Routledge.

Ram, Kalpana, and Christopher Houston. 2015. "Introduction: Phenomenology's Methodological Invitation." In *Phenomenology in Anthropology: A Sense of Perspective*, edited by Kalpana Ram and Christopher Houston, 1–25. Bloomington: Indiana University Press.

Robbins, Joel. 2009. "Value, Structure, and the Range of Possibilities: A Response to Zigon." *Ethnos* 74, no. 2: 277–85. https://doi.org/10.1080/00141840902940500.

Roberts, Tyler. 2013. *Encountering Religion: Responsibility and Criticism after Secularism*. New York: Columbia University Press.

Sartre, Jean-Paul. 1969. "Itinerary of a Thought." *New Left Review* 58: 43–66. https://newleftreview.org/issues/i58/articles/jean-paul-sartre-itinerary -of-a-thought.

Schielke, Samuli. 2010. "Second Thoughts about the Anthropology of Islam, Or How to Make Sense of Grand Schemes in Everyday Life." *ZMO Working Papers* 2: 1–16. https://d-nb.info/1019243724/34.

–. 2015. *Egypt in the Future Tense: Hope, Frustration, and Ambivalence Before and After 2011*. Bloomington: Indiana University Press.

Schielke, Samuli, and Liza Debevec, eds. 2012a. *Ordinary Lives and Grand Schemes: An Anthropology of Everyday Religion*. New York: Berghahn.

Schielke, Samuli, and Liza Debevec. 2012b. "Introduction." In *Ordinary Lives and Grand Schemes: An Anthropology of Everyday Religion*, edited by Samuli Schielke and Liza Debevec, 1–16. New York: Berghahn Books.

Schilbrack, Kevin. 2014. *Philosophy and the Study of Religions: A Manifesto*. Chichester, West Sussex: Wiley Blackwell.

Seeman, Don. 2009. *One People, One Blood: Ethiopian-Israelis and the Return to Judaism*. New Brunswick, NJ: Rutgers University Press.

–. 2015. "Coffee and the Moral Order: Ethiopian Jews and Pentecostals against Culture." *American Ethnologist* 42, no. 4: 734–48. https://doi.org/10.1111/amet.12167.

–. 2018. "Divinity Inhabits the Social: Ethnography in a Phenomenological Key." In *Theologically Engaged Anthropology*, edited by J. Derrick Lemons, 336–54. Oxford: Oxford University Press.

Silva, Sónia. 2011. *Along an African Border: Angolan Refugees and Their Divination Baskets*. Philadelphia: University of Pennsylvania Press.

Smith, James K.A. 2017. "Staging an Encounter between Anthropology and Philosophy: Hits and Misses in the Work of Michael Jackson." *Reviews in*

Anthropology 46, no. 4: 151–63. https://doi.org/10.1080/00938157.2017
.1408394.

Smith, Wilfred Cantwell. 1963. *The Meaning and End of Religion: A New Approach to the Religious Traditions of Mankind.* New York: Macmillan.

–. 1977. *Belief and History.* Charlottesville: University Press of Virginia.

Stoller, Paul. 1997. *Sensuous Scholarship.* Philadelphia: University of Pennsylvania Press.

–. 1998. "Rationality." In *Critical Terms for Religious Studies*, edited by Mark C. Taylor, 239–55. Chicago: University of Chicago Press.

–. 2009. *The Power of the Between: An Anthropological Odyssey.* Chicago: University of Chicago Press.

van de Port, Mattijs. 2011. *Ecstatic Encounters: Bahian Candomblé and the Quest for the Really Real.* Amsterdam: Amsterdam University Press.

–. 2017. "Epilogue: Religion, Lived Religion, and the 'Authenticity' of Failure." In *Straying from the Straight Path: How Senses of Failure Invigorate Lived Religion*, edited by Daan Beekers and David Kloos, 124–32. New York: Berghahn.

Vasquez, Manuel. 2011. *More than Belief: A Materialist Theory of Religion.* New York: Oxford University Press.

Weber, Max. 1958. *The Protestant Ethic and the Spirit of Capitalism.* Translated by Talcott Parsons. New York: Scribner.

Wardle, Huon. 2023. "Anthropology as an Existential Inquiry." In *The Routledge International Handbook of Existential Human Science*, edited by Huon Wardle, Nigel Rapport, and Albert Piette, 36–49. London: Routledge.

Wikan, Unni. 1991. "Toward an Experience-Near Anthropology." *Cultural Anthropology* 6, no. 3: 285–306. https://doi.org/10.1525/can
.1991.6.3.02a00020.

Willen, Sarah S. 2019. *Fighting for Dignity: Migrant Lives at Israel's Margins.* Philadelphia: University of Pennsylvania Press.

Wrathall, Mark A., and Hubert L. Dreyfus. 2009. "A Brief Introduction to Phenomenology and Existentialism." In *A Companion to Phenomenology and Existentialism*, edited by Hubert L. Dreyfus and Mark A. Wrathall, 1–6. Malden, MA: Wiley-Blackwell.

Zigon, Jarrett. 2009. "Phenomenological Anthropology and Morality: A Response to Joel Robbins." *Ethnos* 74, no. 2: 286–8. https://doi.org
/10.1080/00141840902940518.

1 Existential Anthropology and Religious Studies: A Personal Account

MICHAEL JACKSON

If by a religion you mean a single coherent set of doctrines, precepts, and practices, then none of the familiar global religions – nor any of the local folk religions of a thousand societies around the world – would be one religion. It would, at the limit, be a plenitude of religions at every moment, new ones hatching every day.

– Kwame Anthony Appiah (2018, 41–2)

When, in January 2005, I was interviewed at Harvard Divinity School for a visiting professorship, I lacked any academic background in religious studies and had serious doubts about my suitability for the position, despite my friend Bob Orsi's assurances that my ethnographic work in West Africa and Aboriginal Australia contributed important methodological and theoretical insights for the study of lived religion.

Accordingly, I focused my job talk on a single incident from my fieldwork among the Warlpiri of Central Australia, and began with a description of how, following heavy rain in the desert, a gasoline tanker, heading to a remote gold mine, got bogged down on a dirt road. After radio calls for help, the mining company dispatched a grader to haul the tanker out of the mire and create a detour. In doing so a desert walnut tree was knocked over and destroyed – a tree which stood on an important Warlpiri Dreaming track where, according to mythological accounts, an ancestor-hero, Yunkuyirrarnu, and other initiated men camped with their wives and several uninitiated boys during an epochal journey from the north. Because I had firsthand ethnographic knowledge of this locality, I was contracted by an Aboriginal organization to investigate the mishap and find out if the "owners" of the site wanted to seek compensation for damages in a court of law.

36   Michael Jackson

Once word got around that I was investigating the destruction of the site, I had only to mention "that *watiya*" (that tree), and faces would darken with sorrow and anger. Billy Japaljarri, an eccentric individual at the best of times, looked at me as if I were *warungka* (socially inept), and should not need to ask. "We all sad for that *watiya*," he said. "Everyone is full of anger and sorrow, specially the *kirda* and *kurdungurlu*" – those who were patrilineally and matrilineally related to it. "The tree was *tarruku*" (sacred), Wilson Japangardi said. It was not really a tree, but the life essence – the *pirlirrpa* – of a person. The tree was the *yuwirn-ngi*, or Dreaming spirit, of Yunkuyirrarnu. "Everyone was grieving for that old man," Wilson said. Later, I talked to Clancy Japaljarri, who bore the same name as the Dreaming-hero. "If you spoil a Dreaming-place," Clancy explained, "you destroy the people that belong to that Dreaming-place." His argument was that the loss of the life (*pirlirrpa*) of the tree entailed a corresponding loss of life among those who called the tree "father." Both the tree and those who held this patrimony in trust shared the same Dreaming essence. This was why the "fathers" of the damaged site were so worried. They felt that someone would sicken and die now that the tree was dead. Their anxiety was compounded by a suspicion that perhaps they had not done everything in their power to safeguard the site. The words they used conveyed emotions of feeling sick in the stomach and filled with a sense of inner worthlessness. Indeed, the remorse went so deep that there had been talk of people singing themselves to death.

Clancy kept using the word *wajawaja-mani*, which suggested not only the loss of the tree but the loss of a link to the past. "We feel the same way when a person passes away," Clancy said dolefully. "We pity that person, we feel great sadness for them." Clancy touched his abdomen to show me where these emotions were most deeply felt. He paused for a moment, then added: "I'm sad now. I can't show my children that tree. My father told me that Dreaming ... but I can't show it to my son."

Old Lumi Jupurrurla spoke of the Yunkuyirrarnu site as *mukanypa nyayirni* – "really sacred." It was something "money can't buy." "That proper dear one," he told me, "'im dear one." It was exactly the same way one spoke of a person who was near and dear. But this value does not consist solely in the sedimented meanings of the past at a place one thinks of as sacred; it depends on the generative activity of people in the here and now. We owe to Marx and Engels the insight that labour and begetting are both reproductive activities. In the metaphor of birth, Warlpiri recognize the same connection. Hunting and gathering, food-sharing, initiation and marriage, bearing and rearing children, these are all expressions of a mode of activity which is at once social and visceral – the activity of bringing life into being and sustaining it. The Warlpiri metaphor for this life-sustaining activity is of "growing up." To "grow up" (*wiri jarrimi*) implies a process of nourishing and strengthening. The metaphor holds good for rituals of increase, the activity of making boys into men, raising children, and upholding the Law.

The "sacred" is synonymous with this generative power. For Warlpiri, the value of any site is given to it cumulatively through the vital and concentrated activity of those who hold that place in their care. This implies social value, since caring for a site or performing ceremony at the site involves creating and affirming relationships among those who call the site "father" (those patrilineally related it), those who have "drunk the breast milk of that place" (those matrilineally related to it), and contemporaries and countrymen who have been bestowed honorary rights of ritual affiliation. A site thus assumes an ethical and economic value proportional to the social value placed on the networks of people who perennially perform the ritual work of reembodying and reanimating – in stories, songs, body paintings, and dancing – the inherent vitality of the place. In the absence of this activity, a site does not cease to possess value; rather, its value becomes latent. If the site is rarely visited and ceremony never performed there, this latency and silence may take on negative connotations. The site may be seen as the haunt of ghosts, an object of sorrow and loss, a subject of fear. In other words, the intersubjective relation between people and country loses its vitality in the same way that country becomes lifeless if the spinifex grass is not periodically burned, a body wastes away through lack of activity, or the bonds of kinship fall into abeyance when people lose touch with one another, or the deceased become dangerous shades.

But perhaps the most compelling insights Warlpiri informants gave me concerned the existential ground of their feelings for the destroyed site. Displays of grief over the destroyed site were a way of bringing home to me not only the *social* value invested in the site but also the existential loss people had suffered in having their voices ignored, their land trampled on, their views unrecognized, and their pleas dismissed.

How could people make good their loss? I asked.

On this question, Clancy was adamant. Miming the stabbing action of a spear, he made as if to eviscerate himself. Just as the belly (*miyalu*) was the seat of a person's life-force, so a sacred site was the *miyalu* of the land where the life-force of a people was concentrated. The whitefella who had disembowelled the sacred site should suffer in kind, paying for his error with his own life. That was the Law.

38   Michael Jackson

More realistically, Old Jangala said, "We got to hurt those whitefellas, so they're more careful in future. We got to make them pay."

"We say money is the whitefella Dreaming," Clancy explained. "They make a lot of money, they want a lot of money, so if they have to fork out money, that teaches them a lesson."

"How much are you asking them to pay?"

Clancy named a sum. Given everything that he had told me, it seemed a paltry amount.

But neither blood vengeance nor financial compensation were the real issue, which became very clear when I spoke to the older men at an initiation camp a few days after they had performed ceremony at the site in the presence of the white miners, showing them rarely seen "sacred" objects in an attempt to impress upon them the seriousness of what had happened.

Interrupting the card game that was going on, I asked if the miners had understood what was revealed to them.

"Those *kardiya* (white people) alonga Granites, don't understand *yapa* (Aboriginal people)side," Joe Jangala said.

"Those miners have to go through *yapa* first," Frank said. "Sometimes they don't ask no one alongside them. When whites get the OK to come on, they think they are free to do what they like."

The anger cut deep. Japanangka turned from his cards. He was wearing a T-shirt in the Aboriginal colours of black, red, and yellow. His curly white hair was dirtied to rust, and the stubble on his chin was like mica. He too had taken part in the ceremony. "Did they catch that man who knocked that tree over?" he wanted to know. "Did they get 'im? What they goin' to do to him? They bin punish 'im yet?"

Pepper Jupurrurla saved me from having to come up with an answer. Tossing in his cards and struggling to catch his breath, he embarked on one of his long-winded explanations of the Law. "In the old days you signalled with fire smoke if you wanted to cross other people's country. You waited until you were asked. Same if you shared in other people's ceremony. You got to be invited, you got to be asked. But in those days we couldn't stop those whitefellas. We had to be friendly, to get tobacco, matches, and tucker, so we tried to work along together. But they too strong for we."

"We got to put a stop somewhere," Joe broke in. "We know we bin robbed. Whitefellas have to wake up to themselves, to Aboriginal people. They got to work with Aboriginal people and try to make a deal with us when they're going through Aboriginal lands. Whitefellas have to go through Aboriginal people first."

Frank Jungarrayi tilted the Stetson back on his forehead. His voice was harsh and deliberate. "We gotta push im properly. We worry for that business all the time. We worry too much because they bin knock down sacred trees for us. Really worry. They got to pay up. We want that money now!"

Frank's vehemence triggered an angry chorus. The card game was over. Even Zack was awake and listening.

"This isn't bullshit," Joe rejoined. "We not just making this up."

"White people cheating us for money," Japanangka said. "Rubbish money. They gotta pay us properly."

Under this barrage, the last thing I wanted to do was play devil's advocate. But I needed to know what the men thought about the miner's mitigating plea that the destruction of the tree had been a regrettable accident.

The men listened as I stated the non-Aboriginal case. Their expressions were obdurate and unimpressed. When I had finished, Frank was first to speak. No longer belligerent, he now seemed at pains to help me grasp something that was obvious to any Warlpiri. If a "sacred" tree simply grows old and dies, that is all right, Frank said. But if a person damages or cuts down such a tree, that person must pay with his or her own life.

"But what if that person did not know the tree was 'sacred'?" I asked.

"Everyone knows!" Frank said. He reminded me that boys were taken on long initiatory journeys across the country and shown sacred places, instilled with knowledge of the Dreaming and their responsibility for the land.

"But what of whites?"

"Those whitefellas knew about the tree," Frank said.

For Frank and the other men, knowledge was something you lived. It wasn't something you bore in mind and never acted on, something to which you simply paid lip service. And it certainly wasn't something abstract, which you wrote down on a piece of paper, filed away, and then forgot. That was why there was no excuse, no extenuating circumstance, for what had been done. Indeed, the destruction of the tree suggested not ignorance of its significance but negligence, calculated indifference, and possibly malice.

How could the situation be redressed?

Archie rolled a cigarette and lit it. There would have to be payback, he said. "That tree held ceremony."

Wilson explained that people had been shamed by what had happened. *Kurnta* connotes both respect and shame. Only by taking action to exact retribution could a person lift the burden of shame from himself. That was why people were demanding compensation. The whites had acted without any regard for Warlpiri values. Warlpiri had been demeaned.

40   Michael Jackson

By paying compensation, whitefellas would demonstrate respect, and everything would be "level," "resolved," "square and square."

In the ultimate scale of things, the destruction of the tree was transitory. Damage to the bedrock had not been done. Already saplings were springing up from the ground at the site – a sign of the vital ancestral essence embedded there. Even the insult and injury people had suffered would be forgotten once compensation had been paid and whites acknowledged their mistakes. So ran the Warlpiri reasoning. But could one reconcile this reasoning with the scientific rationality invoked by politicians when justifying the nation's pursuit of what they called "the general good" or "the national interest" – a rationality they assumed to be a part of a Western cultural essence (the Protestant ethic and the spirit of Capitalism), and therefore lacking in Aborigines? Much of my anthropological writing has been an attempt to deconstruct this kind of supposed division between premodern and modern mentalities, and the epistemic cuts with which we historically and habitually distinguish them from us.

Earth and Sky

Although, my talk echoed non-Aboriginal usage by referring to "spirits" and "sacred sites," the Warlpiri words, *pirrlipa* and *miyalu* have bodily, emotional, and social connotations that the English terms fail to capture. While my interlocutors rejected the view that Dreaming sites were like holy places or pilgrimage sites, they drew a comparison with the Pool of Remembrance at the National War Memorial Museum in Canberra and road markers commemorating the travels of early white explorers in the Northern Territory. But there was a difference, for remembering was not so much a psychological process as a form of concerted physical and ritual labour in which ancestral life-essences and traces (*yirdi*) lying dormant in the womb or belly of the earth were regenerated and re-embodied by the living. In ritual performances, men and women paint their bodies with ancestral motifs, arouse ancestral essences through the rhythmic stomping of their feet on the ground, re-enact episodes from Dreaming myths, and chant ancestral song-cycles to the clacking of boomerangs. These bodily and often bloody exertions conjure images of birth and rebirth (*palka jarrimi*) and explain why ancestral or Dreaming sites are associated with the belly (*miyalu*) and with places where water and game are abundant.

In contemporary Australia, however, even the concept of the Dreaming (*jurrkulpa*) has become etherealized, reflecting a pervasive post-Enlightenment tendency to associate religious experience with subjectivity and the sublime.[1] Not only has religiosity become increasingly divorced from material, emotional, and bodily forms of life; it has become abstracted from everyday existence in the same way that rationality has become fetishized as a transcendent mode of thought.

As inwardness became synonymous with spiritual and intellectual life,[2] the importance of ritual praxis – sacrifice, possession, initiation, divination, seasonal rites, and festivals – was downplayed and Indigenous cosmologies given exaggerated significance. As Christian conceptions of religion and ritual were projected on to lifeworlds that lacked such identifications, European powers expanded their political spheres of influence throughout the Global South, invoking such contrasts as superstition versus science in order to separate "higher" from "lower" forms of sociality and mentality. Thus was created the rationale for the denigration and exploitation of so called primitive or savage peoples by allegedly more civilized ones.

I have long been convinced that if we are going to move beyond these outmoded and discriminatory typologies, we need to strike a better balance between describing our common humanity and our cultural differences.

How, I wondered, could I participate in the conversations of a divinity school that, despite its celebration of diversity, tended to privilege texts over contexts and proceed as if the complexity, fluidity, and variety of life-as-lived could be meaningfully encapsulated by such categoric terms as Muslim, Hindu, Buddhist, Jew, or Christian? As an anthropologist and humanist, I assumed that the differences *within* cultures were greater than the differences *between* them, and that, by implication, the very concept of a bounded culture, religion, or society was spurious. For me, there was a troubling similarity between the conflation of lived experience with collective representations and the racist reduction of a whole person to the colour of his or her skin. But how would my colleagues react to the application of this critique of identity thinking (glossing over individual variability in order to define entire groups or populations in terms of a single invariant trait) to religion? And how feasible would it be to bracket out the vocabulary of transcendence, spirituality, mysticism, divinity, and sacrality with which we sustain the illusion of religion's sui generis character?

Just as Robert Orsi had been responsible for my position at Harvard, so his *Between Heaven and Earth* (2005) would prove crucial to my entrée into religious studies. Combining empirical and personal accounts of how the elementary forms of religious life are neither abstract concepts, nor ideal types, nor units of meaning, but instead pivotal relationships between mother and child, father and son, or heaven and earth, Orsi shows that relationships of kinship, marriage, and friendship, or relationships between contrasted emotions (love and hate), or

42   Michael Jackson

social conditions (war and peace, hierarchy and equality) are often the grounds on which both real *and* imaginary forms of life are constructed. This defined my starting point for exploring the conditions of the possibility of what we conventionally think of as religion.

In Transit

In the months between being offered a visiting professorship at Harvard Divinity School and moving with my family from Denmark to the United States, I spent two weeks with Sierra Leonean friends in London. Still disoriented by the termination of my contract at the University of Copenhagen and the end of our life in Denmark, I was particularly sensitive to the struggles of Sierra Leonean migrants to reconcile their emotional attachments to their homeland and the exigencies of their lives in England. How did *they* cope with their transitions from a familiar to a foreign world?

Sewa Koroma wasted no time in recounting all that had befallen him since we last saw each other in Freetown two years ago, and we walked for a long time across the city from Paddington Station, where we had agreed to meet, before finally stopping on Westminster Bridge to take in the view. Tourist boats were moving up and down the river whose muddy banks had been exposed by the ebbing tide. Ahead of us lay Country Hall, where I had been interviewed for a welfare job with the homeless in the winter of 1963. A lifetime ago, it seemed, before the London Eye, the Gherkin, and the Millennium Bridge were built, before Sewa had been born. As if suddenly aware of similar anachronisms in his own life, Sewa exclaimed, "You know, Mr Michael, I am thinking that right now my brothers and cousins are all working on their farms back home in Kondembaia, working hard, but I am here in London, walking these streets, living this life here, this different life …"

When I asked Sewa which was harder, life in Kondembaia or London, he replied, "I have to be grateful to God for what he's done for me. Because I couldn't imagine me now on the farm doing that hard, hard labour. It's a blessing for me to find myself here, even though it's hard. It's better, you know …"

"Why is it better here? What makes it better?"

"Well, here, as long as you're hard-working the job is there. You just have to go out and look for it. But back home the jobs are not there."

"What's wrong with farming?"

"Well, you know farming. Overseas, the richest people are the farmers. But back home things are different; the poorest people are the

Existential Anthropology and Religious Studies   43

farmers. They don't have the equipment, the things to do the farming; they make their farms with their bare hands, no machines, nothing. So that's like life and death. It's really hard back home."

Though I pressed Sewa to spell out the differences between the hardships of village life and the hardships of being a migrant, he could not. Was farming *really* more arduous than the menial and minimally paid jobs he had been doing in London as a security guard, a cleaner, a night watchman, and a factory worker, or did the difference lie in the fact that farming condemned one to the repetition of time-old patterns while London offered the promise of new departures? One thing was sure, and this was true to a greater or lesser extent with all the Sierra Leoneans I spoke to in London: although one might rail against many things about Sierra Leone – the endemic corruption, the lack of jobs, the electricity outages and food shortages – one missed other things with a passion that could not be assuaged.

For Sewa, his efforts to create a viable life in London constantly came up against his sense of duty to family back home. As the scion of a ruling house, he wanted to honour the memory of his late father, who was a Muslim and Paramount Chief, as well as keep open the possibility that he or his son might one day assume the chieftaincy. This tension between his personal life and the life of his lineage found expression in Sewa's ambivalence about drinking alcohol. "My dad is still alive," Sewa told me. "It's just that I am not seeing him. I only see him in my dreams, like once a month or so I see him in a dream, but I know he's around me. I have a picture of him in my room. There's one thing he never wants any of his kids to do, and that is drink alcohol. When I go out and drink alcohol, as soon as I come home and step into my room and see that picture, I have to run out of the room again. I want to go and take the picture and put it away, like in my cupboard or box, but I know I have alcohol in my system so I cannot touch the picture. I have to wait for days to take that picture and put it somewhere, so I can walk into my room and not see it straight away. I know it's just a picture, but it's like it's him seeing me, what I'm doing, you know. You see, I've got all these beliefs. So when I stop drinking, I pray to him and ask him for forgiveness."

Sewa was often "seized" by homesickness. It "took hold" of him and would not let him go. He would become preoccupied by tensions within his ruling house and the lack of communication among his cousins, and he phoned many of them on his mobile every day. As soon as he had completed his studies in automotive engineering, he intended to return home and pursue a career in politics, following in his father's footsteps.

I had known Sewa's father well, and remembered how, as a small boy, Sewa was nicknamed "walking-stick" because of the way he followed

44 Michael Jackson

his father everywhere, dogging his heels, head down, concentrating on placing his feet exactly where his father placed his, literally walking in his father's footsteps.

That Sewa was sustained emotionally in exile by the "belief" he had inherited from his father (by which he meant both Islam and a sense of what in Kuranko is known as *bimba che* – ancestral legacy or birthright) was made very clear in the way he responded to my question, "Do you think of yourself as a Muslim?" "I am a Muslim. I was raised in a Muslim home. My father was a Muslim, and my mother too. And I believe in the Muslim religion because ..." Sewa hesitated, as if searching for the right word.

In what Sewa now shared with me lay the key to understanding religion, not as a systematic theology or metaphysics of existence, but as a practical coping skill.

"A lot of the time I get bad dreams," Sewa said. "The only thing that saves me when I get these bad dreams, every month or two weeks, the thing that comes up straight in my mind is *La illaha il Allah. Allahu Akbar, Allahu Akbar*, God is great, God is great. Then I am relieved of that bad dream. Because sometimes I am struggling in my dream, fighting in my dream, not able to shake it off. But that is the first thing that comes into my mind. *La illah il Allah*. I say it for a minute or so, and my fear goes and I am fine." "What kind of dreams are these?" "Mostly they are fighting dreams, people trying to stab me ..." "In England here?" "Back home. Most of the dreams I get, I find myself back home. Someone is trying to give me poisoned food, you know. Some bad dreams like that. But the one that bothers me the most is I'm fighting with people, you know. It might be like someone I know, maybe one of my brothers or cousins or friends will always appear in my dreams fighting me. That really bothers and pains me."

The Palm at the End of the Mind

When I gave my job talk at Harvard Divinity School I proposed a thought experiment that involved bracketing out conventional academic ways of framing analysis with a priori concepts like religion, ethnicity, gender, class, or culture. Such a phenomenological suspension of customary frameworks, I argued, might bring our attention back to the lived complexities, practical difficulties, and ethical quandaries that preoccupy people's everyday lives without necessarily, or only occasionally, finding expression in abstract forms of understanding. Thus, Sewa prays to Allah in his hour of need, but his turn to religion is conditional on the desperation of his situation and the depth of his attachment to his father rather than an unwavering commitment to a doctrine. Some mornings, he would fill a bowl with cold water and beg God and the ancestors to help in his family's struggle for the chieftaincy, but these appeals were made only when the situation back home seemed especially dire. I hesitated to characterize this existential mobility as opportunistic because human consciousness is always shifting as circumstances change. Thus, in Devaka Premawardhana's account of how the Makhuwa of Mozambique adopted Pentecostalism for a while only to reject it, or paid lip service to it in one context only to distance themselves from it in another, convertability is the issue, not conversion. As Premawardhana argues, this existential mobility suggests a pragmatic attitude towards belief that calls into question a widespread tendency in the academic study of both anthropology and religion to assume that a person's avowals and affiliations are reliable guides to his or her lived experience, and that a person remains fairly constant over time (Premawardhana 2018). But in the continual and strategic search for viable ways of interacting with the world all manner of material, spiritual, and social resources may be called upon, including religion, as when Sewa was oppressed by bad dreams.

An existential perspective is not only sensitive to this fluctuating and adaptable nature of consciousness and action but implies that privileging stable states, received wisdom, or institutionalized settings – a mosque, temple, church, shrine, or sacred site – may lead us to overlook the vitality and inconstancy of life-as-lived. By shifting our focus from extant texts and collective representations to questions of what Hubert Dreyfus calls skillful coping – how people in a variety of situations struggle to strike a balance between being actors and being acted upon, between competing imperatives or allegiances, between "magical" and "rational" actions, between freedom and necessity, between their singularity and their shared humanity, and between their private and public lives – an existential perspective avoids the illusion of thinking that forms of being correspond to forms of thought (Dreyfus and Wrathall 2014).

Though I had touched on these themes in earlier books, I now embarked on writing a book that I hoped would demonstrate the relevance of existential anthropology for religious studies. Drawing on my recent fieldwork in London, my mother's journals, various literary and biographical sources, and works by Talal Asad, Agehananda Bharati, Wilfrid Cantwell Smith, William James, Jacques Derrida, and Karl Jaspers, I outlined a psychodynamic approach to liminality that encompassed theological questions about the relation between the human and the extrahuman, social issues centred on relations between the familiar and the foreign, ethical questions concerning the relation between self and other, and philosophical questions regarding the relation between microcosm and macrocosm. Jaspers's concepts of the Encompassing (*das Umbreifende*) and of Limit Situations (*Grenzsituationen*), were as crucial to this project as William James's notion of "the more" that lies around us like the sea beyond the fringing reef of an atoll, evoking all that exists beyond our immediate horizons, exceeding our grasp, eluding our common knowledge, and confounding our ordinary sense of who and what we are. I would subsequently use the concept of the limitrophe to further develop this perspective, for it recognized that limit experience is potentially both destructive and creative (Jackson 2015).[3] Connoting the vital relationship in African thought between town and bush as well as the classical tension between logos and phusis, the term limitrophe conjures the life-giving potential of places, people, and powers that lie beyond the pale of our established lifeworlds, and suggests that existential vitality depends on going beyond what has been prescribed by custom, internalized as habit, or enshrined in received ideas of truth and reality.

In every society, people come up against the limits of what can be said, conceptualized, counted on, or controlled – experiences excluded from the dominant discourse, penumbral phenomena lying beyond empirical reach, resisting our attempts to tame and symbolize them in language, regions where words fail us, leaving a "remainder" that haunts us (de Certeau 1984, 61). Wallace Stevens speaks of "the palm at the end of the mind," standing "beyond thought," on "the edge of space," while a gold-feathered bird sings in the palm "without human meaning, without human feeling, a foreign song." This became, for me, the existential matrix from which religion springs but to which it cannot be reduced, for just as a tree has roots, trunk, and canopy, it would be absurd to claim that either the roots or the leaves are the sole source of life for the tree, since it is their vital relationship on which the tree's existence depends.

The Palm at the End of the Mind (2009) inaugurated a series of books that I published over the next decade, exploring the indeterminate relationship between life and thought in a variety of ethnographic and autobiographical settings.

Consider, for example, Sewa's daily "sacrifice" to his late father. It would be tempting to see in this practice traces of some premodern theology or mentality. Yet honouring one's father, and recognizing a debt to one's forebears is, despite the cultural variations in the way genealogical connections are expressed, evident in every human life. Nor should Sewa's personal struggles seem foreign to us, whether protecting his birthright or seeking to reconcile his father's strict prohibition on drinking alcohol with the drinking habits of English friends.

Existential Anthropology and Religious Studies 47

And when, at the end of a long day together, we repaired to Sewa's apartment and he donned his Kuranko gown, kicked off his trainers and slipped into his Kuranko sandals, played Sierra Leonean highlife, and cooked Sierra Leonean food, I glimpsed a strategy I would come to use in surviving the academic and social formalities of life at Harvard. I was also consolidating my view that coping is less a matter of affirming belief or conforming to custom than deploying whatever resources lie at hand for creating a life within limits, getting around obstacles rather than overcoming them, accepting contradictions rather than resolving them, and finding a way of making ends meet rather than grasping the meaning of life.

Beyond Belief

In a recent critique of the intellectualist bias in academic writing, Kwame Anthony Appiah observes that religion is not "centrally about the things we believe," and that "at the heart of religious life across space and time are matters other than creed" (Appiah 2018).[4] Ethnographic research lends strong support to this argument. Consider, for instance, Alfred Gell's celebrated study of religious vertigo among the Muria of Central India where ritual swinging not only induces trance but carries the swinger into an intimate relationship with the gods. Gell observes that the Muria are less concerned with elaborating a theodicy than with the ritual practice itself whose basic building blocks are drawn from everyday life.[5] As he puts it, "particular activities are abstracted from their routine contexts and are focused on and so to speak 'savoured'" (Gell 1980, 232). Thus, mundane acts of riding and balancing on an elephant, or inducing vertigo by whirling and swinging, become means of attaining an ecstatic state of consciousness in which one surrenders to the divine, and one's sense of self becomes at one with the gods themselves. In proceeding to explain ecstatic experience in terms of "the disruption of vestibular modulation of input-output relations in the central nervous system," Gell anticipates what is sometimes called a naturalistic approach to religious experience. Rather than extrapolate from sacred texts, our experience of supernatural phenomena is traced to neuropsychological processes, or what Justin Barrett calls "natural human perception and cognition" (Barrett 2000). These processes are phylogenetically given, and pre-exist the cultural, conceptual, and interpretative schema with which we apprehend them.

There are echoes of this view in Ann Taves's argument that religion is not a sui generis phenomenon. Rather, some of us ascribe certain inner experiences to the cultural category "religion," just as others ascribe comparable experiences to the unconscious or describe them as spiritual

48   Michael Jackson

or sublime (but not divine) (Taves 2009). We then reify the categories, as if they were as real as the experiences they supposedly mirror, or we claim that our experiences confirm the validity of the categories to which we have assigned them. For Agehananda Bharati, however, the emotional intensity and subjective authenticity of an experience does not necessarily confirm the objective reality of what is experienced. The strength of a believer's faith, a mystic's ecstasy, or an atheist's scepticism proves neither the validity nor invalidity of the ontological claims made on the basis of these experiences (Bharati 1976). Religion is therefore a manner of speaking rather than a matter of fact. This is why Hent de Vries suggests that we avoid defining religion in terms of "an irreducible realm of being called divine" or as "belief in certain articles of faith, let alone obedience to some ecclesiastical or scriptural authority." Rather, he argues, religion is a semantic strategy for signalling what lies beyond logos ("reason," "word," "rational principle") and cannot be readily thought, said, or seen (de Vries 1999, x, 5–6).[6]

John Dewey sums up this approach to what is existentially given rather than conceptually constructed, either theologically or scientifically, in these words:

> The visible is set in the invisible; and in the end what is unseen decides what happens in the seen; the tangible rests precariously upon the untouched and ungrasped. The contrast and the potential maladjustment of the immediate, the conspicuous and focal phase of things, with those indirect and hidden factors which determine the origin and career of what is present, are indestructible features of any and every experience. (1958, 43–4)

Nor is it only the encompassing world that is refractory to comprehension and control; it is also the world within, as William James noted, for "whatever it may be on the *farther* side, the 'more' with which in religious experience we feel ourselves connected is on the *hither* side of the subconscious continuation of our conscious life" (1958, 386).[7]

More recently, Devaka Premawardhana has articulated an argument against logocentricity by pointing out that it reinforces structures of social inequality in the Western world. "The most sustained meaning of *logos* in Hellenistic thought," he writes, "particularly that of Heraclitus and the Stoics, is that of a 'unity behind plurality,' the universal ordering principle and law that is as applicable to the cosmos as it is to humans." Premawardhana goes on to make a case for *loco* over *logo*, suggesting that the "*logos* (especially its associations with purity and textuality) should be balanced by the *loco*, with its accents on hybridity (*mestizaje*) and orality" (Premawardhana 2018, 401). It is precisely the possibility of the marginal Latino *loco* decentring the hegemonic Greek *logos* that will keep theology relevant in an age in which, Edward Said writes, "the huge waves of migrants, expatriates, and refugees ... have become the single most important human reality of our time the world over" (Said 2004, 47).

Worlds Within and Worlds Without

Critiquing the logocentric focus of religious studies invites us to think relationally rather than reductively, and to recognize the mutually constituting dynamic of subjective and objective realities.[8]

Whether we consider our relationship to the world without or the world within, we confront the same existential dilemma of how best to imagine and manage the gap between these seemingly antithetical domains. One of humanity's recurring strategies is to anthropomorphize inner and outer spaces, thereby making it possible to act as if the world in its entirety is governed by the same principles of exchange, reciprocity, and responsiveness that govern everyday social life. This is not to endorse Durkheim's thesis that God is a projection of society writ large. Rather, it is to argue that by assuming that the same laws hold true in both the extrahuman and human worlds, we reduce our anxieties over our ability to control and comprehend things lying beyond our ken. In imagining that remote times and places – the depths of the sea, lakes or forests, mountain heights, the heavens, or even distant planets – are peopled by wights, spirits, divinities, and other quasi-human life forms, we close the gap between the familiar and the foreign and open up the possibility of relating to all living and non-living things as if they shared some common properties. Accordingly, the relationships between inner and outer, self and other, or microcosm and macrocosm are all of a piece.

All human experience, whether deemed religious or existential, involves a dynamic relationship between concepts that appear exterior to us and sensations that seem to well up from deep within.[9] For D.W. Winnicott our task is therefore one of exploring the "intermediate area of experiencing to which inner reality and external life both contribute" (1971, 3). In so far as a general notion of religiosity or spirituality is in circulation, people will avail themselves of this notion in apprehending their inner experiences, just as some of these experiences will cause them to confirm, revise, or dismiss these notions. In short, the relation between inner and outer realities remains indeterminate since each has to some extent the power to shape how the other is interpreted. This causes considerable ambiguity over how we interpret both external and inner reality.

50   Michael Jackson

Consider for instance the painter Mark Rothko's view that art dramatizes the struggles of human existence, and though these struggles may find expression in religious texts and ancient myths they are grounded in recurring human anxieties and dilemmas "no matter in which land or what time, changing only in detail, but never in substance."[10] Ironically, Rothko falls back on a notion of religion in espousing this view.

> I'm not interested in relationships of color or forms ... I'm interested only in expressing basic human emotions – tragedy, ecstasy, doom, and so on – and the fact that lots of people break down and cry when confronted with my pictures shows that I *communicate* those basic human emotions ... The people who weep before my pictures are having the same religious experience I had when I painted them. And if you, as you say, are moved only by their color relationships, then you miss the point![11]

Rothko never defined himself as a religious painter. 'He'd always say, "I'm not a religious man"'[12] It is as if the line between art and religion is never clear cut, so one is not surprised that fourteen of Mark Rothko's paintings are displayed in an octagonal non-denominational chapel in Houston, Texas, or that there are six similar artist chapels in the South of France alone, dedicated to works of Chagall, Matisse, Cocteau, Picasso, Bonnard, and Le Corbusier. Nor should we find it odd that art galleries, like museums, are often hushed, reverential spaces in which art devotees move as in a shrine, attentive to the presence of sublime genius in the same way that respect is paid to God in a church, temple, or mosque. Indeed, a vandalized Rothko painting, finally restored and replaced among kindred works in the Tate Modern, became the focus of fervent discussion as to whether an art gallery should be allowed to become an interactional amusement arcade whose atmosphere incites irreverence or considered consecrated ground that demands that bodily functions, self-centred passions, and the trappings of mundane life be left at the door before one enters.

To repudiate monothetic conceptions of religion is also to acknowledge that religion, art, and even personhood are not coherent, internally consistent categories that hold true for everyone in exactly the same way, all the time, but are deployed as shorthand terms to mask the phenomenological diversity and multiplicity of experience. Thus in Kenneth George's illuminating account of the celebrated Indonesian painter, A.D. Pirous, the painter himself admits to a somewhat arbitrary relationship between his faith and his art. *Who* he is as an artist is both connected to and separable from *what* he is by dint of being born a Muslim in Indonesia. Speaking of his twenty-year friendship with Pirous,

George observes that "Islamic art and Islamic aesthetics are not settled matters, but arenas of intense debate, conflict, and, of course, creativity," by which he means that "Muslims ceaselessly rethink and rework their arts as they respond to the shifting currents of culture, politics, and history, and as they negotiate their varied allegiances to – and identifications with – nation, ethnicity, kin, and ideology" (2010, 11). Something of this paradox of being faithful to a tradition, whether artistic or religious, while selectively and creatively making it speak to one's particular life concerns, is also captured in Naveeda Khan's study of Islam in Pakistan where people may aspire to and espouse religious and national ideals though no "clear, consistent relation to Islam" or the state exists (2012, 5).

In my 2016 book, *The Work of Art*, which both echoes and expands on themes I first addressed seven years earlier in *The Palm at the End of Mind*, I argued for shifting our focus from cultural, religious, or ethnic diversity to *human* diversity, and to accept that human thought and action are never entirely reducible to the terms with which we classify, categorize, and conceptualize it.

To this end we need ethnographic methods that explore lived experience not from afar or from above, but through participation and conversation. Rather than proceed from a priori assumptions, whereby the other is seen solely from our point of view, we begin in media res, as one human being among others, seeking common ground. Hannah Arendt speaks of training the imagination to go visiting, but ethnography means training ourselves to do more than *imagine* what it is like to be in the place of another; it involves actually living with others, sharing their lives, and speaking their language in order to glimpse what matters most to them in their struggles to achieve a life worth living, for themselves and for those they love.

Accordingly, the question of religion devolves into the question of ethics, by which I mean the strategies whereby human beings struggle for viable lives between the poles of moral or politico-economic givens and personal or existential desires. In this view, individual lives are never simply instantiations of some shared identity, be it gendered, ethnic, religious, or political, but perpetually oscillating between internal and external imperatives, lived realities and collective representation, certainty and uncertainty, the face that is turned to the world and the face that is kept in the shadows, the time claimed for oneself and the time given to others. Our allegiances, affections, and attention are constantly shifting between different places, people, and possibilities. An ethical life is seldom a matter of slavish adherence to custom or belief, or of surmounting obstacles, but more a matter of how we struggle to get an edge over adversity, to get around the obstacles in our path, to live with sorrow, endure loss, and survive life's setbacks. To do justice

52   Michael Jackson

to this ethical negotiability in our relationship with life, this constant switching of moods, emotions, and thoughts in the course of everyday life, William James developed his method of radical empiricism. Rather than focus on intransitive states of mind or points of view, James emphasized the transitive, transitory, and transitional aspects of human existence, and he used the homely image of the life of a bird, alternatively resting and moving, nesting and flying, to make this point. In theorizing personhood, James took the same approach. We sometimes act and experience ourselves as singular and unique beings, sometimes as if we were identical with others, birds of a feather flocking together. Our sense of self is seldom settled for very long. We constantly shapeshift in relation to the situation in which we find ourselves, the person or persons we are with, and the notions we have internalized in the course of growing up in a particular family or society. It isn't that we are divided selves, uncommitted to any worldview, or possess multiple personalities; rather it's that we have a remarkable capacity for transitivity, and without this capacity sociality would be impossible, for to be social one has to not so much be oneself but to become the person who, in a given situation, can relate to others and to whom others can relate.

If life is constantly in flux, so too should our writing reflect this and not create the illusion of fixed forms, determinate causes, and finalized meanings. Science and religion both address the human dilemma of comprehending and controlling realms that lie beyond our immediate reach and working out ways of relating to those realms. Whether the world beyond is depicted in terms of its material, spiritual, or personal characteristics (scientifically, religiously, or anthropomorphically) may be less *existentially* significant than the trial and error that characterizes our everyday relations with it.

NOTES

1   See, e.g., Herbert Marcuse (1968).
2   In Hannah Arendt's terms, this is a shift in emphasis from the vita activa to the vita contemplativa, from the life of work and labour to the life of the mind (1958).
3   Limitrophe derives from the Latin *limes* ("boundary") and the Greek, *trophos* ("feeder") and *trephein* ("to nourish"). In its original meaning, *limitrophus* designated lands that provided food for troops defending an outpost of Empire.
4   Appiah's argument is presaged in the work of Wilfred Cantwell Smith, *The Meaning and End of Religion* (1963: 37–50).

Existential Anthropology and Religious Studies   53

5 Cf. Ann Taves's approach to what she calls the "building blocks of religious experience" (Taves 2009) and Jonathan Z. Smith's search for "the bare facts of ritual" (J. Smith 1982, 1–18).
6 De Vries acknowledges his debt to Derrida's critique of a "globalatinized," Greco-Roman bias in our thinking about religion (de Vries 1998, 4, 30).
7 There are, of course, profound similarities between James's notion of "the more" and Jaspers's notion of "The Encompassing" (*das Umgreifende*) (Jaspers 1997).
8 William James noted, since "whatever it may be on the *farther* side, the 'more' with which in religious experience we feel ourselves connected is on the *hither* side the subconscious continuation of our conscious life" (1958, 386).
9 As John Dewey puts it, experience "recognizes in its primary integrity no division between act and material, subject and object, but contains them both in an unanalyzed totality" (1958, 8).
10 Cited in Polcari (1988, 34).
11 Cited in Rodman (1961, 93).
12 Cited in Breslin (1993, 484).

WORKS CITED

Appiah, Kwame Anthony. 2018. *The Ties That Bind: Rethinking Identity, Creed, Country, Color, Class, Culture*. New York: Liveright.
Arendt, Hannah. 1958. *The Human Condition*. Chicago: University of Chicago Press.
Barrett, Justin. 2000. "Exploring the Natural Foundations of Religion." *Trends in Cognitive Sciences* 4, no. 1: 29–34. https://doi.org/10.1016/S1364-6613(99)01419-9.
Bharati, Agehananda. 1976. *The Light at the Center: Context and Pretext of Modern Mysticism*. Santa Barbara: Ross-Erikson.
Breslin, James R. 1993. *Mark Rothko: A Biography*. Chicago: University of Chicago Press.
de Certeau, Michel. 1984. *The Practice of Everyday Life*. Translated by Steven Rendall. Berkeley: University of California Press.
Dewey, John. 1958. *Experience and Nature*. New York: Dover.
Dreyfus, Hubert, and Mark A. Wrathall. 2014. *Skillful Coping: Essays on the Phenomenology of Everyday Perception and Action*. London: Oxford University Press.
Gell, Alfred. 1980. "The Gods at Play: Vertigo and Possession in Muria Religion." *Man* 15, no. 2: 219–48. https://doi.org/10.2307/2801669.

George, Kenneth. 2010. *Picturing Islam: Art and Ethics in a Muslim Lifeworld*. Chichester, West Sussex: Wiley-Blackwell.

Jackson, Michael. 2009. *The Palm at the End of the Mind: Relatedness, Religiosity, and the Real*. Durham: Duke University Press.

–. 2015. *Harmattan: A Philosophical Fiction*. New York: Columbia University Press.

–. 2016. *The Work of Art: Rethinking the Elementary Forms of Religious Life*. New York: Columbia University Press.

James, William. 1958. *The Varieties of Religious Experience: A Study in Human Nature*. New York: Signet.

Jaspers, Karl. 1997. *Reason and Existenz*. Translated by William Earl. Milwaukee: Marquette University Press.

Khan, Naveeda. 2012. *Muslim Becoming: Aspiration and Skepticism in Pakistan*. Durham: Duke University Press.

Marcuse, Herbert. 1968. *Negations: Essays in Critical Theory*. London: Allen Lane.

Orsi, Robert. 2005. *Between Heaven and Earth: The Religious Worlds People Make and the Scholars Who Study Them*. Princeton, NJ: Princeton University Press.

Polcari, Stephen. 1988. "Mark Rothko: Heritage, Environment, and Tradition." *Smithsonian Studies in American Art* 2, no. 2: 32–63. https://www.jstor.org/stable/3108950.

Premawardhana, Devaka. 2004. "Between Logocentrism and *Loco*centrism: *Alambrista* Challenges to Traditional Theology." *Harvard Theological Review* 101, no. 3–4: 399–416. https://doi.org/10.1017/S0017816008001922.

–. 2018. *Faith in Flux: Pentecostalism and Mobility in Rural Mozambique*. Philadelphia: University of Pennsylvania Press.

Rodman, Selden. 1961. *Conversations with Artists*. New York: Capricorn.

Said, Edward. 2004. *Humanism and Democratic Criticism*. New York: Columbia University Press.

Smith, Jonathan Z. 1982. *Imagining Religion: From Babylon to Jonestown*. Chicago: University of Chicago Press.

Smith, Wilfred Cantwell. 1963. *The Meaning and End of Religion: A New Approach to the Religious Traditions of Mankind*. New York: Macmillan.

Taves, Ann. 2009. *Religious Experience Reconsidered: A Building Block Approach to the Study of Religion and Other Special Things*. Princeton: Princeton University Press.

de Vries, Hent. 1998. "Faith and Knowledge: The Two Sources of 'Religion' at the Limits of Reason." In *Religion*, edited by Jacques Derrida and Gianni Vattimo. Stanford: Stanford University Press.

–. 1999. *Philosophy and the Turn to Religion*. Baltimore: Johns Hopkins Press.

Winnicott, D.W. 1971. *Playing and Reality*. Harmondsworth: Penguin.

2 Eye and Mind Revisited: The Work of Art in Ethnography

PAUL STOLLER

Maurice Merleau-Ponty's brief text, *Eye and Mind*, is undisputedly one of the most influential philosophical essays of the twentieth century. In it, the great phenomenologist suggests that the work of art is a pathway to an embodied enlightenment that can enable us to practise what Michael Jackson (2016b) has called "the art of life." In this essay I intend to use Merleau-Ponty (hereafter M-P) and Jackson's ideas on embodiment, art, and religion to discuss "the art of ethnography," a slowly developed practice that in time can reveal deep-seated insights about human being-in-the-world. Using this framework, I consider how gradually developed anthropological knowledge can lead us to produce a more artful ethnography that illuminates in a powerfully accessible way the wisdom of the people that we describe in our works.

While much of M-P's philosophical writing may appear to be far removed from the concerns of ethnographic writers, I would suggest that his orientation to the phenomenal world marks a path towards social and cultural illumination – towards a more experimental and artful representation of social and cultural life. In what follows, I describe the fundamentals of M-P's approach to the phenomenal world and to art. I then focus upon how this kind of phenomenology relates to what Michael Jackson calls the work of art. In the concluding parts of the essay, I probe how an artistic gaze can help future anthropologists to negotiate with finesse the social and cultural turbulence of our contemporary world.

Eye and Mind

The key premise of M-P's *Eye and Mind* is that nature, as the artist Paul Cezanne suggested, is on the inside. To know nature, then, is to know

---

This chapter is adapted with permission from Stoller, Paul. 2023. *Wisdom from the Edge: Writing Ethnography in Turbulent Times*. Cornell University Press.

56 Paul Stoller

the texture of inner space. As M-P (1964, 22) wrote the "quality, light, colour, and depth which are there before us are there only because they awaken an echo in our body and because the body welcomes them." Such an orientation is a critique of scientific positivism. For M-P and Cezanne there is an inner reality of things that supplement the "objective" reality that scholars have extracted from their observations of the world. To operationalize this inner reality into hypotheses, formulae, and laws condemns us to a superficial apprehension of the physical and social worlds. M-P believed that the painter is our guide on the path to what he called the "there-is." The painter savours the life that resides in the inner dimensions of things. Indeed, the painter, like other artists, feels the "reverberations" that can create awareness in the eye and mind of the person who confronts the sensory splendour of the world.

M-P's writing about art is not some vague mystical journey into the unseen or the sensory unconscious. In *Eye and Mind*, he suggests that artists are our guides to the "there-is" because they open their being to the world. "Indeed, we cannot imagine how a *mind* could paint. It is by lending his body to the world that the artist changes the world into paintings" (Merleau-Ponty 1964, 16). Put another way, the act of painting is a metaphor for sensing the world from the inside. This idea is underscored by the great Swiss-born painter Paul Klee, whose lectures on art and design were published in *The Paul Klee Notebooks*. In his book *Monologue du peintre* Georges Charbonnier discussed Paul Klee with the painter Andre Marchand, who paraphrased Klee's painterly approach to the world:

> In a forest I have felt many times over that it was not I who looked at the forest. Some days I felt that the trees were looking at me. I was there, listening ... I think that the painter must be penetrated by the universe and not penetrate it ... I expect to be inwardly submerged, buried. I paint to break out. (Charbonnier 1959, cited in Merleau-Ponty 1964, 31)

Are artists alone in their inner sensibilities? M-P charts a course towards a sensuous turn in our observations and our representations of those observations. Such a turn, of course, can be applied to anthropologists and their representations. How do we make the indeterminacies of existence intelligible? How can we bring them to life? Consider Nietzsche's thoughts on scientific intelligibility. He wrote that the mission of science

> Is to make existence intelligible and thereby justified ... Socrates and his successors, down to our day, have considered all moral and sentimental

The Work of Art in Ethnography 57

accomplishments – noble deeds, compassion, self-sacrifice, heroism ...
to be ultimately derived from the dialectic of knowledge and therefore
teachable ... But science, spurred on by its energetic notions, approaches
irresistibly those outer limits where the optimism of logic must collapse ...
When the inquirer, having pushed to the circumference, realizes how logic
in that place curls about itself and bites its own tail, he is struck with a new
kind of perception, a tragic perception, which requires, to make it tolerable,
the remedy of art. ([1876] 1956, 93)

By way of Nietzsche, Cezanne, and Klee, M-P suggested that scholarly
discourse is limited. Denotation or telling has a limited capacity to describe the inner dimensions of nature or the deep recesses of the human
existence. The deep exploration of the human condition requires, for
M-P, the remedy of art (evocation or showing). He has much to say
about the power of evocation in art and in artful prose.

The words, the lines and the colours which express me come from me as
my gestures are torn from me by what I want to say, the way my gestures
are and by what I want to do ... In the art of prose, words carry the speaker
and listener into a common universe by drawing both toward a new signi-
fication through their power to designate in excess of their accepted definition. (Merleau-Ponty 1964, 139)

Merleau-Ponty (1969, 20) goes on to suggest that the "words most
charged with philosophy are not necessarily those that contain what
they say, but rather those that most energetically open upon being, because they more closely convey the life of the whole and make our habitual vibrate until they disjoin." In this way, writers – or painters, for
that matter – use what M-P calls "the indirect voice" to evoke the "brute
and wild being" of the world.

Experience and the Work of Art

We live in complex and unstable times. There are no quick-fix answers
to the political, social, and intellectual problems of the current era.
Given the multiplex whys and wherefores of contemporary life, is it
still possible to make sense of the human condition? Can we apprehend
M-P's brute and wild being? And if we can experience such a revelatory
and brute consciousness, will it deepen our sensibilities, our capacity to
understand the imponderables of living-in-the-world? Do artists and
anthropologists have a role to play in this important contemporary en-
deavour? What can M-P's *Eye and Mind* teach us about confronting the

58   Paul Stoller

darkness that has swept over contemporary social life? Can we squeeze small measures of well-being from the speedy chaos of social life? Can anthropological insight chart a path that leads to a life well-lived? In two of Michael Jackson's latest books – one on reinventing philosophical anthropology and one on the power of art in shaping the contours of social life, the anthropologist-poet explores these vexing questions with powerful perspicacity.

In *As Wide as the World Is Wise*, Jackson (2016a) elegantly explores the spaces between things – murky spaces in which human beings are always already, to borrow from Jacques Derrida, situated. These are spaces that escape brute categorization. They are spaces that are defiantly non-concrete – spaces that require the evocation of art and artful scholarship. For his epigraph, Jackson quotes Jacques Derrida.

> The logocentrism of Greek metaphysics will always be haunted … by the "absolutely other" to the extent that the Logos can never englobe everything. There is always something which escapes, something different, something other and opaque which refuses to be totalized into a homogeneous identity. (Derrida 1984, 117)

In this wonderfully crafted work, Jackson is our guide to those existential spaces in which, according to Nietzsche "logic curls up and bites its own tail." These are spaces that are different and opaque. After more than forty years of fieldwork in West Africa and Australia, after a lifetime of reading, reflection, and writing about living-in-the-world, Jackson describes how his experience directed him to follow the sinuous, non-totalizing path between things – between the one and the many, between identity and difference, between ourselves and others, between the personal and the professional, between belief and experience, between being and thought, between fate and free will, between centre and periphery. *As Wide as the World Is Wise*, then, is a book that artfully explores the imaginative spaces between anthropology and philosophy. Indeed, in this rich, deep, and textured book, Jackson's erudition demonstrates with eloquence how the messy specificity that characterizes ethnography enriches our thought. Consider this thought-provoking passage:

> Are philosophy and anthropology not also ways of creating appearances – whether of order and understanding – that provide us with a sense of purchase on the elusive face of human existence? And are not philosophers and anthropologists the cousins-german of the trickster heroes who figure in all traditions? (2016a, 50)

The Work of Art in Ethnography   59

Indeed, Jackson provides a plethora of ethnographic and experiential examples that demonstrate how our anthropological and philosophical cogitations "never englobe everything," to return yet again to Derrida (1984). "There is always something that escapes." (Jackson 2016a, 117). Things are always impermanent. Our experience, feelings, thoughts are continuously evolving. Our lived reality is one that confounds everyday certainty. We are all in "the between." In life, we find ourselves in

> a perpetual oscillation between engaging with the world and seeking distance, respite, or release from it. No matter what vernacular idiom is employed to capture this oscillation – philosopher's hut, the open field, the contrast between town and bush, theological images of earth and ether, existential tensions between home and the world – the dilemma persists of how to balance and reconcile these competing imperatives, or discover how one can live with their incommensurability. (2016a, 204)

How can we live in the intellectual and experiential turbulence of "the between?" How can we bear the intellectual and existential fruits of cultivating what Keats called "negative capability," the capacity to live with incommensurability, the inchoateness of which stretches the imagination and sparks creativity?

Jackson considers these questions in another recent work, *The Work of Art* (2016b), in which he rethinks Durkheim's *The Elementary Forms of Religious Life* ([1912] 1995) from a decidedly phenomenological perspective. Drawing inspiration from the aforementioned *Eye and Mind* (1964), Jackson tacks between personal reflection and an interpretation of a varied group of artists, including the mesmerizing productions of Australian Aboriginal artists. By way of his analysis and his personal reflections, Jackson demonstrates how art is not an inert element of representation but a dynamic force that can transform life. The work of art, then, can enable us to open our being to the world, prompting writers and painters to see–think from the inside.

In the end, Jackson extends his analysis of artistic works to write about the art of life:

> The art of life is thus an art of making the world appear perennially new by what Rimbaud called *"un long, immense et raisonne dereglement de tous sens"* – an endless play of light and dark, bitter and sweet, sound and silence, hard and soft, acrid and fragrant. Against the grain of inscribed habits of thought, action, and perception, art – whether graphic, sculptural, musical, verbal, gestural or kinesic – involves a honing, a practicing, a play of our sensibilities, which bring us to a place that seems to surpass

60   Paul Stoller

the familiar, the known, the expected, surprising us, taking our breathe away, opening our eyes, transforming our understanding, and, ultimately, re-creating ourselves. (2016b, 186)

Between the lines of this book, Jackson demonstrates that art can transport us to the creative and imaginative spaces between things. He shows us how art can reshape our being-in-the-world, transforming our inner turmoil into the outward beauty of prose, poetry, drama, sculpture, and painting – works that move us.

As Wide as the World Is Wise and *The Work of Art* are works that demonstrate the power of M-P's "indirect language" as expressed through voice and style. The evocativeness of the "indirect language" connects writers and readers in profound ways. In both works, Jackson tacks between the personal and professional, between Australia and Sierra Leone, between the inner and outer dimensions of art – all to create a textual form that mirrors his central message: that in life we find ourselves in "a perpetual oscillation between engaging with the world and seeking distance, respite, or release from it" (2016a, 204).

There are passages in these books that sometimes "take our breath away," that give us a sense of existential renewal. There are passages that are "as wide as the world is wise." In the end, the rich texture of these books underscores the wisdom of Songhay elders who have always advised patience on the path of knowledge. If you are patient, they liked to tell me, your path will open, and you'll be able to meet your greatest obligation: to pass on what you've learned to the next generation.

The Art of Ethnography

Can anthropologists, most of whom have conducted extensive ethnographic research, follow the partially obscured tracks through the deserts of academic discourse and find illumination? Can we, following the embodied insights of M-P's *Eye and Mind* and the wisdom found in Michael Jackson's *The Work of Art*, embrace the art of ethnography? In the end, can we learn how to convey to the public our important and slowly developed insights about the human condition?

Many scholars reduce ethnography to a set of practices. Ethnographers, after all, conduct fieldwork in a variety of settings. Fieldwork consists of Malinowski's celebrated, if not conceptually flawed, notion of participant observation – "being there." Trying to observe while you participate is no easy feat. Even so thousands of ethnographers have attempted this oxymoronic method as they struggle to conduct a census, engage in informal and semi-formal interviews, or attend a ritual which they may photograph or film. In the same vein, ethnographers are supposed to record their participant-observations in fieldnotes, some purely observational, some more personal. These fieldnotes combined with field photographs and field films become the foundation for constructing a representation. In the end these ethnographic texts or films contribute to the ethnographic record. Is this not the set of procedures that we teach our graduate students?

For me, the sink or swim context of anthropological graduate study seems to be designed much like an apprenticeship in sorcery: the master initiates the journey, but the apprentice must find his or her own on the path to illumination (Stoller and Olkes 1987; Stoller 2008; Stoller 2014). In this disciplinary arena, the notion of art or the art of ethnography is little mentioned. In the institutional context of (social) science, neophytes often have little guidance about how to find their distinct voices.

Beyond the rigorous set of rules that define ethnographic research, the potential distinctiveness of ethnographic texts often gets lost in the fog of institutional expectation. The "expected" anthropological monograph should have an introduction, a review of the relevant literature, presentation of data, a discussion of the data, and a conclusion in which the work's disciplinary significance, which the author has stated in the introduction, is reaffirmed. These academic conventions of representation usually lead to the production of turgid texts of limited appeal. Given the economic privations of contemporary publishing, publishers now have a less than enthusiastic interest in publishing anthropological works. One way to change this representational dilemma is to engage in the art of ethnography, in which writers sensuously articulate dimensions of locality, language, and character. Borrowing techniques from film, poetry, and fiction, artfully inspired ethnographers can craft ethnographic descriptions such that readers come to know the dynamic idiosyncrasies of the people and place. In so doing an artful ethnography has the potential to spread slowly developed, important anthropological insights far and wide.

Space and Place in Artful Ethnography

An artful ethnography can to bring to life ethnographic spaces and places. It can give readers a sense of locality – one of the great gifts that ethnography brings to the world. How can writers use words to sensuously describe a landscape, a wall, a road, a house, or a room? For me, writers should try to describe a space or place as if it were alive – with feelings and memories. As strange as it may seem, writers should attempt to let the sights, smells, sounds, texture of a space/place dictate how to describe it. This technique borrows from Paul Klee's

62   Paul Stoller

aforementioned technique of opening his being to the forest and painting it to "break out." In this painterly style of describing ethnographic spaces, it is important to highlight salient features. It is also important to imagine what a particular room, house, tree, or pathway has witnessed. When I recently observed a majestic baobab tree, which grows next to the Institute of African Studies at the University of Ghana, Legon, I wondered what history that tree had witnessed.

Sensuously setting an ethnographic scene can captivate readers. Sensuous scene-setting is one way to compel contemporary readers to turn the page. Here are some examples in which writers evoke space and place. Consider how James Agee, author of *Now Let Us Praise Famous Men* (1941), an ethnography of life in rural Alabama during the American Depression, described a sharecropper's house:

> Every few minutes George would get up and open the door a foot or so, and it showed always the same picture; that end of the hallway mud and under water, where the planks lay flush to the ground; the opposite wall; the open kitchen; blown leaves beyond the kitchen window; a segment of the clay rear yard where rain beat on rain beat on rain beat on rain as would beat out the brains of the earth and stood in a bristling smoky grass of water a foot high. (1941, 365)

A more contemporary example of sensuous ethnographic scene setting comes from Anna Badkhen and her 2018 ethnography, *Fisherman's Blues: A West African Community at Sea.* Follow how Badkhen describes a dawn at sea near Joal, Senegal's largest "artisanal" fishing port.

> Dawn spills astern: lavender, violet, golden. Capillary waves gently scale the ocean all the way to the horizon. Winds clots low fog. The *Sakhari Souaré* glides at full throttle west-southwest, rolls over lazy six-foot swells. The shore's low skyline of baobab and eucalyptus and doum palm flashes in the light, sinks into the sea. Its bruised cumulus vanishes, too. Black against the banded east a seabird, an early riser, falls out of the fog and scoops something out of the water and banks away. The pirogue's six crew balance spreadlegged on the thwarts and on the foredeck, dig their bare soles into the slippery wood, lean into one another, watch the sea for fish. (2018, 1–2)

Here's how I attempted to sensuously set the scene for my ethnography of Songhay spirit possession, *Fusion of the Worlds* (1989):

> Clack! A sharp sound shattered the hot, dry air above Tillaberi. Another clack, followed by a roll and another clack-roll-clack, pulsed through

The Work of Art in Ethnography 63

the stagnant air. The sounds seemed to burst from the dune that over-looked the secondary school of the town of a thousand people, mostly Songhay-speaking, in the Republic of Niger.

The echoing staccato broke the sweaty boredom of a hot afternoon in the hottest town in one of the hottest countries in the world and, like a large hand, guided hearers up the dune to Adamu Jenitongo's compound to witness a possession ceremony.

The compound's three-foot millet stalk fence enclosed Adamu Jen-itongo's dwellings: four straw huts that looked like beehives. At the compound's threshold, the high-pitched whine of the monochord violin greeted me. Inside, I saw the three drummers seated under a canopy be-hind gourd drums. Although the canopy shielded them from the blister-ing Niger sun, sweat streamed down their faces. Their sleeveless tunics clung to their bodies; patches of salt had dried white on the surface of their black cotton garments. They continued their rolling beat. Seated behind them on a stool was the violinist, dressed in a red shirt that covered his knees. Despite the intensity of the heat and the noise of the crowd, his face remained expressionless as he made his instrument "cry." (1989, 1)

The sensuous description place and space, then, is a key ingredient in the recipe for an artful ethnography. In the art of ethnography it evokes the "there-is."

Dialogue in Artful Ethnography

In artful writing what can be more difficult than crafting dialogue? The distinctive way that a person speaks is a window into her or his charac-ter, motivations, and emotional states. Important as it is, artful dialogue is often absent in ethnographic texts. "Informant" talk is often relegated to the indented block texts of transcribed interviews, which usually gives no indication of the idiosyncrasies of said "informant's" talk. In addition, "informant" talk is often transformed into indirect speech, in which the "informant's" talk is summarized in the ethnographer's explicative prose (See Geertz 1988). In artful ethnography, scholars bor-row dialogue techniques from fiction and creative non-fiction writers who use them to convey important information and build character.

But is it possible to write dialogue that perfectly captures every as-pect of a person's speech? I have found that crafting dialogue is the most challenging aspect of writing both fiction and ethnography. In my experience, West Africans tend to speak to one another with a com-plex formality. Depending upon the time of day, there are multiple for-mal greetings. People often refer to one another indirectly – even in

64   Paul Stoller

the context of the speech situation. Rather than calling one another by name, West African interlocuters often refrain from mentioning names. Instead they might refer to "the man from Bonfebba," or "the spirit priestess of Mehanna," or the "cousin of the blacksmith." To a reader in the US, UK, or France such expression may seem quite stilted. When I wrote my novel, *The Sorcerer's Burden*, I tried to replicate the formality of Songhay speech, which provoked the following response from a young hotshot literary agent in New York City:

> [I've] read much of your book, and I wanted to be in touch. Fact is, I think the idea, the setting, the story here is really awesome. Really interesting and different and intense. But if I'm honest, I think there are a few problems that became big issues for me. I think Omar's tone is meticulous and perfect, but he speaks in the same way he thinks, which is dry and lacking of emotion, and then, everyone else speaks in the same way, polite and careful and it feels like there's only one voice all the way through, which is pretty hard for me. If the dialogue had more spark to it, more interactiveness and individuality, I think this book could be really, really great. I know this is just me, others might think differently, but I'll tell you – I don't write comments like this unless I think there's merit.
> So I do wish you the best of luck, Paul. (Author's Files)

Although I didn't appreciate his wet-behind-the ears arrogance, the comments convinced me to seek a middle-ground in my dialogue, which, in the end, made the novel more accessible to a broader audience of readers.

It is always good to read masterful dialogue. In what follows I present dialogue from Walter Mosely, a master of dialogue in fiction, Joshua Hammer, who presents memorable dialogue in creative non-fiction, and Ruth Behar, one of our finest ethnographers, who knows how to construct powerful dialogue.

Walter Mosley writes fabulous crime novels. His major protagonist who appears in many of his books is Easy Rawlins, an African American private detective who knows a thing or two because he's seen a thing or two. In Mosley novels the plots and characterizations are often articulated through dialogue. Here's a short example from his 2005 novel, *Cinnamon Kiss*, which features a conversation between Easy Rawlins and Cynthia Aubec:

> "Hi. My name is Ezekiel Rawlins." I held out my hand.
> A big grin came across her but somehow the mirth didn't make it to her eyes. She shook my hand.
> "How can I help you?"

The Work of Art in Ethnography   65

"I'm a private detective from down in L.A.," I said. "I've been hired to find a woman named Philomena Cargill ... by her family."

"Cinnamon," the woman said without hesitation. "Axel's friend."

"That's Axel Bowers?"

"Yes. He's my partner here."

She looked around the storefront. I did too.

"Not a very lucrative business," I speculated.

The woman laughed. It was a real laugh.

"That depends on what you see as profit, Mr. Rawlins. Axel and I are committed to helping the poor people of society get a fair shake from the legal system."

"You're both lawyers?"

"Yes," she said. "I got my degree from UCLA and Axel got his across the Bay in Berkeley. I worked for the state for a while but didn't feel very good about that. When Axel asked me to join him, I jumped at the chance."

"What's your name?" I asked.

"Oh. Excuse my manners. My name is Cynthia Aubec."

"French?"

"I was born in Canada," she said. "Montreal." (2005, 87–8)

Notice how Mosely's dialogue contains both speech and descriptive action both which lend themselves to the flow of the interaction.

The second example is a dialogue from Joshua Hammer's stunning work of creative non-fiction, *The Bad-Ass Librarians of Timbuktu* (2016), which describes how a Timbuktu guardian of his family's collection of ancient manuscripts saved those irreplaceable texts from the fires of radical Islamicists who had sacked and occupied his fabled city. Here is a conversation between Haidara, the aforementioned guardian, and some Libyan officials, representing Muammar Al Qaddafi. After looking through the manuscripts the Libyan officials wanted to buy the collection.

"We have a proposition for you," they said.

"I'm listening," Haidara replied.

"We want to buy everything we see here." They opened a briefcase, and showed Haidara stacks of bills in various currencies."

...

"Thanks, but no thanks," he told the Libyans. "You never said that you were coming here to attempt to purchase the manuscripts."

"What do you mean? We will pay you in any currency you want."

"It's not for sale."

"Why not?"

66 Paul Stoller

"Because this isn't for me. This is the heritage of Mali. It belongs to a great nation."

"But we can make you comfortable for the rest of your life."

"No," he said. (2016, 50–1)

Here again, the dialogue underscores the rhythm of a tense interaction between Haidara, the central character of the work, and the cash-carrying Libyan officials.

The third example is from Ruth Behar's classic ethnographic memoir, *The Vulnerable Observer* (1996). The conversation is between Polonia, Rufi, and Ruth Behar and takes place in rural Spain. The topic is how to shroud a cadaver.

Polonia began: "When it was my mother, we [she and her sister] shrouded her. And Junta. She died at night, at four, at three or so in the morning. We shrouded her between the three of us my sister Junta and I. Florencia [her brother-in-law] was here, too, my husband was also here, which was curious, it was fiesta—"

Rufi interrupted her to ask a generalizing question. "But how did you wash them?"

Her mother shrugged. "You wash them."

"With a towel, a sponge?"

"You wash them very well. No, nothing, it doesn't mean anything, because it is a normal body."

Rufi, playing the ethnographer, offers an explanation. "Why do you wash them, so that they will be clean when they go to heaven?" Rufi's zeal to interpret and draw conclusions – perhaps because it offers too close a mirror of me in ethnographic costume – makes me cringe in my seat.

"I don't know. These are customs."

Rufi turns to me and says: "It's folkloric, isn't it, Ruth?"

I, trying my best, intercept with a snatch of information I have picked up from an old will. "Yes, customs. Sometimes they dress them up in nun's or monk's clothes." (1996, 45)

In this short dialogue the reader not only learns something about mortuary customs in rural Spain but also about the tangled complexities of the ethnographer's subject position in the field.

Crafting Character in Artful Ethnography

A central element of any artful ethnography is that of character. All too often the people in ethnographies remain obscure. What do they look like?

The Work of Art in Ethnography 67

What physical features do they possess that distinguish them from other people? Might it be the way their faces are set in a frown, a grimace, or a grin? Is their posture particular? Do they walk rapidly with a stiff-legged gait, or do they skip or limp? Are they unsteady on their feet?

Do they have a distinctive way of speaking? Do they repeat a phrase regularly, a phrase that is a window into their state of being? When readers have read an ethnographic text, will they remember the people describe in the book? In artful ethnography sensuously descriptive words evoke the idiosyncrasies of character to create an alluring and hard-to-forget portrait. I here present brief portraits from Michael Chabon's 1995 novel, *Wonder Boys*, from Anna Badkhen's ethnography of Fulani transhumance, *Walking With Abel* (2015), and from my own work-in-progress, *African Dreamscapes*.

Here is a scene from *Wonder Boys*. Grady Tripp, a prodigy novelist, suffering from writer's block, goes to the airport to meet his famous literary agent, Terry Crabtree.

> "Tripp," said Crabtree, approaching me with his free hand extended. He reached up with both arms to embrace me and I held on to him for an extra second or two, tightly, trying to determine from the soundness of his ribs whether he loved me still. "Good to see you. How are you?"
>
> I let go of him and took a step backward. He wore the usual Crabtree expression of scorn, and his eyes were bright and hard, but he didn't look as though he were angry with me. He'd been letting his hair grow long as he got older, not, as is the case with some fashionable men in their forties, in compensation for any incipient baldness, but out of a vanity more pure and unchallengeable: he had beautiful hair, thick and chestnut-colored and falling in a flawless curtain to his shoulders. He was wearing a well-cut olive-drab belted raincoat over a handsome suit – an Italian number in a metallic silk that was green like the back of a dollar bill – a pair of woven leather loafers without socks, and round schoolboy spectacles I'd never seen before. (1995, 7–8)

In *Walking With Abel*, Anna Badkhen describes Fanta, a rural Fulani woman in Mali:

> Fanta nestled the calabashes on top of her hand and set off on the southbound path toward Wereka. She did no farewells; this was a ritual she performed every other day and it did not merit ceremony. Nor did she ease gradually into her walk. She started right out of the camp at a quick steady stride that never changed until she reached the village. It was the tempo of her last walk, and of her walks before that, and of her mother's,

68   Paul Stoller

and of all the milkmaids' past recall who had fixed their footsteps to the trail before. She simply picked it up. She would have picked up a dropped calabash that way, or a grindstone she had loaned to a neighbor.

At first Fanta walked with her right hand raised to hold the straw lids so the wind wouldn't blow them away. After a hundred paces the arm and wrist drained of blood and began to ache. She stopped and shook off her right plastic flipflop and with her toes scooped up from the ground a flat stone. She flexed the right leg at the knee and stood on her left unbending leg and without leaning, without looking, reached behind her with her right arm and picked the stone out of her foot. Neck perfectly straight the calabashes steady on her head. She had done this a thousand times before. Her bubble-printed shawl flapped against her cheek. She placed the rock on the topmost lid and let both arms fall like a marionette's armsby her sides and walked again. Around her ankles night moisture rose cold from the drying fields. Pied crows hopped in low labyrinths of manure. (2015, 49–50)

Finally, I provide a description of Amadu Zima, one of my Songhay mentors, who lived in the village of Mehanna, on the west bank of the Niger River:

One evening, like most of my evenings in Mehanna, I walked to Alfaggeh Adboulaye's study for more conversations about science, healing and religion. On the way I once again saw an old man standing by his compound door, which had been fashioned from a sheet of corrugated tin. As had been our practice, we exchanged warm greetings. This time, though, he waved for me to approach. It looked like he had once been a tall man. But age had bent him like a water-logged tree branch. Deep lines crisscrossed his square face. His eye whites, yellowed from years of exposure to dust and wind, teared with irritation. Even in that dire condition, his eyes suggested a deep kindness.

"You know I've been watching you."

"I didn't know. Watching me?"

"You've come here for many years."

"True."

"And each time you greeted me with kindness and respect."

I nodded.

"You never asked anything of me."

"True."

"I know your name, but you don't know mine."

A moment of silence filled the space between us.

"My name is Amadu Zima. I like you."

Not knowing what to say, I remained silent.

The Work of Art in Ethnography   69

"Come into my house so I can tell you my story."

The old man invited me into his compound, which was barren – not a bush or tree growing, no chickens or sheep or goats – just sand, dirt, a few scattered tin bowls, a laundry tub, and an outdoor hearth, three blackened stones, forming a pyramid on top of which sat a large cast iron pot. There was one rectangular mudbrick house for the old man's wife and daughter, who weren't there. I followed the old man into his house, a conical hut with a mudbrick base covered by a thatch roof. The hut's thick walls kept it cool. Amadu Zima slept on a metal framed single bed with a straw mattress. We sat down on a frayed palm frond mat he had unrolled in the center of the hut. Smooth and clean wadi sand made the hut floor soft and cool.

In all three examples character is constructed through physical description of faces, movements, dress, speech, and space. It is also constructed through what is said and unsaid, what is stated and what is left to the reader's imagination.

The Art of Living in the World

Whenever I visited Paris, I tried to sit in on screenings in Jean Rouch's projection room, which was above his cluttered offices on the second floor of the *Musee de L'Homme.* When young filmmakers arranged to show Rouch their unfinished films, he would routinely invite a motley assortment of people – scholars, other filmmakers, an occasional patron of the museum, and one or two students – to comment on the film-in-progress.

"But I don't know anything about film," one of the invitees once said at one of the screening sessions.

"That's good," Rouch replied. "It doesn't matter."

After the projection, Rouch, who always sat in the front row, turned around, faced his invitees, and facilitated a discussion – impassioned debate on film technicalities, sound quality, editing techniques, and post-production problems. The person who had proclaimed her ignorance of film found the film "uninspiring."

Rouch then began to ask questions that I had heard before.

"Where is the story in this film?"

"How can you fix the story?"

"What can you do so that the film connects with the audience?" (Stoller 2020)

For Jean Rouch story was always prior to theory. That is not to say that theories are not useful and important. They are. It is to say that in the world of scientific theories, given the instabilities of scientific truths, they have short shelf lives. In the wake of erstwhile theories, though, we seem to always come back to the story, the foundation of the ethnographic record, which is the anthropological gift to the world. The narratives that comprise the ethnographic record are texts and films that can, if they are well crafted, remain open to the world. As Jean Rouch well knew, stories create a bond between the filmmaker and the audience or the author and her or his readers. Through the power of evocation stories can move us to think new thoughts, construct new realities, and feel new feelings (see Bruner 1991). They are the catalyst for social change.

> Story – sacred and profane – is perhaps the main cohering force in human life. A society is composed of fractious people with different personalities, goals, and agendas. What connects us beyond our kinship ties? Story … Story is the counterforce to social disorder, the tendency of things to fall apart. Story is the center without which the rest cannot hold. (Gottschall 2013, 138)

Indeed, stories are windows through which we encounter the human condition. They demonstrate how we are all connected. That is the power of the story. That is the work of art in ethnography.

So how do you learn to craft a good story?

Why are some films and/or ethnographic texts more memorable than others?

Maurice Merleau-Ponty and Michael Jackson might say that memorable ethnographies are the ones in which the sensuous projection of image – in prose and film – compels an audience to sense the drama of social life. Stories that poetically showcase the lived and un-lived environment, that feature idiosyncratic dialogue, and that underscore the vulnerabilities of character have the capacity to create connections between authors and audiences. They have the capacity to remain "open to the world."

But in the art of ethnography, there is something more profoundly existential at play.

> Songhay elders love to recite the following proverb:
> *Kumba hinka ga charotarey numey.*
> "It takes two hands to nourish a friendship."

Indeed, the sensuous evocation of space, dialogue, and character present a necessary but not sufficient condition for crafting the kind of stories that comprise an artful ethnography. In the end, the artistic quality of ethnography devolves less from technique and more from how you live your life. Do you live in the moment? Do you walk with confidence on your path? Do you "open your ears" and listen to elders? Are you willing to enter the stressful arena of representational vulnerability? These life choices implicate ethnographers among their others and enable them to tell a good story. For me, the depth, texture and staying power of an ethnographic film or ethnographic text emerges directly from the depth of the relationships that the ethnographer has developed. No matter the sophistication of technical practice or philosophical nuance this deceptively simple principle sets the foundation for the future of an artful ethnography the insights of which chart a course for living well in the world.

It takes two hands to nourish a friendship.

WORKS CITED

Agee, James, and Walker Evans. 1941. *And Now Let Us Praise Famous Men.* New York: Houghton Mifflin.

Badkhen, Anna. 2015. *Walking with Abel.* New York: Riverhead Books.

–. 2018. *Fisherman's Blues: A West African Community at Sea.* New York: Riverhead Books.

Behar, Ruth. 1996. *The Vulnerable Observer.* Boston: Beacon Press.

Bruner, Jerome. 1991. "The Narrative Construction of Reality." *Critical Inquiry* 18, no. 1: 1–21. https://doi.org/10.1086/448619.

Chabon, Michael. 1995. *Wonder Boys.* New York: Picador.

Charbonnier, Georges. 1959. *Le monologue du peintre.* Paris: Julliard.

Derrida, Jacques. 1984. "Deconstruction of the Other. Interview with Richard Kearney." In *Dialogues with Contemporary Continental Thinkers: The Phenomenology of Heritage*, edited by Richard Kearney, 107–26. Manchester, UK: Manchester University Press.

Durkheim, Emile. (1912) 1995. *The Elementary Forms of Religious Life.* Translated by Joseph Swain. London: Allen and Unwin.

Geertz, Clifford. 1988. *Works and Lives: The Anthropologist as Author.* New York: Polity Press.

Gottschall, Jonathan. 2013. *The Storytelling Animal.* New York: Houghton-Mifflin.

Hammer, Joshua. 2016. *The Bad-Ass Librarians of Timbuktu.* New York: Simon and Schuster.

Jackson, Michael D. 2016a. *As Wide as the World Is Wise: Reinventing Philosophical Anthropology.* New York: Columbia University Press.

–. 2016b. *The Work of Art: Rethinking the Elementary Forms of Religious Life.* New York: Columbia University Press.

72   Paul Stoller

Merleau-Ponty, Maurice. 1964. *Eye and Mind (L'Oeil et l'esprit)*. Paris: Gallimard.

–. 1969. *La Prose du monde*. Paris: Gallimard.

Mosely, Walter. 2005. *Cinnamon Kiss*. New York: Little, Brown.

Nietzsche, Friedreich. (1876) 1956. *The Birth of Tragedy out of the Spirit of Music*. Translated by Francis Goffling. Garden City, NJ: Doubleday (Anchor Books).

Stoller, Paul. 1989. *Fusion of the Worlds: An Ethnography of Possession among the Songhay of Niger*. Chicago: The University of Chicago Press.

–. 2008. *The Power of the Between: An Anthropological Odyssey*. Chicago: The University of Chicago Press.

–. 2014. *Yaya's Story: The Quest for Well-Being in the World*. Chicago: University of Chicago Press.

–. 2020. "Conclusion: The World According to Rouch." In *Routledge Handbook of Ethnographic Film and Video*, edited by Phillip Vannini, 348–54. Spring.

Stoller, Paul, and Cheryl Olkes. 1987. *In Sorcery's Shadow: A Memoir of Apprenticeship among the Songhay of Niger*. Chicago: University of Chicago Press.

3 Blood, Flesh, and Emotions: An Anthropologist and Her Fieldwork in Meat-Packing Plants

KRISTY NABHAN-WARREN

Cattle

They have come here to die. While most humans in the industry say that the animals are unaware of their fate, others say that *they know*. It is the crack of dawn and they are brought in by the truckloads before the sun rises. They continue to arrive throughout the morning and early afternoon in loud trucks. They are dirty, thirsty, and tired from the journey. They have been driven here in semi-trailers and have felt the wind through the openings. They have heard the sounds on the highways and backcountry roads. The wind rustles their hair as the fast-moving trailers move towards their final destination. Once they arrive at the intake barn in rural Iowa, the hundreds of steer (male) and heifer (female) Black Angus cattle with their distinctive black tongues, will be taken out of the trailers and put into the barn. They are given water and are talked to by handlers like Scott, who says he loves cattle and can't imagine a life where he isn't taking care of them.[1]

These powerful creatures are highly prized in the cattle industry for their distinctive marbled flesh. The ones who come to this Iowa slaughterhouse have been cared for by Iowan, Nebraskan, and Wisconsinite farm families. Black Angus cattle are known for their genial temperament. Their hair is soft and thick. The truckloads that arrive at the slaughterhouse have been corn fed since they were weaned, which industry insiders say provides for the juiciest, most flavourful meat. They are expensive and priced according to market value. The steers and heifers slaughtered today will be de-hided and put into a massive cooler, where they will remain for forty-eight hours, the USDA required amount of time to allow the carcass to chill to prevent bacteria growth.

The cattle that make their way to Iowa Premium Beef (IPB) and the slaughterhouses that dot the rural Midwest and other rural parts of the country exist to feed humans. This is the core belief about animals in the protein industry, whether we are talking about chicken, turkeys, hogs, or cattle. Industry CEOs promote the belief that the animals who come to their vertically integrated farm-slaughterhouse-fabrication-distribution centres are on earth to maintain human existence. Protein industry CEOs and CFOs want to ensure that more humane methods such as knocking or stunning are used to kill the beasts, but they do not feel "sorry" that the animals are killed for human consumption because "that is what their purpose is," as Mike, the supervisor for Iowa Premium Beef's slaughter floor, also called "kill floor" and "hot side," says. At IPB in Tama, Iowa, 1,100 Black Angus steers and heifers are killed by captive bolt pistol (CBP) and processed each day.

Labour and Faith

"If it weren't for my faith in Dios y la Virgen, and my wife and kids, I would have gone to a dark place," Fernando shares over coffee in his parish basement one Sunday morning. As we sip our coffees, Fernando shakes his head as he recounts the various jobs he has worked at the nearby hog processing plant. He says that while his work at the packing plant has afforded his family a more secure economic status, his body and mind have suffered over the years. The chemicals used at the hog plant where he has worked for over twenty-five years caused a "terrible rash" on his hands, and he has suffered from sore hands and pulled muscles on a regular basis. When he assumed what proved to be a less physically demanding supervisory position, he had intense panic attacks from the stress and had to start taking a pill a day to manage his anxiety. Yet despite the physical difficulties and injuries sustained over the years, Fernando says that he takes a lot of pride that he has been able to endure hardship for his family. Yet this pride does not include a naïve embrace of the world as it is. Lest I come away from our conversations with the idea that he hoped his kids would follow in his footsteps and work at the plant, Fernando made sure to emphasize that he would "never want" his sons or daughters working in the packing plant. His lived, working class Catholicism is a practical one, informed by the realities of anti-Latino/a "build-the-wall" racism, and living in a segregated church and society. Fernando says he hopes and prays that he has suffered enough to ensure that his children and future grand-children have expanded work opportunities. As I pored through my field journals, Fernando's emphatic hopes were shared by almost every single Latino/a and refugee meat packer I had interviewed.[2] The sufferings of parents like Fernando are embodied religious pay-it-forwards, so that children and future grandchildren do not have to work in an industry of death.

Packing plants are places of dynamic, embodied intersubjectivities between humans and animals.[3] For humans to exist and to thrive, thousands of animals must die in today's global economy. For many of my interlocutors, including the mostly white CEOs and upper management team, as well as the Latino/a, Sudanese, Congolese, Vietnamese, and Burmese labourers – line workers and shift managers – religion is what keeps them from going over into the abyss of continual disorientation. Religion keeps them centred, and gives them assurance that the blood, bones, and flesh in which they are immersed daily has a purpose. Fernando, who has worked many jobs in the hog industry, gives thanks to the real, divine figures in his life for protecting him and ensuring that his children will have more options. For white managers and higher-ups at the packing plants, men like Steve Armstrong, IPB's human resources manager, the belief in "servant leadership" and having "the heart of a servant" is crucial to the success of their business.[4] Steve's religiously infused belief in serving the workers who care for and kill the animals, and the animals themselves, keeps him centred, and is echoed by other white packing plant managers I spent time with. During the course of my fieldwork in churches and meat-packing plants, the language and praxis of faith linked the majority Latino/a and African labourers to the animals they killed and butchered as it did the majority white CEOs and upper management to the Brown and Black workers and animals killed to maintain a society where animals, humans, and religious belief and praxis are intimately related.

For the remainder of this essay, I will take an experimental approach to existential anthropology by detailing my emotions and bodily sensations during my week of work at Iowa Premium Beef and my time at a Tyson hog processing plant. I will reflect on my own religio-spiritual orientations and thoughts as an anthropologist of religion. I will attempt to follow in my mentor Michael Jackson's footsteps, and will focus on my own anthropologist body in the field, my raw emotions, affect, and overall existential condition. To wit, the fieldwork for this essay and larger book project was the most difficult work I have ever done. It literally brought me to my knees in exhaustion. It humbled me.

For weeks after the fieldwork, which took place in 2017 and 2018, I was emotionally, physically, and mentally exhausted. Writing about my experiences was difficult, if not impossible, for months after. I couldn't seem to get the smell of the slaughterhouse off my body; my notebooks smelled of blood and offal, and the sounds of blades and saws haunted me. I washed my hair twice a day, attempting to rinse out the spectre

76   Kristy Nabhan-Warren

of smell, so much so that it became dry and brittle. I felt the heavy carcasses brush up against my own body, saw the beheaded torsos move along the line, and saw the black tongues propped up on racks. Black Angus cattle and hogs haunted me and continue to haunt me.

The research I conducted for this essay was for a larger book project, *Meatpacking America: How Migration, Work, and Faith Unite and Divide the Heartland* (Nabhan-Warren 2021). In the book, I allude to, but do not delve as deeply into the existential, phenomenological, or embodied challenges I encountered during and after the fieldwork. This essay has afforded me the opportunity to dig more deeply and to push myself to phenomenologically and existentially engage with the cattle and the workers, and to reckon with my own post-fieldwork existence. My goal in this essay is to engage with existential anthropologists and with what Michael Jackson calls the "shock of disorientation" that reoriented my own mind and body being-in-the-world (Jackson 1983).

Knocking Emotions

After the cattle are cleared by the USDA inspector, they are brought to the loading area that is connected to one end of the plant. This process starts at approximately 6:30 a.m. They are led, one by one, first down a ramp from the trailer and then up a ramp that leads to the holding cell. The cattle are in line and are spaced apart from each other. While the language of "slaughter" and "kill" is used on the floor and in the plant, the language of "knocking" and "stunning" is also used. Once the animal is in the cell, the walls are closed in around it so that there is a snug fit. The plant employee known as the "knocker," holds the metal CBP up to the animal's forehead and presses it into the creature's head firmly so that the metal rod inside penetrates the cattle's skull and renders it "senseless." The killing that is done here is called percussion stunning.

It smells musky, like fear. The room is dimly lit and it is warm. It smells like shit, blood, and hair. I climbed the stairs to stand on top of the small metal platform, legs shaking, where I watched as several cattle were stunned, one by one. I watched as their bodies slumped to the floor of the trolley system. Once the animal had been struck by the electricity, its 1,700-pound body fell over on the metal floor, not moving, and on its side. The trolley system then moved the heavy body up the line, as it was designed to do. According to my informants at the plant, the animal is not "technically dead" yet as the heart continues to pump the blood out of the body. Because its skull has been crushed, it supposedly feels no pain. But I found myself wondering. Did it not feel pain?

Blood, Flesh, and Emotions   77

How do we really know? The carcass literally "bleeds out," and the blood runs down the floor, squeegeed down a large drain by a kill floor worker. It will make its way to make blood meal for farmers' fertilizer. The floor is slick with blood and is a dark, blackish-red. By the time the carcass reaches the end of the slaughter room line, mere minutes later, it is technically dead. An intricate process then ensues which transforms the whole, hided body into the hairless, red and white, fat-marbled carcass that hangs by the Achilles tendon from a large hook. It is quite an engineering sight to behold to see a thousand-pound carcass hanging from the tendon, the strongest in the body. I am told by kill floor workers that the Achilles is the toughest tendon and "can take" the weight of the carcass.

I came to my research on slaughterhouses and religion in the Midwestern United States as someone with ample experience cooking and serving meat, and as someone who has known the realities of working class America. But I had never seen or experienced what it is like to be part of the supply-side of the massive US meat industry before conducting fieldwork in two Iowa packing plants. As with the majority of Americans, I had been raised to not think much about where the meat that my family consumed came from. Like most Americans, I am not from a family of farmers or producers, and my association with meat was mostly as plastic-wrapped red packages at the grocery store. Before my conversion to vegetarianism in college, I had long been part of hogs', cattle's, turkeys', and chickens' afterlives as a consumer, but I rarely stopped to think about them when they were alive.[5]

There was no getting around the brutal reality that my university and graduate education was funded in part by the slaughtered animals that I cooked and served. The afterlives of animals continued to haunt me, and my fieldwork for *Meat America* forced me to face my own complicity in an industry of death, what the veterinarian and animal behavioralist Michael Fox has called "bioconcentration camps of the agribusiness food industry" (Fox 2006, xix). Never did I anticipate that my research on religion and migration would take me into the bowels of two Iowa meat-packing plants. I felt a growing sense of urgency, a moral obligation if you will, to immerse myself within a packing plant. I had been immersed in fieldwork within rural Iowa for a few years and had been hearing story after story about work in the packing plants. My predominantly Latino/a and Central and East African interlocutors shared stories of their injuries, their mental anguish, and the difficult necessity of "getting used to" the bloody work. Most of my interlocutors said they never got used to the work and had nightmares of blood and body parts. And labourers like Scott, introduced earlier, says he "could not imagine" ever being part of the slaughter of the animals he cared for at the intake barns. While workers like Scott say they do not have nightmares, they still feel what Scott referred to as the "guilt" of being part of a business that is built on the deaths of thousands of living creatures.

Following in the footsteps of my religious studies mentor Robert Orsi, I have situated myself within the "lived religion" orientation of religious studies ethnographers – focusing on the productive as well as messy interplay of "popular" and "official" piety and praxis. As an anthropologist of religion, I have focused on the methodology of ethnographic fieldwork my entire career. I had been conducting fieldwork inside rural Iowa parishes for several years and wanted to understand what happened inside packing plants and how religion – if at all – was at work inside the slaughterhouses. One of my interlocutors, Father Joseph Sia, a rural parish priest, encouraged me to take this important ethnographic step and accompanied me to Tyson hog processing in Columbus Junction, Iowa. Father Sia helped me realize that I needed to enter into the packing plants to see, feel, and hear the quotidian realities of work that the vast majority of my interlocutors – his parishioners – performed six days, forty to fifty hours a week. Seeing, smelling, and experiencing the blood and flesh as it splattered on my own body, the hard physical labour, and the killing and processing of animals was necessary for me to grasp the precarity and hiddenness of migrants and animals in today's protein industry.

Thousands of animals are killed every day in slaughterhouses across the United States, and thousands of migrant and refugee Brown and Black workers kill, harvest, and package the meat for humans' breakfast, lunch, and dinner plates. Both the animals and workers are hidden from the public eye and are fungible commodities – replaceable bodies and parts. The technological domination of cattle, hogs, and human animals was there right in front of me. I felt sick, dizzy, and overwhelmed in a way I had never experienced during fieldwork, or any place else, before. Giant machinery roared all around me, and along with the various saws and whizzer knives, made a cacophony. The experience was at first profoundly disorienting and sensuous. It was humiliating, as I did not know where to step, what to avoid, and what to say. I was terrified, disoriented in a place I had never known before (Stoller 1997, 137). My emotions were jumbled, and I didn't know whether to scream, cry, or to say nothing at all – I experienced what the existential anthropologist Paul Stoller calls a "mixing of head and heart" (Stoller 1997, xviii). Thinking back, I mostly stared, overwhelmed, and wrote furiously in my notebook.

Years before I undertook the radically disorienting fieldwork for *Meatpacking America*, I urged ethnographers of religion to turn to their bodies as sites of knowledge as much as to their interlocutors' bodies (Nabhan-Warren 2011). My graduate work with Michael absolutely impacted what became this essay, a reflective piece on religious studies ethnographies and what a turn to embodied knowledge might mean for the discipline. In his classic essay "Knowledge of the Body," Michael Jackson cautions anthropologists against interpreting embodied experience as "symbolic," thus making what is concrete and sensuous into empty signifiers of academic-speak, cognitive, and/or linguistic meanings (1983, 328). Jackson's career has been devoted to the development of what he refers to as a "grounded and common-sense mode of analysis which lays emphasis on patterns of bodily praxis and the immediate social field and materials world" (1983, 328).

Aligning myself with Jackson and anthropologists who have followed in his footsteps, Jacksonians – those phenomenologically and existentially oriented anthropologists – I continue to maintain the firm belief that our bodies are sites of knowledge, and that we must turn to our bodies to see, feel, hear, taste in the field. Our bodies are sites of wonder and take in the world around us through feelings. We need to watch and hear others' bodies but also our own as it is a source of knowledge and what Ludwig Binswanger calls "Being-in-the-World." We must breathe in, smell, see, and hear, and trust what our senses tell us. My body in the packing plants taught me about the intertwined, intersubjective realities of humans and animals, and that the deaths of some animals mean a future for others/refugees/humans. Untangling these entanglements became one of my core missions in the book. I wanted to understand how humans who were vulnerable economically, socially, and politically reconciled their own being-in-the-world with the animals they slaughtered and processed. How did they make sense of their own existence and survival in relation to the cattle? How do they transcend the other-worldly disorientation of the packing plants and orient themselves to the world?

My fieldwork in Iowa slaughterhouses led me to ask these questions about bodies and meaning. And, because this essay is part of an edited volume on existential anthropology in honour of a dear mentor whose impact on my intellectual and personal growth cannot be measured in mere words, a core question, it seems, is: *What does it mean for existential anthropology when we take a step back and consider human animals and their relationships and intersubjectivities with non-human animals?* I wonder whether phenomenological and existential anthropologists have focused too much on humans and not enough on other animals and living creatures. Reflecting on my own research, humans have been my primary interlocutors up to now. I wonder about what might be gained when anthropologists explore intersubjectivities of human animals and non-human animals – in this case, cattle. In his "Prologue: Loneliness and Presence," the late theologian Thomas Berry writes, "The presence of other, nonhuman beings – the creatures with whom we share the planet – helps us see preoccupation with humans alone as not just debilitating, but also a betrayal of human possibility" (2006, xvii). What possibilities are missed when we focus on human animals and/or the non-human animals and not the intersubjectivities between humans and other enfleshed creatures?

As I listened to my human interlocutors talk at length about their Catholic and Protestant faith lives, their migration experiences, and their work at the plants, it became clear to me that violence and precarity were constant themes for these women and men. Maurice, a South African refugee who came to the United States with his wife and sons after winning the Diversity Lottery, says that his job as a "head dropper" at the hog plant was the job that almost broke him. He worked five ten-hour shifts a week for several months before moving on to a less physical position at the plant, but the embodied memories stay with him. Maurice recalls the pain in his hands and shoulders, along with the severed heads and the horror if the job. At work, he would put himself in a meditative mode where he would focus on his love for Jesus, his love for his wife and sons. He says that he came to believe that his job had a purpose and that the animals were there for humans. He focused on his gratefulness to the animals for providing a job and livelihood for himself and his family. By focusing on his gratitude for Jesus, his family, and the hogs whose bodies his family depended upon to live, Maurice was able to find meaning in the blood and carnage at the meat-packing plant.

Blood and Tears

One can be a steward of/over another living animal, and can acknowledge a shared kinship, but there is an assumed relationality of dominance and dependence. This anthropocentrism, which religious studies scholars such as David Haberman, Kimberley Patton, and Donovan Schaefer, along with the ethicist Paul Waldau, have committed themselves to critiquing and dismantling, places human animals over other creatures of the animal kingdom. Existential anthropologists, with our attention to the fine-grained lives of humans, and our searching inquiries into our own sense of self, community, and meaning, must look to animals and species as like us.[6] That I was emmeshed in an epistemology that placed me over non-human animals quite literally hit me in the face during my fieldwork. As I stood shoulder to shoulder with hanging carcasses, blood and fluids splattering on my notebooks, my face, and near my mouth, I experienced what Donovan Schaeffer has described as an "animality of affect" (2020). Words and thoughts were muted, and I *felt*, I *experienced*. I was enveloped in animals' bodies. Their blood was on me: the smell in my nostrils, slippery under my work boots. As Jackson has written extensively, I wasn't thinking so much as I was feeling in a challenging circumstance: "human beings, faced with nonnegotiable, overwhelming, or degrading situations, attempt to salvage some semblance of comprehension and control such that in some measure they govern their own lives, are complicit in their own fate, and not simply insignificant and impotent creatures of circumstance" (2017, 15).

What I was feeling wasn't necessarily remarkable, but it was beyond my ability to name it linguistically. I had tried to capture my thoughts in my notebook that I carried with me through the plant. That notebook is full of my observations and words that indicated what I was seeing and feeling. More eloquent words and thoughts came much later. The thinking came at night – scattershot – when I was in my motel room a couple of miles up the road from the plant. After the shift was over, I would drive from the plant to the motel, where I would stumble into my room, shower, and put on clean clothes. I placed my soiled clothes in a dirty pile and laid out my work clothes for the next morning's shift. I had a cooler full of snacks. It took me awhile to have an appetite. I forced myself to eat some fruit, crackers, and nuts. Nothing tasted good. I felt sick and was not able to articulate what I was thinking or feeling. I just felt sick. I felt guilt, remorse, sadness; "sensations and pulsations for which we do not have adequately calibrated language" (Bray and Moore 2020, 2). I had witnessed hundreds of once living, breathing animals die that week. I witnessed their deaths and their formerly alive bodies sliced, cut, and packaged. I wasn't thinking but feeling, and it was the "raw, jumpy, bullish, quivering matter of subjectivity" that ran though my animal body (Schaefer 2020, 33). Sounds of the kill floor haunted me at night, and I woke up crying. I dreamt of blood.

Months after the fieldwork, when I sat down to process the experiences and to write, I would start to cry. The smells and splatters were still on my notebook, smudged here and there, and I shuddered when I looked at them. While I had washed away the remains of blood and flesh from my body, it remained in my fieldnotes as a reminder of the fieldwork and its lessons. When the anthropologist Franz Boas wrote up his fieldnotes during his 1883 trip to the Arctic with Inuit interlocutors, he reflected on the "spot of blood" on the back of the paper that indicated the raw seal he had ingested.[7] He writes about the importance of "joining in" customs and rituals with one's interlocutors, writing, "their mouths filled with raw seal liver (the spot of blood on the back of the paper shows you how I joined in)" (Seeman 1997, 10). Joining in the culture of slaughter and situating my body amid the blood and other fluids of the kill and fabrication floors, I took home blood spattered fieldnotes, a mark of culture and my place in it.

Yet the disorientation of the fieldwork lasted. Vivid images of cattle being slaughtered, having their hides ripped and their eyes gouged out of their skulls kept me up at night. I woke up sweating and shaking. I felt sick with guilt and complicity. Why had I assumed that human lives and moreover, human interlocutors, were more important to study? Here, on the kill floors and hot and cold sides of packing plants, I saw how we human animals kill, slice, cut, and package other animals for our consumption. I observed how efficiency and detachment works. The kill floor employees I talked to all said that "you get used to it" but when I would ask them to elaborate, most admitted that "you never really get used to it." As Fernando said to me, "you just do what you have to do, but it is terrible work. It hurts your mind, body, and soul." What all of the slaughterers and fabricators told me was that you have to "get used to it" – the killing industry that is – because you have a job to do. Fathers and mothers have bills to pay and family members back home to support via remittances. Meat-packing in Iowa and the rural United States is usually the highest-paying job available to Latinos/as and refugees, but the work is brutal and most of my interlocutors say that they never really get used to the difficulty and demands of their jobs.

The jobs that those who work for slaughterhouses do is hidden from society. Today's packing pants are located not in dense urban areas as they were in the nineteenth and early twentieth centuries, but in remote, rural areas that have access to highways. As the anthropologist Alex Blanchette has recently noted in *Porkopolis*, it is rare today to see a living pig outside (2020). And, just like the animals whose lives are determined by the intensive vertical integration from insemination to death, the majority migrant and refugee workers at most meat-packing plants across the United States today are hidden from plain sight, at work and at home, out of fear. During my fieldwork, I experienced the enfleshed visibility of animals and what the anthropologist Timothy Pachirat has called the "utter invisibility of slaughter, the banal insidiousness of what hides in plain sight." In describing today's slaughterhouses, Pachirat goes on to assert, "Facing outward, this industrialized

Blood, Flesh, and Emotions 83

slaughterhouse blends seamlessly into the landscape of generic business parks ubiquitous to Everyplace, U.S.A., in the early twenty-first century" (2011, 23).

Wonder

To my great surprise, I found that my fieldwork at Iowa Premium Beef was as wondrous as much as it was disorienting. In spite of the blood, the noise, and the extreme heat and cold, and my own thirty years as a vegetarian, I felt alive on the kill floor. The smells, sounds, and sights were pungent and raw. Here, surrounded by flesh, blood, and sinew, I didn't have to prove my intellectual worth as I did in my everyday job, but I did have to learn through my senses. I had to sidestep offal and the hanging carcasses, and I had to rely more on my bodily senses than my mental intelligence. When I turned my mind off and refused to overthink, following my body and its ducking and sidestepping, I was in greater sync with the rhythms of the plant. This reorientation of my body-mind and senses was somewhat thrilling. I bobbed and weaved through and around the hanging carcasses, careful to avoid being hit in the side or in the face. Quoting the phenomenologist Maurice Merleau-Ponty, Jackson notes, "my body has its world, or understands its world, without having to make use of 'symbolic' or 'objectifying' function." My awakened senses were neither symbols/symbolic nor semantic/semiotics – the meaning was in my body's doing (Jackson 1996, 30). I learned to close my mouth when the mists of water sprayed around me, lest animal fluids enter my mouth.[8] My body had yet to grow accustomed to "habits instilled within a shared environment" (Jackson 1983, 334). I was in a new space and my body and mind were adjusting to the disorientation. Yet accompanying the radical disorientation of environment was a freeing sense of my body in motion. As the existential anthropologist Paul Stoller has written, "The most important and difficult lesson that a sensuous scholarship provides is that of humility. No matter how learned we may become, no matter how deeply we have mastered a subject, the world, for the sensuous scholar, remains a wondrous place that stirs the imagination and sparks creativity" (Stoller 1997, 136).

The plant was a wondrous place. My nose, eyes, and ears were my teachers. I was acutely aware of my senses. Inside the plant, the clear lines of communication and lack of pretention at IPB was refreshing. I knew what was expected of me, I was treated with respect, and my conversations with women and men in a variety of positions at the plant were candid. I was even told that I had a job there if I wanted it – if I got tired of the academic grind. In some ways, I'll be honest, it was an intriguing offer. At risk of romanticizing the work and the place, the lines of communication seemed clear – you work hard but clock out and go home at the end of the day. Slaughterhouse work is in sharp contrast to the otherwise sedentary and privileged life of a white academic. Work is hard, dangerous, and intense, but it is over at the end of the day in the slaughterhouse. At the packing plants, people work to live and put their families and lives outside of work first. Unlike the work of an academic whose work upholds the reification of mind over embodiment, and in which the work of the mind is enshrined above all else, slaughterhouse work is embodied. Yet not to romanticize – it is also dangerous, dirty work that harms workers' bodies and kills non-human animals' bodies.

During a shift at the packing plant, White, Latino/a, and African refugee supervisors walk back and forth on the line, making sure their charges are doing quality work. Their work is hidden and unknown to the vast majority of us. I watched as the kill floor employees' chiselled arms sawed through the hogs and the cattle. I saw the deft movements of the all-female trimmers, who expertly trim fat away from the valuable flesh. I watched, entranced, at the highly skilled work that Pachirat describes as a labour "considered morally and physically repellent by the vast majority of society … sequestered from view rather than eliminated or transformed" (2011, 11). I was watching women, men, hogs, and cattle "sequestered from view," and the intersubjectivity of the hidden human and non-human animals was palpable. The refugees and migrants who work the line at the rural packing plants I observed are considered expendable and fungible commodities just as are the hogs and cattle.

As an anthropologist at the packing plant, I was like a "new hire" but not quite – for I wasn't able to *actually* work the line for legal and insurance reasons, though I was allowed to stand alongside line workers while carefully observing, making mental notes and literal notes with my pen. By the end of my IPB workweek, my notebook was splattered with blood droplets and retained the smell of the factory for weeks after. When I opened it to go over my fieldnotes, I detected a vague scent of flesh. Dried blood darkens the pages.

It was 6:30 a.m. and I had been in the plant since 5 a.m. that morning. After I let myself in through the revolving doors with my visitor badge and walked over to the main plant building, I walked up to the third floor and met Mike in his office. After several slurps of coffee, we suited up in our white frocks, which resemble hospital scrubs tops, hairnets (plus a beard net for Mike), earplugs, and helmets. Once we reached the door that would take us "on the floor" of the plant, we sanitized our hands, dipped our boots in the requisite boot sanitizer station, and entered the "hot floor" or "hot side." As with all businesses and companies, there is an insiders' language and I had much to learn this week. The hot floor is also called the slaughter floor, the kill floor, and the harvest or harvesting floor. In the end, the truth is that a live animal has recently been killed and it is up to the one hundred and twenty women and men who work on this floor, also known as the "kill floor," to strip the beast of its hide and to prepare the carcass to be refrigerated for forty-eight hours. The offal, which includes intestines, kidneys, and other parts, will be removed here and cleaned and packaged for use. Intestines, for example, are cleaned and hand processed by workers, becoming tripe for dishes like menudo, the popular Mexican stew.

Mike took me on a tour of the hot side before the killing had begun for the day. It was clean – spotless, even. Mike showed me each aspect of the kill floor and pointed out special features such as the self-sanitizing conveyor belt that moved along primal parts of the meat, and the individual sanitizing stations where 180 degrees Fahrenheit water was in constant supply to clean the workers' hooks, knives, and hands. Processing a freshly killed animal is both a science and an art form. Hot side employees have their knives ready to perform their individual tasks, and once the hide is ripped off the body with a huge state of the art machine, known simply as the "hide ripper" machine, the tail is cut and loosened in what is called "bung dropping"; bellies are sliced open, and the viscera is removed. Organs are removed and placed on hooks; the carcass moves along on a specially designed self-sanitizing table. The USDA employees on this line wear special white boots which are designed to be worn on the table where they walk around inspecting the carcass parts.

The first thing that you hear when you enter the kill room/knocking room through the screen door is the clicking and whooshing sound of rolling metal from the trolley system moving the cattle upwards. A muffled metallic-sounding "click click click click click click." It is a lot like the sound of a rollercoaster, but softer, the clicking of metal and moving of parts working in tandem to move something towards a destination, in what I had associated with a scary if thrilling ride. The clicking is muffled in accordance with the famous animal behavioralist Terry Temple Grandin's recommendations and protocols for more humane killing of factory animals (Grandin 2020).

The cattle are taken on a ride, and one that will soon end. When I was up on the platform, mindful that my knees were slightly bent and breathing deeply through my mouth so as to not faint, I heard only the muffled moving of the hide against the metal walls around the animal's body. The smell is musky and faecal-tinged. There was no sound from the cattle, no crying, just an audible shuffling of the body. Then, in the last seconds, the animal started moving a bit more quickly ... its body told me, at least, that it *knew*. And that is when I began to cry softly, saying under my breath, "oh she knows, she *knows*." I had to sit down, overcome with emotion.

Then suddenly, it was over: the knocker "knocked" her in the centre of her forehead, and she fell over seconds later, on her side. The animal is killed by a captive bolt pistol (CBP), a pneumatic device which, as Mike, the hot side supervisor informed me, "causes the cattle to be brain-dead and senseless" so that it does not feel any pain.

The ritual knocking is instantaneous. The creature then slumps to the side and bleeds out, which is called "exsanguination." John Berger's description of slaughter in *Pig Earth* is apt. He writes: "Her legs fold and her body collapses instantaneously. When a viaduct breaks, its masonry – seen from a distance – appears to fall slowly in the valley below. The same with the wall of a building, following an explosion. But the cow came down as fast as lightning. It was not cement which held her body together, but energy" (Berger 1979, 1).

The blood comes from the hole in the animal's head and from its nose. As the now-dead animal moves along the trolley, electric shocks pulsate through the body and push whatever blood is remaining in the body outward. As Berger has written, the "fibres of meat are still quivering from the shock of slaughter, exactly as the skin of a cow's neck does in summer to dislodge the flies" (1979, 3). This killing technique was pioneered and championed by Temple Grandin, who is considered a celebrity at IPB, as many of the workers have met her personally and admire her for her knowledge and plain-spokenness about animals and humans.

The ritual of slaughter was a solemn one. Raúl and Edith, the amazingly patient and generous quality assurance supervisors who let me shadow them all day on the hot as well as cold side, brought me up the ladder to the platform to watch. Our eyes met and we all bowed our heads out of respect. I found myself whispering a soft prayer of thanks to this creature whose life was being taken to feed people. Tears rolled down my face and I felt my throat constrict out of sympathy and empathy for this creature. I prayed that whoever tasted this steer's or heifer's meat would give thanks too.

A little while later, Raúl and I talked later about watching the killing and how it affected us. He asked me if I was "ok" and I said "yeah, but it was pretty intense." We talked about our sadness for the animals who were killed for their meat. Even though Raúl has watched cattle die many times at the plant and has been part of the cattle industry for

Blood, Flesh, and Emotions   87

over twenty-five years, it is still hard for him to watch and to process. I wondered aloud if the cattle knew what was going to happen to them. He nodded and said that yes, he thinks they do know. We both looked down, contemplative. He shared a story of growing up in Jalisco, Mexico and being on his uncle's cattle ranch. "I used to be amazed because when my uncle would call each cow by name, she would run up to him. They know their names and are so smart. I have to think that they know what is happening to them when they are brought here."

The Black Angus cattle that are born and raised on small to medium-sized Midwestern farms are very well taken care of by the families and producers that raise them. When they are twenty-four months old on average, the steer and heifers are rounded up and loaded onto a truck that will deliver them to this Eastern Iowa plant. Then they are unloaded and brought to the barn outside of the plant, where they are penned, fed, and watered. An on-site USDA certified veterinarian goes though "pre-op" ritualism also known as "Ante-Mortem inspection" that ensures the animal is healthy enough to be killed for human consumption. When it is time, the cattle are brought in small groups to the receiving door and put in a trolley which wheels them up to the platform, called a "knock box," where they will be killed, or as it is referred to here, "stunned" or "knocked." The knocking continues all day long, until all 1,100 cattle that were penned that morning are killed and are on their way to processing. The now-deceased cattle move down the serpentine trolley-way, towards the next station which includes de-hiding, beheading, and de-jowling.

It is called the "hot side" and "hot floor," as well as "slaughter floor" and "kill floor," for a reason – it is *hot* in here. Damn hot. The smell is a pungent odour of hot fresh blood mixed with scalding water; steam full of this smell rises from the blend of the two elements. The recently killed, very large hanging animal carcasses are hot. The water used for cleaning and rinsing is always a USDA-mandated 180 degrees Fahrenheit, and the air is hot and moist. The human labour required is very physical, and working bodies emit a lot of heat. While the entire business of slaughtering animals and boning meat is a very bloody one, the hot room is especially bloody. The carcass is fresh and the women and men who work on the slaughter floor work amid blood for ten hours a day. It takes a certain kind of person to thrive in the environment, one who can handle a peculiar kind of intensity, massive amounts of blood, fat, and flesh in close quarters moving at rapid speeds with saws, knives, and hooks.

Hot side workers have job titles that leaves little to the imagination – jobs like "hide ripper," "head ripper," "belly ripper," "tongue ripper," "gutter," and "kidney popper." Each worker has a highly specialized job that she/he does day in and day out. And each body part is valuable – whether it is for human or non-human consumption. Livers and hearts hang suspended from large meat hooks and eventually make their way to be processed for human and animal consumption. The hearts are quite large, the size of a large papaya, and the livers are impressively large as well.

As in all packing houses, an animal is disassembled into many parts and companies like IPB strive to waste as little of the animal as possible. "We are a unique industry really, because instead of putting something together, we take it apart," said IPB's chief safety officer Sue, affectionately called "Safety Sue," by her co-workers. Indeed, what happens is a kind of bloody magic. A, 1,000–1,700-pound animal is brought to the plant, killed, and processed for consumption; it is quite a sight to behold.

Eloida, a young and vivacious young Latina in her early twenties, is the plant's main dentician. Her job is to inspect the teeth of each carcass to rule out Bovine spongiform encephalopathy (BSE), also known as mad cow disease. Cattle that are over thirty months old are more susceptible to BSE, and a telltale sign, in addition to lethargy when alive, is three front teeth on top. If three teeth are detected, the carcass is deemed unfit for human consumption and marked for incineration at the landfill. Eloida, wearing blue latex gloves, expertly and deftly swipes the inside of each carcass's mouth. After each mouth swipe, she manages to gracefully do a 180-degree turn and wash her hands off in the hot running water, ready to inspect the next head. I watch, fascinated with her grace and precision. I'm told that Eloida did not start at the plant as a dentician, but that she is "the best" and has a perfect record so far. Her job, like all jobs here on the kill floor, is hot, bloody, and invasive. For hours on end, Eloida stands and inspects the insides of carcasses' mouths for disease, and she must be efficient as well as careful. Mike says she is "one of the best" he's ever seen and that she is "a natural" at the job, much better than her predecessor. Eloida tells me that it is a tiring job, but one that helps her family out financially and that gives her more responsibility in a workplace that she has ever had before.

Intersubjectivities and Humility

I entered my fieldwork determined to gain an understanding of vulnerable humans in a bloody industry. Yet once I stepped foot inside the slaughterhouses, the smells, sounds, and sight of the cattle forced me to confront the intersubjectivities of the hogs and cattle with humans.

I became acutely aware of what Jackson calls the "complementarity of phenomenology and existentialism," and the roughness and readiness that led me to "oscillations in consciousness" that reflect changing life situations (2012, 293). As I was writing this essay and the book, *Meat America*, I closed my eyes and thought about the intake farm. I thought about the cattle grazing there, hours before they were killed. I inhaled, and wondered if they heard the muffled sounds of their fellow steers and heifers. Did they feel? Did they cry? Were they aware of their impending deaths? Raúl believes that they have this awareness, and so do I.

Reflecting on humans' understandings of non-human animals' sufferings, the alt-rock band Nirvana's lead singer-songwriter Kurt Cobain crooned, "It's ok to eat fish 'cause they don't have any feelings" (1991). At IPB, kill floor workers have internalized and rationalized the message of "they exist to feed us" and "it's ok to kill them." Yet most of my Latino/a and African interlocutors who work on the line admitted that they never really got used to the killing and felt remorse for the animals. They are the ones who do the hard labour and are surrounded by animal carcasses for their entire work shift. Unlike the predominantly white upper management, who work in Febreze-scented, air-conditioned offices and visit the line from time to time, these women and men are in the thick of the animals' afterlives and are existentially as well as phenomenologically plagued by the implications of their labour. They stay up at night wondering, much like Morrissey, the lead singer of the '80s band The Smiths, who lamented animals' deaths by factory farm in the band's 1985 song "Meat Is Murder." "Heifer whines could be human cries, closer comes the screaming knife. This beautiful creature must die. This beautiful creature must die. A death for no reason. And death for no reason is murder. And the flesh that you fancifully fry. Is not succulent, tasty, or kind" (1985).

After my time in the slaughterhouses, I understand how the livelihood of vulnerable humans in the US and global economies – refugees and the working poor – is dependent on killing other living, breathing creatures. Most importantly, the labourers feel it and see it, too. They know that their survival and ability to succeed economically is because some animals have been deemed to die, and they are part of the cycle. They wish they were not caught up in the cycle but they are and their lives depend on the animals and their afterlives. The slaughterhouse intersubjectivities are mirrored in everyday life with its maintenance of white privilege and a de facto caste system where the status of migrants and refugees is kept below that of native-born white Americans like the upper management team and academics like me. Those who last in the packing plants manage to deal with the physical and emotional pains so that they can economically provide for their families. The radical embodied and existential disorientation I experienced at the packing plants led to a reorientation of my understanding of intersubjectivities of hogs, cattle, and humans, as well as the necessity for anthropologists to enter deep into the places where our human and non-human interlocutors inhabit. It was a reminder to me that "Religious Studies ethnographers can gain a deeper appreciation of the myths, rituals, and symbols we encounter in the field if we relax our dependence on the theories we bring with us to the field and let our hands, feet, eyes, and hearts lead the way" (Nabhan-Warren 2011, 402). Yet I cannot get away from what Jackson calls the "painful paradox" of ethnographic fieldwork, in which the ethnographer enters into others' lifeworlds "without hindrance" and should "return to his or her own with such bounty" (2017, 201).

I hope that this essay has prompted the reader to consider what a more expansive existential anthropology might look like. I agree with Berry, who urged us to pay greater attention to the lifeworlds of non-human animals and living creatures as much as we focus on human animals – necessary for a more capacious understanding of the human condition. As Jackson has noted in his wide-ranging work, an existential anthropology that endeavours to understand both human and non-human conditions, is an anthropology that honours living, breathing intersubjectivities. An existential anthropology that takes seriously as nodes of epistemology emotion, embodiment, and our interwovenness with those of our interlocutors is experimental as it is one that ultimately aims for a capacious view of knowledge that is rooted in humility. Humility is a necessary check on our own importance and ego in the field and forces ethnographers to consider our own being-in the-world and why our ethnographies matter. In his recent *How Lifeworlds Work* Jackson lays emotions and existentialism bare in his conclusion, "Coda: Emotions in the Field," asserting, "Indeed, it sometimes seems that the ethnographer's professional success in life is a studied insult to those who made his success possible, a betrayal of hospitality received and a cruel confirmation that understanding makes no difference to the social divisions that separate those who have and those who have not" (2017, 201).

I think I – we – anthropologists must take Jackson's penetrating language as a challenge to the future of our academic endeavours. Is it enough for us to advance professionally and to not do something about the emotions and affects we experienced in the field? For me, the answer is no. I think that anthropologists have an ethical responsibility to our interlocutors and that we must repay their hospitality with concrete measures and in ways that they would welcome.

My fieldwork in rural Iowa and in the meat-packing plants made me wonder what the "next step" could be. What would I do with the new embodied and existential awareness and knowledge I gained from my time in the packing plants? Would I advocate for and help ensure changes in the packing industry? Would I help draft policies that would lead to better lives for migrants and better working conditions? Would I focus on individual families and assist them in ways that improved their existence? These are important questions of praxis for anthropologists to ponder, with so much at stake in the world today. For my part, in the course of the fieldwork, I have financially assisted a couple of refugee families, and given rides to and from school, music lessons, and the mall. Once the book is published, I will donate half of the proceeds to local organizations that work directly with migrants and refugees who work at the packing plants and in agriculture. I will offer to assist those agencies with my scholarly expertise should they request it. I recognize with great humility that these efforts fall short of the substantial, systemic efforts needed to improve the lives of workers and to make changes to the US and global industrial meat production. Yet I believe, moved by Jackson's ruminations and sitting with the hard truths, that we must do something and more.

NOTES

1 Scott, interview with author, Iowa Premium Beef. Tama, Iowa. January 2018.

2 The African refugees I interviewed during fieldwork that spanned 2013–18 include Congolese, Sudanese, and South African women and men.

3 In his recent and stunning ethnography *Porkopolis: American Animality, Standardized Life, & the Factory Farm* (Durham: Duke University Press, 2020), the anthropologist Alex Blanchette focuses on the inseparable lifeworlds of the hogs and humans in today's pork industry.

4 Steve Armstrong was the human resources manager at IPB during my October 2017 and January 2018 fieldwork. He has since retired.

5 I have worked in many kitchens and restaurants, as a cook, server, hostess, and caterer. From fast food restaurants in America's Rust and Sun Belts, to high end eateries in Midwestern college towns, I have prepared, cooked, and served meat. While I officially I stopped eating meat my freshman year of college, I continued to live off of animals' lives. Working at fast food and casual dining eateries such as Taco Bell and Pizza Hut helped pay for my

92 Kristy Nabhan-Warren

books and living expenses as a college student. Animals' flesh helped pay for my college expenses and helped put me through graduate school. I was aware of the contradictions of my vegetarianism (and for two years veganism) and my willingness to serve animals as food. I was a vegetarian who cleaned, roasted, and sliced turkeys at a now-defunct gourmet sandwich shop in Tempe, Arizona, in the summers during my MA program in religious studies.

6 David Haberman, in his *People Trees: Worship of Trees in Northern India* (2013) and *Loving Stones: Making the Impossible Possible in the Worship of Mount Govardhan* (2019), explores the human-extra-human intersubjectivities that are nurtured. He takes seriously humans' relationships formed with non-human living (trees) and non-human, non-living, seemingly inanimate objects (stones and mountains) and shows how an ecocentric view of life is lived and nurtured. Paul Waldau and Kimberley Patton's edited volume *A Communion of Subjects: Animals in Religion, Science, and Ethics* (2006) is an excellent examination of how animals have been thought of and treated over time. The authors take synchronic as well as diachronic perspectives, providing broad sweeps as well as focused ethnographies of animals and how humans have crafted problematic and conflictual relationships to creatures from whom they have worked hard to detach themselves existentially.

7 I thank Don Seeman for alerting me to his essay where he writes of Boas's life-changing journey to the Arctic and the significance of the blood.

8 I learned quickly as a mist of water mixed with animal fluids entered my mouth on the first day in the plant. After this experience I closed my mouth when I walked through the hot and cold sides of the plants.

WORKS CITED

Berger, John. 1979. *Pig Earth*. New York: Random House.

Berry, Thomas. 2006. "Prologue: Loneliness and Presence." In *A Communion of Subjects: Animals in Religion, Science, and Ethics*, edited by Paul Waldau and Kimberley Patton, 5–10. New York: Columbia University Press.

Blanchette, Alex. 2020. *Porkopolis: American Animality, Standardized Life, & the Factory Farm*. Durham: Duke University Press.

Bray, Karen, and Stephen D. Moore. 2020. "Introduction: Mappings and Crossings." In *Religion, Emotion, Sensation: Affect Theories and Theologies*, edited by Karen Bray and Stephen D. Moore, 1–18. New York: Fordham University Press.

Fox, Michael. 2006. "Agriculture, Livestock, and Biotechnology: Values, Profits, and Ethics." In *A Communion of Subjects: Animals in Religion, Science, and Ethics*, edited by Paul Waldau and Kimberley Patton, 556–67. New York: Columbia University Press.

Grandin, Terry Temple. 2020. "Recommended Captive Bolt Stunning Techniques for Cattle." Dr. Temple Grandin's Website. Accessed 5 January 2022, https://grandin.com/humane/cap.bolt.tips.html.

Haberman, David. 2013. *People Trees: Worship of Trees in Northern India*. Oxford: Oxford University Press.

–. 2019. *Loving Stones: Making the Impossible Possible in the Worship of Mount Govardhan*. Oxford: Oxford University Press.

Jackson, Michael. 1983. "Knowledge of the Body." *Man* 18, no. 2 (June): 327–45. https://doi.org/10.2307/2801438.

–. 1996. *Things as They Are: New Direction in Phenomenological Anthropology*. Bloomington: Indiana University Press.

–. 2012. "Afterword." In *Phenomenology in Anthropology: A Sense of Perspective*, edited by Kalpana Ram and Christopher Houston, 293–304. Bloomington: Indiana University Press.

–. 2017. *How Lifeworlds Work: Emotionality, Sociality, and the Ambiguity of Being*. Chicago: University of Chicago Press.

Nabhan-Warren, Kristy. 2011. "Embodied Research and Writing: A Case for Phenomenologically Oriented Religious Studies." *The Journal of the American Academy of Religion* 79, no. 2 (June): 378–407. https://doi.org/10.1093/jaarel/lfq079.

–. 2021. *Meat America: The Work of Faith in the Heartland*. Chapel Hill: The University of North Carolina Press.

Nirvana. 1991. "Something in the Way." *Nevermind*. DGC Records.

Pachirat, Timothy. 2011. *Every Twelve Seconds: Industrialized Slaughter and the Politics of Sight*. New Haven: Yale University Press.

Schaefer, Donovan. 2020. "The Animality of Affect." In *Religion, Emotion, Sensation: Affect Theories and Theologies*, edited by Karen Bray and Stephen D. Moore. New York: Fordham University Press.

Seeman, Don. 1997. "Anthropology and the Religious Student: Between Love and Respect." *Bekhol Derakhekha Daehu: Journal of Torah and Scholarship*, no. 4 (Winter): 5–22. https://www.academia.edu/7434498/Anthropology_and _the_Religious_Student_Between_Love_and_Respect_Rav_Kook_and _Franz_Boas_.

The Smiths. 1985. "Meat is Murder." *Meat is Murder*. Sire Records.

Stoller, Paul. 1997. *Sensuous Scholarship*. Philadelphia: The University of Pennsylvania Press.

Waldau, Paul, and Kimberley Patton, eds. 2006. *A Communion of Subjects: Animals in Religion, Science, and Ethics*. New York: Columbia University Press.

4 Recesses of the Ordinary: Michael Jackson's Reinvention of Philosophical Anthropology

TYLER ROBERTS

Introduction

One of the ethnographic sites Michael Jackson returns to repeatedly in his writings is Sierra Leone, where, off and on for many years, he has lived with and studied the Kuranko people. Jackson is fascinated by Kuranko storytelling, particularly by their stories about venturing out from the village and the *nomos* of its settled domesticity to encounter the antinomian energies of the wild (2016, 190–1). As Jackson hears them, these stories tell of and even help engender a "renewal of life," for "[i]t is only through transgressing the boundaries of custom and convention that a person can tap into the vital sources of life itself" (2016, 181). Yet, Jackson also cautions us that such vital energies are dangerous, for they can threaten the very orders that give necessary structure to the lives they energize. These stories, then, point to the necessity of negotiating the boundaries between the closed orders of home and the antinomian openness of the wild. This work in, on, and about boundaries and Jackson's appeal to the storytelling of a non-Western, Indigenous people are keys for understanding his ongoing efforts to reshape philosophical anthropology. The efforts go back at least to his 2005 *Existential Anthropology* but perhaps finds their most forceful expression in the more recent *As Wide as the World Is Wise: Reinventing Philosophical Anthropology*. Following, among other sources, Levi-Strauss's dictum that people always have been thinking equally well, Jackson criticizes what he sees as Western philosophy's tendency to distance itself from ordinary human life and to privilege concept and logical argument over storytelling, art, and ritual. Taking cues from the Kuranko and others, Jackson's goal is a philosophical anthropology "answerable to experience rather than some extra-empirical standard" such as the abstract principles, ideals, and ideas of Western philosophical traditions (2016, 10). Doing so, he shifts "our focus from logos to life and [anchors] philosophical debates in the immediate and pressing issues of everyday existence" (12).

It is worth pointing out that the Kuranko are at least in one respect like the Western philosophers Jackson criticizes: they recognize that the reality they inhabit for most of their lives – the reality of the village, structured by cultural, moral, and other categories – is not the only reality. The key difference for Jackson, though, is that much of Western philosophy and theology has been constructed on the idea that the other reality, a transcendent logos, is *more* real than what human beings experience in their daily lives. By contrast, it seems that the Kuranko do not posit the reality of the wild as any more real than the reality of the village; instead, they believe that life is found in working *between* these different realities. Following this cue, Jackson works at the boundaries between dominant and marginal strands of Western philosophy, between Western philosophy and other forms of human thought, and between concept and the non-conceptual, pursuing, in *World,* what in an earlier work he described as a "phenomenology of liminality" (2009).

Each chapter of the book explores two concepts, such as "Identity and Difference," that a reader might be tempted to understand as binary opposites. The chapters undermine this expectation by performing an "oscillation" (2016, 22) between the concepts, a deconstructive movement of thought that, like Kuranko storytelling, plays between investment in neat categories and concepts and attention to the "non-conceptual" life that underlies all thinking. This borderland work is the object of my enquiry in what follows. I affirm the general trajectory of Jackson's reinvention, particularly his efforts to direct philosophical and ethnographic attention to the "everyday" and "ordinary" of human life. But I also argue that Jackson's deployment of distinctions between the "conceptual," on the one hand, and the "non-conceptual" and "immediate" or "lived" experience, on the other sometimes obscure the complexities of the "ordinary" as a site of the mutual energizing of life and logos. I argue, further, that we can usefully work out these complexities by thinking through Jackson's work in conversation with the philosopher Stanley Cavell.

For Jackson, ethnography and anthropological interpretation have two primary tasks. First, to understand their subjects, ethnographers must attend as closely as possible to what is distinct about the ways of living, thinking, and imagining of their subjects. Ethnography, in this respect, is a matter of marking the differences between peoples. At the same time, Jackson also views ethnography as bearing witness "to the humanity of the other" (2016, 20), and so it is a matter of commonalities between human beings. Ethnography, in other words, is always bound up with tensions between difference and similarity, the particular and the general; it entails the work of comparison and translation (51). Proceeding from the conviction that anthropological translation across difference is possible, he also wants to ask: what does "their" way of living have to teach us about how "we" live and how we think? And how does a reinvented philosophical anthropology enable such learning?

Despite his criticisms of Western philosophy, Jackson does find resources for answering these questions from within Western philosophical traditions. The carnivalesque in Mikhail Bakhtin and the *elan vital* in Henri Bergson help Jackson think about the Kuranko stories about the wild energy of the bush. And in his efforts to make philosophy answerable to experience Jackson assigns prominent roles to William James, Maurice Merleau-Ponty, and Theodore Adorno. From James's radical empiricism, Jackson takes the idea that reality is found as much in the transitive as it is in the substantive: reality is not just things but also the relations between things (2016, 64). With James and Merleau-Ponty, Jackson views experience as "constantly oscillating between a mode in which we act without much conscious thought and another mode in which we consciously think about or reflect on our actions" (95). For my purposes, Adorno is the most interesting and the most problematic of Jackson's influences, for it is Adorno's effort to free ourselves from "the autarky of concepts" that guides Jackson's work at the boundary of the conceptual and non-conceptual. There is, Jackson argues, an aporia between "our lived experience and the ways that we conceptualize, narrate, and represent it" (181), an unnameable "more" shadowing all our concepts. For Jackson, the philosopher venturing to keep in mind this "more" is analogous to the Kuranko venturing out into the wild. This is interesting and productive, but I think we should examine critically Jackson's closely related claim that making philosophy "answerable to experience" means understanding that "our humanity is often compromised by moral codifications, religious dogmas, and the generalizations and abstractions of social science [and philosophy]" (19).

1. Recesses of the Ordinary

Following these philosophical pathways and taking the Kuranko as a model, Jackson urges us to resist ethnographic and philosophical tendencies to reify concepts and categories, to invest in tidy narratives, and to employ other strategies to close off thought from "lived experience." These tendencies are one reason for the traditional academic emphasis on religious and ethical principles as the route to understanding why people do what they do. Attending instead to the transitive, the non-identical, and the incessant movement of thought and life makes it possible, Jackson argues, to see more clearly how people actually think and act in the world, to see what he calls "everyday" or "ordinary" life. Most of us, he contends, don't live our lives in ways that match up with the clear, articulate demands of our religious obligations or ethical theories. This is not due to some failure on our part, but to the fact that we always are negotiating complex existential imperatives. Attending closely to how people think in their everyday efforts to find a place for themselves in the world, to survive and, to the extent possible, to achieve "well-being" (2016, 136), reveals that ordinary thought responds to these imperatives pragmatically, situationally, and in relation to others and with "wider fields of being" (2016, 3). Ordinary thought takes different forms in different contexts and not always, perhaps rarely, does it match the philosophical norms of consistency and principle. Ordinary thought is grounded in the way that "we move through life" and take on different identities or emphasize different sides of ourselves in different contexts as we respond to the demands placed on us or the possibilities that open up for us.

This is the theme of an early section of *World*, entitled "Recess of the Ordinary." There, Jackson borrows Veena Das's notion of a "descent into the ordinary" to argue that anthropologists and ethicists need to pay less attention to moral principles and systematic ethics and more to the "gritty and gruesome realities" of life and to the way people ordinarily work through them (2016, 13–14). Kant's categorical imperative or Levinas's "face," for instance, as powerful and as compelling as they might be, fail to take serious account of the "ambiguity and uncertainty" that characterizes human life and constrains responsiveness to self and other and to the surprises that life inevitably brings (2016, 18). It is important to register that here Jackson writes in both analytic and normative registers. That is, even as he sketches a particular anthropological approach to understanding how people actually live their lives, he argues for what I'd call an ethics of responsiveness. Both registers bring him to the conclusion, in this section, that it is necessary to "redeem" our tendencies to distance ourselves from the ordinary in "a return to the particular" (2016, 19). What does this mean? If, as the trajectory of this section of Jackson's book suggests, we equate this move to the particular with the "descent into the ordinary," and if we keep in mind that in this section Jackson is moving back and forth between ethnographic and normative registers, we might say two things. First, from the point of view of the ethnographer, being attentive to others in the context of their ordinary lives means not being so attached to our own conceptual categories that we fail to see the particularity of these lives and our own place in relation to them. Second, from the normative perspective, it means that "our humanity is realized" in responsiveness to the particularities of our lives and those of others and that this responsiveness depends, in part, in recognizing how "moral codifications and religious dogmas" distance us from these particularities. In short, Jackson equates attention to the particular with "freedom from the autarky of concepts" (2016, 19).

Things get more complicated, though. Jackson writes that returning to the particular entails "remembering the non-conceptual soil from which concepts spring in the first place" (2016, 19). What does this mean? The answer certainly starts with the lessons Jackson learns from the Kuranko about the bush, from James about the transitive, and from Adorno about the aporetic nature of our concepts. But then what is the relation between the particular and the ordinary, on the one hand, and the non-conceptual, on the other? Or what is the difference between freeing oneself from the *autarky* of concepts and encountering the *absence* of concept? How is it possible to identify the differences that make something "particular" without words and concepts? One way to think about these questions is to consider that Jackson is working with what he describes as the always "unresolved tension between openness and closure," which he characterizes as "universal" (2009, 10). From this perspective, freedom from the autarky of concepts might simply entail keeping in mind that no particular conceptual grid fully captures reality. Then "remembering" the limits of the conceptual would entail practising an openness that exceeds one's own particular personal and cultural principles, customs, and moral commitments.

How is such remembering related to the "ordinary"? One might argue that from both the ethnographic and the general human perspective, such remembering is anything but ordinary. That is, it requires disciplined training in ethnography or the ethical work of attention to the wild or the transitive that Jackson finds in the Kuranko, some of the migrants he works with, or in religious and other forms of transcendence. People often close themselves off from one another, fail to be responsive by falling back on rote and habitual forms of engagement. We do this routinely. It is also the case, however, that people in their ordinary lives do sometimes open themselves to one another and the world with critical and creative forms of engagement. From here, we start to see a certain doubling of the meaning of "ordinary." Early in the section "Recesses of the Ordinary," Jackson treats as ordinary the fact that people sometimes disengage from the ordinary. Jackson invokes the anthropologist Veena Das and her ethnographic attention to "the small disciplines that ordinary people perform in their everyday life"

(Das 2012, 139). Jackson writes that we should think about these "disciplines" in terms of "storytelling, ritualization, experimentation, and dialogue," as "ways of transforming one's immediate experience in order to make life more bearable and fulfilling, a way of creating models or homologues of reality that allow one to momentarily disengage from everyday situations, the better to reengage with them" (2016, 14). But of note here is that such "disengagement" seems to be less about remembering the non-conceptual than the work of "transforming one's immediate experience." Wouldn't such labour involve reflecting on or conceptually engaging one's experience? However we might answer this and other related questions, what seems clear is that in Jackson's writing the terms *everyday* and *ordinary* sometimes refer to the object of philosophical and ethnographic thought, sometimes to a particular kind of approach to such objects, sometimes to the simple facts of human life and its routines, and sometimes to a normative ideal for human life – and sometimes all or some combination of these. In what follows, I try to untangle some of this complexity by considering different ways of thinking about "disengagement" and by exploring the concept of the ordinary in the work of other anthropologists such as Das and Michael Lambek, and especially in Stanley Cavell, whose philosophical work on the ordinary informs both Lambek and Das. Jackson's criticisms of the abstraction and reifications of traditional philosophy are mostly on target, for, as Cavell will argue, they often represent a refusal of or an escape from both the routine and the richness of the ordinary. For Cavell, this marks them as forms of scepticism, which, in its broadest sense, he understands as a dissatisfaction with being human. But scepticism is not just a philosophical problem, for Cavell sees it at work in ordinary life as well. And it is here that we find crucial differences between Cavell and Jackson. For now, I will put it simply by saying that where Jackson emphasizes the non-conceptual ground of experience, Cavell stays with ordinary words and concepts. Indeed, Jackson's appeal to the non-conceptual and associated ideas such as "immediate experience," I will argue, expose a trace of scepticism in his work. But, in the end, Cavell differs from Jackson not by proposing a radically different vision of the ordinary but by bringing to it nuances that are not clearly marked in Jackson's work. This suggests that Jackson's project could be strengthened by incorporating Cavellian insights.

2. Ordinary Ethics

According to Didier Fassin, the first decades of the twenty-first century have seen a shift in anthropology from a focus on moral codes and the reproduction of moral order to "the formation of ethical subjects" and the recognition of "moral freedom" (Fassin 2012, 7–8). This entails a shift from the long-standing focus in social and cultural theory on structure, function, power, and interest to consideration of how human beings, in the midst of their lives, exercise freedom and agency in their ethical relations with themselves, others, and the world. This is a useful context for understanding a closely related shift: the turn to the "ordinary" in anthropological explorations of speech, violence, self-fashioning and, more generally, ethics. Like Jackson, anthropologists such as Veena Das, James Laidlaw, and Michael Lambek argue that although studying ethics from the perspective of principles, rules, or religious commands is not unimportant, there is much to be learned from the ways in which ethics is embedded in everyday practices of language and social engagement.

All this has meant renewed attention to ethical theorists and philosophers such as to Aristotle, Arendt, Wittgenstein, Foucault and, most important for my work here, Stanley Cavell. Cavell is central to the work of Lambek and Das. For Lambek, ethics is largely tacit, embedded in "everyday comportment and understanding," and "grounded in agreement rather than rule, in practice rather than knowledge or belief and happening without calling undue attention to itself" (Lambek 2010, 2). The word *agreement* points to Cavell's view of meaning and language as grounded in deep-seated agreements that are the conditions for words to be meaningfully said, concepts to be meaningfully applied, for us to be able to count a particular event as an instance of, say, marriage. Following Wittgenstein and Heidegger, Cavell understands these agreements as emerging from the complex, multifarious practical relationships that constitute forms of life. Ordinary language philosophy, as Cavell inherits it from Wittgenstein and Austin and which entails the close examination of "what we say when," understands our words as the site of these agreements and relationships. These "knots of agreement," as Cavell puts it, are the medium of our "attunement" with each other (Cavell 2005, 139).[1] "Words," Cavell writes, "come to us from a distance; they were there before we were; we are born into them. Meaning then is accepting that fact of their condition" (Cavell 1992, 64).

These agreements, as Lambek stresses, are implicit in the things we say and do. Thus, our sense of what to do, of the right thing to do, often is relatively obvious, and we do it routinely. But ethics is also sometimes a matter of judgment, reflection, and discernment. "Judgment," Lambek writes, "entails discerning when to follow one's commitments and when to depart from them, or how to evaluate competing or incommensurable commitments" (2010, 28). Here, again, he follows Cavell, for whom there are two primary types of situation that call for judgment. In situations of misunderstanding or ideological mystification, the "mutual attunement" that allows us to communicate and live together relatively seamlessly can become an issue. Here, the procedures of ordinary language philosophy, attending to the way we actually use our words, might help us to resolve the misunderstanding, or demystify certain uses of language. In other situations, of deep disagreement or conflict perhaps, one finds oneself out of joint with the people with whom, in most respects, one shares a form of life. This might result in changing one's life and, accordingly, one's use of certain words. So, although our ethical lives are grounded in tacit agreements and commitments, we encounter situations in which we come up against the limits of our agreements and must creatively reflect on what the situation calls for. Doing so, we may end up departing from what, at least from some established perspectives, would be understood as the "ordinary" thing to do. But such departure is also "ordinary" – we do it all the time.

It is these two intimately related yet opposed senses of "ordinary" that require our attention. How do we negotiate the move from the tacit to the explicitness and reflexivity of judgment in ethical life? In what sense is disengaging from the routine also routine, that is, still included under the concept of ordinary ethics? Above, I noted that Jackson invokes Veena Das's discussion of "the small disciplines that ordinary people perform in their everyday life." For Jackson, this points to the need for people to sometimes "momentarily disengage from everyday situations, the better to reengage with them." As I also have noted, Jackson's primary form of disengagement is to turn to the non-conceptual. Like Jackson, Das contrasts her way of thinking about ethics with those whose ethical reflections take place in the appeal to "transcendental, objectively agreed-upon values." However, rather than appealing to the non-conceptual, Das argues that ethical work is a matter of "the cultivation of sensibilities within the everyday," and, borrowing a distinction from Cavell, involves "the labor of bringing about an eventual everyday from *within* the actual everyday" (Das 2012, 134). Das works out this doubling of the everyday in her treatment of "moral striving" in a Hindu family in Delhi grappling with the challenges presented to them by a son's marriage to a Muslim woman (Das 2010). Turning briefly to this treatment will allow a more precise account of the differences between Jackson, on the one hand, and Das and Cavell, on the other.

The main figures in Das's story are the married couple, Kilpar, the son, and Saba, the daughter-in-law, as well as Kilpar's mother and Das's primary interlocutor, Leela. This family's story takes place in the midst of many decades of religious, political, and cultural tension, which sometimes flares into violence, between Hindus and Muslims in India. These tensions frequently find expression in the context of inter-religious marriage. It is a matter of "routine and habit" for Hindus and Muslims to treat such marriages with suspicion and to intervene to prevent them, make them difficult to sustain, or, failing those efforts, to cut off relations with the married couple. However, Leela's family, according to Das, works creatively at the edges of community and convention to make space for the couple and their new life together. For them, everyday life becomes a site where "the projects of state power or given scripts of normativity can be resisted" (2010, 376). Leela's family resists this script not through the application of ethical principles or rules, but in an everyday work of discovery, openness, and responsiveness, the "labor of opening oneself to a different vision of what it might be like to receive the other" (2010, 397). Not the result of a decisive appeal to moral or religious principles, this openness develops slowly, as the result of accumulated ordinary interactions and "small disciplines" of attention and relation "to the concrete specificity of the other" (2010, 377).

Relevant to the moral sensibility Leela and others in her family manifest is the story of Kildup's grandfather, Leela's father-in-law. Through a series of events that culminated with a dream of a figure whom he understood as a Muslim saint, the grandfather, a Hindu, had become the keeper of a Muslim shrine. He also for many years had dreamt Qur'anic verses, which he would then recite to effect cures for various medical ailments. So, Leela's home, even before Kildup's marriage, was one in which "the identities Hindu and Muslim are in an unstable relation to one another" (2010, 396). This suggests that the family's willingness to play with religious boundaries was not extraordinary in sense of an abstract ethical commitment to something like religious pluralism, held to despite external social pressures, but rather a working out of dynamics and sensibilities already embedded in their everyday lives. At the same time, Das makes it clear that the family members were not simply following the model of the grandfather in their willingness to make space for the couple. Rather, they were actively trying to find their way in a confusing situation by "inhabiting the everyday," that is, attending "to minute shifts in actions and dispositions" in an effort to "discern," to use Lambek's word, or "divine," to use Leela's word, what was going on and what they should do (Das 2010, 357, 396). For Das, one aspect of this work of discernment was the ritual and prayerful efforts of the family to work out their relationship to the Goddess, in the case of Leela, and Allah, in the case of Saba (2010, 392). Just as important, or perhaps simply the other side of the coin, the members of the family reworked their relationship to one another in responsiveness to the "concrete specificity" of one another. Here, attention to the concrete other, in love, made possible the emergence of the eventual everyday. As Das puts it, it is "salutary to understand that, in this urban environment, in this household struggling with everyday wants and needs, this labor of opening oneself to a different vision of what it might be to receive the other should be performed" (2010, 397).

We can consider this family's work to "divine" a way forward by returning to Cavell's treatment of scepticism, understood as disappointment with our ordinary words and relationships that results in the denial of our conditions. One mode of this denial is to try to make words work outside the contexts of ordinary language. Cavell's target here is not certain technical uses of language but what he sometimes describes as the "fantastic" use of language. His frequent target is the philosophical sceptic who turns away from the ordinary use of the word *certainty* in a fantasy of knowledge "that goes beyond *human* sense and certainty" (Cavell 2005, 4). But scepticism is not just found in philosophical (or religious) efforts to transcend our forms of life. It is also found in ordinary life as the "natural" expression of the fact that "we are endlessly separate" from the world, from things, from one another (Cavell 1979, 369). In other words, scepticism emerges from an inherent existential ambivalence about the limits of our condition marked by this separateness. This is the "truth" in scepticism and the reason that for Cavell efforts to refute scepticism are misguided. Even though we are bound together by deep agreements, we are routinely disappointed with this ordinary intimacy and routinely seek or wish for more direct contact or more direct knowledge of them. From this perspective, scepticism is ordinary language's own repudiation of "its power to word the world, to apply to the things we have in common" (Cavell 1994, 154), a form of "faithlessness" to our shared commitments and language (1992, 66).

In our faithless hopes for fantastic, extra-human connections and intimacies, we close ourselves off from ordinary, human connection and intimacy, and so we fail to be fully present to ourselves, to others, and to the world. Cavell's response to this sceptical faithlessness is a reinvestment in or a "resuscitation" of the ordinary in which we move deeper into our conditions by actively inhabiting them and so coming to "a new reception of [our] own experience" (1984, 240). This is the labour of opening, reception, and discernment that Das finds in Leela's family. Like the ordinary language philosopher who inhabits language by receiving words anew, the members of Leela's family engage in small disciplines of attention to one another and to their gods with a patience and openness that allows them to receive new possibilities of being. This is, as Jackson says, a "return to the particular." But Das and Cavell view this return differently than Jackson does, for rather than seeing this return as remembering the non-conceptual, they see it as a "descent into the ordinary," a movement deeper into the words and concepts that matter in the moment and movement into the future. Cavell conceives of this orientation to the future as a form of faith: "To learn to await, in the way you write, and therewith in every action, is to learn not to despair of opportunity unforeseen. That was always the knack of faith" (1992, 61).

3. Abandoning the Quotidian?

Cavell, like Jackson, is concerned to distinguish between philosophy that is attentive and responsive to ordinary life and philosophy that, for existential, moral, epistemological, or metaphysical reasons, tries to find a stance beyond life in some kind of logos. Further, both understand philosophy as an existential or spiritual practice: that is, philosophy not just as a quest for knowledge but as a practice of attentiveness and responsiveness to the particularity of self, others, and the world. For Jackson, this is also true of ethnography. Interestingly, the same could be said of Cavell, for ordinary language philosophy has always been a kind of ethnography, that is, a study of what we say and do when making the familiar strange and the strange familiar. Thus, both exercise a disciplined, phenomenological exactness with respect to language and culture. In addition, the writing of both thinkers is deeply autobiographical. It has become a commonplace for ethnographers to bring themselves into their writing, to cultivate self-consciousness about how their placement in the world shapes their relationship to their subjects. In many respects, Jackson himself is as much the object of his philosophical and ethnographical work as the people he studies. For his part, Cavell's perfectionism brings to philosophy an especially intense existential and autobiographical inflection: philosophy is as much a study of what I (should or need) to say when, as it is a study of what we say when. Cavell puts it best when he writes that philosophy "confronts the culture with itself, along the lines which it meets in me" (1979, 125). For both Jackson and Cavell, philosophy and ethnography work between scholarly analysis and spiritual practice, the strange and the familiar, the social and the individual, logos and life.

Despite these parallels, there are important differences between Cavell and Jackson. In this regard, Jackson's 2009 book *The Palm at the End of the Mind*, subtitled "Relatedness, Religiosity, and the Real," is instructive. There, through a "phenomenology of liminality," Jackson explores the idea of transcendence in terms of what he describes as "connectedness and crisis" (2009, 101). Jackson's notion of crisis is an expansive one, ranging from experiences of catastrophe and extremity to the uncertainty that comes with any face-to-face relationship (2009, 105). It may be too expansive, for there is something of a disjunction between Jackson's ethnographical and autobiographical reflections, on the one hand, and the theoretical and somewhat abstract attention he gives to extreme experiences, on the other. In the former, I find something much more like what Das describes as the "small disciplines" of ordinary life that enable people to persevere and even experience renewal in difficult times. For example, Jackson shares and reflects on entries from his mother's journal, some of which concerns her efforts to live with the suffering of rheumatoid arthritis. We see his mother, Emily, coming up against her limits and her difficulties and meeting them with resilience and humour, self-reflection and gratitude – but also with little drama or anything we'd be inclined to call transcendence (2009, 90–4). Similarly, when Jackson shares his conversations with and reflections on some of the migrants from Africa that he has worked with in Europe, we get difficult stories of struggle and perseverance that are as ordinary as they are rich and insightful (2009, 77).

Elsewhere, though, Jackson writes of "extreme experiences": he reflects on death, figurative and literal, as enabling "new life" (2009, 36), writes of the "insatiable" desire of the ethnographer to "be reborn in the fires of the new" (2009, 82), and affirms transgressive "impulses to destroy, renounce or abandon the quotidian," such as running wild and degrading oneself, and ritual *communitas* that "magically deconstruct[s] the order that is imposed on us in our everyday lives" (2009, 161). In some respects, his later treatment of Kuranko stories about the village and the bush echo these ideas: the "deconstruction" of order that takes place in such extreme experiences allows us to return to the ordinary enlivened. Yet these appeals to extremity press against Jackson's affirmation of the ordinary. They convey the sense that there is something too quotidian, mediated, and even impure about our ordinary lives. In particular, Jackson is suspicious of ordinary language, which he equates with settled order; it is, he writes, "just words." And, he goes on, these words "fail us" (2009, 51). Apparently, what our words fail to do is connect us with the reality of our experience: Jackson frequently distinguishes between experiences he characterizes as "artifacts of language," on the one hand, and "immediate" or "pure experience," on the other (2009, 132). He claims that "words are arbitrary" and that what really matters "is only the phenomena to which they allude" (2009, 37).

Words mire us in convention by reifying the categories and principles of past social orders, thus inhibiting us from "exploring fields of experience that overflow and confound the words with which we conventionally describe the world" (2009, xiii).[2]

From a Cavellian perspective, Jackson's claims about language being "just words" and "failing us" expose a trace of scepticism in his work, for it amounts to a conflation of ordinary language with the "slavish repetition of what has been decided by others at other times" (2016, 181). This conflation flattens our understanding of the social history of language, as evidenced by the word "decided" in this passage. Yes, we must account for power and domination in thinking about the history of language and meaning, but the practical social conditions out of which our words and criteria emerge is far more complex than is indicated in this passage.[3] More important for thinking about scepticism, Jackson's position on ordinary language also displays a sceptical fascination with the purity of experience ("we share, for a moment, the first idea"). I write "trace" of scepticism because I do not want to over-emphasize the difference between Jackson and Cavell on these issues even as I do want to suggest that Jackson's approach to the ordinary would benefit from a Cavellian view of the doubled sense of the ordinary as both actual and eventual. Nor do I dismiss the idea that new life can be found in extreme situations, that such situations can also help us understand more ordinary kinds of experiences, or even that poetry can't usefully point us beyond language. Rather, I want to avoid a conceptual or rhetorical opposition in which the ordinary is identified with deadening or repressive reification and order and the transgression and transcendence of order are identified with life-giving imagination and creativity. Cavell offers us a way of thinking about the richness and the depth of ordinary language, and thus about practices of attention, responsiveness, and creativity *within* the ordinary. Cavell certainly is at times critical of the way we deaden our lives with routine words and habits. Indeed we all, to some degree, are "imprisoned" in the everyday (2005, 297). But his criticism finds its ground in and not beyond ordinary words: "the meaning we give [our words] is rebuked by the meaning they have in our language" (1992, 92). We must, then, continually rededicate ourselves "to the inescapable and utterly specific syllables of our words upon which we are already disposed" (1992, 16). This is a reinvestment in or a "resuscitation" of the ordinary, in which we move deeper into our conditions by actively inheriting and inhabiting them (1984, 240).

This is not to say that Cavell does not also understand the importance of working at the limits of our words and our criteria. Even as

108   Tyler Roberts

our attunement with others goes deep, we are also separate from one another. Coming to our own experience, then, entails working in the liminal space between myself and my culture, or between the multiple forms of life of which I am a part, or between myself and very different forms of life (as in the case, perhaps, of the ethnographer). And this may lead us, as Jackson says of poetry, to "stretch" our language. But to make the obvious point, poetry stretches language with words. For Cavell, the use of a word that might seem at first glance to deny its conditions might in fact be a creative expansion of them, giving the word and us new life, like a fresh metaphor that allows us to see things in a new way: "What makes metaphor unnatural is its occasion to transcend our criteria; not as if to repudiate them, as if they are arbitrary; but to expand them, as though they are contracted" (1994, 147). As the word "contracted" suggests, the test of a new use of an old word is whether it creates bonds between people, whether others take it up. Of course, it may be that no one takes up my words and my efforts to give them meaning. This may lead me to question myself or to mark my distance from the common life of my neighbours. But it may also revivify old bonds or create new ones. Again, though, the point is not to transcend language but to immerse oneself deeply in it in an effort to hear our words differently.

Jackson's focus on extreme experience beyond the conceptual pairs well with a view of religiosity as transcendence in an encounter with something other that wrenches us from our ordinary life. But this is not all he does with religion. He also endorses Robert Orsi's concept of "lived religion," that is, religion as practised by ordinary people in their everyday lives. From this perspective, religion is not so much a matter of texts, systematic theologies, and transcendence but of lived "relationships between heaven and earth" (2009, 100; Jackson quoting Orsi). An outstanding example of Orsi's approach is his study of twentieth century Catholic women's devotion to St. Jude, the patron saint of hopeless causes. There, Orsi works from Church documents, popular Catholic periodicals, and interviews with the devout to weave a rich social history of the cult of St. Jude and to argue that many of the women he studied were able, in their relationship to Jude, to move from extreme and hopeless situations to a sense of renewal. For Orsi, Jude is a liminal figure operating in between the Church and the lives of his devout. On the one hand, Jude was a religious force of discipline embedded in authorized scripts by means of which the Church keeps women in a subservient position. On the other hand, Jude as engaged with by the devout women became a friend to whom they wrote and prayed and a medium through which they connected with each other. Moreover, and most important for my purposes here, their relationship with Jude enabled them to experience "everyday life in a new way" (Orsi 1998, 186–7) by acting as a "solvent of the givenness of experience" (211). Here, however, religion is not a matter of extreme experience. The situations these women found themselves in were already "hopeless." Rather, their relationship with Jude enabled them to rework the ordinary stuff of their lives, the religious and other materials they had at hand, to dissolve, at least to some degree, the bonds that tied them to particular authoritative social and religious scripts, and so to come to new experiences of hope.

Cavell, like Jackson, directs us to practices by which human beings learn to rework culturally authorized scripts of normativity embedded in our everyday lives that serve as "givens" for our experience. But Cavell, along with Das and Orsi, teaches us that it is possible to find new life in and not beyond these everyday lives. This is something we also see, at times, in Jackson, but perhaps not consistently or precisely enough. Jackson follows up his brief discussion of lived religion with a return to his reflections on his mother's journals. Although "Emily never invoked God," Jackson believes that she might have "felt a kinship" with Martin Buber's view that what really matters is "not the 'experiencing' of life (*Erleben*) – the detached subjectivity – *but life itself*" (2009, 102). What really matters, Jackson goes on to write, is not whether one is "religious" or not, but that for all people

> it is in border situations when they are sorely tested, where they come up against the limits of what they can control, comprehend, and cope with, that they are most susceptible to those epiphanies, breakthroughs, conversions, and revelations that are sometimes associated with the divine and sometimes simply taken as evidence of the finitude, uncertainty, and thrownness of human existence. (102)

As a way of thinking about the limits of our concepts, and particularly the limits of distinctions we make between the religious and the nonreligious, there is much to affirm here. My purpose here, however, has been to argue that attention to the ordinary, especially as we see it developed in Cavell and applied anthropologically by Das and Orsi, helps us explore "life itself" between the activity of "control" and passivity suggested by the word "susceptible" in the passage above. The members of Leela's family or the women Orsi writes about may not control or fully comprehend, but they do "cope." And they do so not by abandoning the quotidian or giving themselves up to dramatic experiences of transcendence but by working on their everyday lives.

110 Tyler Roberts

NOTES

1 Cavell often notes that the fact that this attunement is "based on nothing more than our sharing of (and our capacity for imagining)" a wide range of human activities and states of mind makes the fact of language "seem like a miracle" (Cavell 2005, 139).

2 Jackson does make an exception for "great writing," especially poetry. But even there, the point seems to be that poetry points us beyond language, it "stretches language to the limit and points beyond, helping refresh 'life so that we share,/ for a moment, the first idea'"(2009, 51; quoting Wallace Stevens). Again, the idea is that we must transcend the ordinary and language in order to "refresh" or revitalize it.

3 This brings up the issue of critique in Cavell and Jackson. Much more than Cavell, Jackson engages with the lives of the marginalized and disempowered. Cavell by contrast, tends to focus on selfhood and other "first-world" problems. Moreover, Cavell's emphasis on the role of social agreement and ordinary language might be considered critically ineffectual in the face of entrenched relations of power. This isn't the place to work out these differences, but I will open up one avenue for further thought on these issues. Especially in his later work, culminating in *Cities of Words*, Cavell developed his conception of moral perfectionism in a political direction. There, a central focus is the question of *consent*: do I, can I consent to the "we" of which, to this point, I have thought myself a part? The quick point here is that perfectionism calls for decision, which is often the blind spot of our most powerful modes of critique. Jackson relates a story of an interview with Adorno in which he spoke of being "harassed" in the 60s by student activists who condemned his "quietism." Adorno responds that in face of the question "What is to be done?" he can only say "'I do not know.' I can only analyze relentlessly what is." Jackson glosses this response by writing that "critical thought refuses to pretend that the task of thinking is to deliver judgments" (2016, 62). It isn't at all clear to me that Jackson embraces this perspective wholeheartedly, but it is a common one among purveyors of "critique," raising the question for me whether the more we orient critical thought to the "more," "aporia," and "exile" (2016, 83), the more difficult we find it to make the critical moral and political decisions that we constantly must make in our ordinary lives.

WORKS CITED

Cavell, Stanley. 1979. *The Claim of Reason*. Cambridge: Harvard University Press.

–. 1984. *Pursuits of Happiness*. Cambridge: Harvard University Press.

–. 1992. *The Senses of Walden*. Expanded edition. Chicago: University of Chicago Press.

–. 1994. *In Quest of the Ordinary*. Chicago: The University of Chicago Press.

–. 2005. *Cities of Words*. Cambridge: Harvard University Press.

Das, Veena. 2010. "Engaging the Life of the Other: Love and Everyday Life." In *Ordinary Ethics*, edited by Michael Lambek, 376–99. New York: Fordham University Press.

–. 2012. "Ordinary Ethics." In *A Companion to Moral Anthropology*, edited by Didier Fassin, 133–49. Chichester, UK: Wiley Blackwell.

Fassin, Didier. 2012. "Introduction: Toward a Critical Moral Anthropology." In *A Companion to Moral Anthropology*, edited by Didier Fassin, 1–18. Chichester, UK: Wiley Blackwell.

Jackson, Michael. 2005. *Existential Anthropology: Events, Exigencies and Effects*. New York: Berghahn.

–. 2009. *The Palm at the End of the Mind: Relatedness, Religiosity, and the Real*. Durham: Duke University Press.

–. 2016. *As Wide as the World Is Wise*. New York: Columbia University Press.

Lambek, Michael. 2010. "Introduction." In *Ordinary Ethics*, edited by Michael Lambek, 1–38. New York: Fordham University Press.

Orsi, Robert. 1998. *Thank You St. Jude*. New Haven: Yale University Press.

5 *Ruta Graveolens*: Open and Closed Bodies in a Bahian Town

MATTIJS VAN DE PORT

It all started in Santo Amaro, in the temple of a priest called Pai Ro. The candomblé ceremony was in honour of a spirit called Gira Mundo, which means "The World Turns." It is an aptly dizzying name for this wild character, who runs around frantically, non-stop shouting obscenities and cracking dirty jokes, while keeping himself going by drinking large quantities of hard liquor from the bottle. In my fieldnotes I refer to him as "libido unleashed." At some point during the ceremony, Gira Mundo had taken me by the hand to lead me into his shrine, a small room adjacent to the ceremonial hall. Away from all the noise he basically told me I should be less of a control freak.

"You have to throw yourself!" he insisted in the semi-dark, repeating it over and over again. A goat and numerous chickens had just been slaughtered where we stood. The smell of blood hung heavy in the heat. He had shining eyes. He was sweating all over.

"Tem que se jogar!"

I knew all too well what Gira Mundo was talking about. The temple community – both humans and spirits – have come to know me over the years as the anthropologist-with-the-camera who just does not stop looking, and by looking puts himself at a distance. Sure, they have seen that I am trying to blend in, abiding by the temple's dress-codes; that whenever I am around I am present at the ceremonies; that I help out in all kinds of ways; and that I really enjoy their friendship and company. But this has not blinded them for the fact that I also maintain, and jealously guard, a level of non-involvement. I refuse to fully hand myself over to their life world. I keep withdrawing myself. "Next time you come to visit, you can stay in my house, I have a spare room," the priest, Pai Ro, has told me many times, to find that again I booked a room in the nearby hotel. Just so, members of the community are familiar with my ever more elaborate argumentations as to why I do not want to be initiated to Oxóssi, the spirit who is the master of my head. But I don't think they have bought into the arguments. After all these years, they must have sensed that self-monitoring and trying-to-keep-control are my second nature, the inerasable remnants of a middle-class education that offered *politeness* (one's withdrawal behind a façade of social conventions) as the prime tool to deal with the turmoil of social life, and that instructed me, over and over again, to always consider the impact of my actions on others. "Instead of acting on impulse, count till ten!"

The advice of Gira Mundo to loosen up struck a chord. And so it happened that, when some time after the ceremony I visited my friend Lucas in São Paulo, I woke up one morning and decided to have a tattoo.

Lucas, a young artist who has his body inked all over, was totally in for it.

"I'll draw you one!"

He had two twigs of arruda tattooed on his chest. Arruda is known as *Ruta graveolens* in Latin; in English it is known as rue or herb-of-grace. In Bahia this plant is frequently used in rituals to close one's body against evil energies. I said I'd love to have one like that. On the inside of my lower left arm.

"Let's not make it a *florzinha*," Lucas said. "A little flower doesn't do it with that big body of yours." He was drawing the arruda right there at the breakfast table, just before we set off to the nearest tattoo shop.

"Could you do like a really fine line?" I asked Julio, the tattoo artist, who had just told me he had never practised his art on pork skin. I could hear the edge of squeakiness in my voice.

"Sure," Julio said.

Yet such aesthetic worries were gone the moment the needle started moving in and out of my body. I watched the production of an irreversible fact. I fully enjoyed the fact that I had not counted till ten to ponder the possible consequences of walking around with a big tattoo on a highly visible body part. I relished the sense of "having thrown myself."

Me joguei.

The Dangers of the Street

Although I had never really considered having a tattoo, the idea did not appear out of thin air. I was in Bahia to work on a new film on magical and religious practices through which bodies are opened and closed in the Recôncavo area of Bahia (Van de Port 2021). I was drawn to the topic because of a theoretical interest in the way bodies are imagined

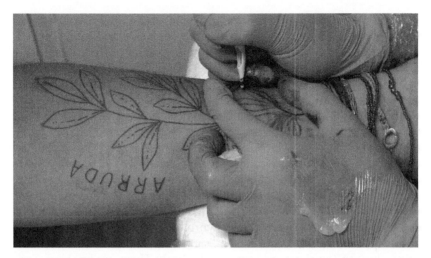

Figure 5.1. Lucas's drawing of an arruda in the process of being drawn into my body.

and "culturally produced" (Van de Port 2015; cf. Jackson 1983, 1996), more in particular those bodies in candomblé that need to be able to receive spirits. People in candomblé take bodies to be permeable and porous containers, which allow for the coming and going of different entities. This conceptualization stands in marked contrast with the way many Europeans understand their bodies, which – in flaunting denial of their leaking and dripping capacity – are imagined as closed vessels that contain (or rather, produce) what Charles Taylor famously called a "bounded, buffered self" (Taylor 2008; cf. Taylor 2007).

Given the precariousness of life in places such as Santo Amaro, it is probably no surprise that Bahians are heavily invested in practices to *fechar o corpo* – closing one's body. For porous, open bodies are vulnerable bodies. When I brought up the topic of *o corpo fechado*, people would immediately talk about the need to close their bodies to protect themselves from the omnipresent dangers "on the street": envious gazes of false friends (known as *olhado*, the evil eye); magical spells cast by ill-intending neighbours; curses that families have "inherited" from previous generations; malignant spirits; as well as slander and gossip, lethal viruses, violent gangs, drug lords, and blinded police cars that drive around late at night with a licence to kill. To close one's body is the attempt to not let those things "get to you."

116 Mattijs van de Port

Shops where religious products are being sold vividly demonstrate the concern to close one's body. On the shelves stand long rows of mass-produced statues of saints – Catholic avatars of African spirits – many of which boast armours, helmets, and shields, rendering their fragile plaster bodies impenetrable. Iron plates tightly follow the bodily curves of such muscled saints as São Expedito ("the saint for urgent matters") or São Jorge ("the warrior saint"). The crown on Santa Bárbara's head looks like a fortress. Throngs of protective necklaces, in all the colours that represent the different *orixás*, hang on the walls. On the counter stand boxes containing such items as woven bracelets with cowry shells attached to them, called *contra-egum*, which are worn on the upper arms to prevent attacks by the spirits of the dead; amulets, which in Bahia are called *patuá*, and take the form of little sewed bags containing herbs and prayers, to be worn on a necklace, or in one's bag; and scapulars, the necklaces which "sandwich" the body between two saints, one on the chest, and one on the back. There are booklets containing *orações fortes* ("strong prayers"). The many products to break evil spells and cast off the evil eye include incense and perfumes; dried leaves for herbal baths; fresh leaves to beat the "evil dust" out of bodies or the walls of one's house; plants to be put near doors and windows to bar evil from entering, with names such as the sword-of-Ogum, sword-of-Oxóssi, with-me-no-one-can, who-watched, and little-broom; various cactuses, whose leathery green skin is protected by rows and rows of spines; and of course the aforementioned arruda, from which people take a little twig to put behind their ears so as to close their body. The fact that these shops are thriving businesses is a telltale sign of the way locals take their bodies to be vulnerable and under threat.

The weekly prayer sessions in Pai Ro's temple reveal a similar concern: songs and prayers are endless calls for divine protection, expressive of a yearning to be "shielded" and "sheltered."

> I will go dressed and armed with the weapons of Saint George
> so that my enemies, having feet will not reach me;
> having hands will not trap me;
> having eyes will not see me,
> neither with thought can they cause me harm.
> Firearms will not reach my body;
> knives and swords will break without touching my body,
> ropes and chains will break without tying my body.
> Jesus Christ protects and defends me
> with the power of His Holy and Divine Grace.
> The Virgin of Nazareth covers me

Figure 5.2. Almiro wearing a twig of arruda. "Against the evil eye," was his immediate response as to why he was wearing it.

> with her sacred and divine mantle,
> protecting me in all my pains and afflictions.
> And God, with His Divine Mercy and great power,
> is my defender against the evils and persecutions of my enemies.
> Glorious Saint George, in the name of God,
> extend to me your shield and your powerful arms,
> defending me with your strength and your greatness;
> and may my enemies underneath your feet
> become humble and submissive to you.

After the prayers, *caboclo* spirits are called out to possess their mediums. They walk around carrying big bushels of freshly picked *aroeira* branches, with which they beat the "evil dust" out of people's bodies – a dust that one accumulates "on the street." And to the street is where the branches go after having been used.

Illness is obviously another danger to the bodily organism. In the small town of Candeias, a faith healer called Seu Capelinha enumerates all the illnesses he can think of in his litanies, a sheer endless list of bodily afflictions. "I cannot miss out on one," he told me. "For that would then be the weak spot of the person I am healing." Strikingly, the litanies are interspersed with emotional calls for the Holy Virgin to cover human bodies with her "mantle of love." The image once again attests to the centrality of body boundaries in fighting off omnipresent dangers.

Alerted to these never-ending calls for protection and ongoing attempts to fortify the body against evil, I began to wonder how it could have been that I had been largely side-tracking the violence and dangers of "the street" in my previous ponderings of Bahian religiosities – mentioning them in passing, for sure, yet not letting them weigh in. For it is not as if I did not know Bahia to be a violent society. In the early stages of my fieldwork, I lost a dear friend, Joel, who was brutally stabbed in his own home. Over the years, many people told me they had lost loved ones through violence. Via social media I keep being notified of yet another friend of a friend who has fallen victim to homophobic attacks or police violence. And there were direct confrontations as well. I was assaulted various times when out on the street. I was told that the friendly man I had been drinking beer with the night before was known to be a murderer. And not too long ago I was involved in a near fatal incident, when Lucas and I, touring the Bahian interior, ended up passing by a bank robbery. A .38-calibre bullet pierced the front window of the rental car we were driving and ended up right in front of me on the dashboard.

"*O anjo de guarda do senhor é muito poderoso,*" was the comment by the policeman who later inspected the car. "You have a really strong guardian angel."

So yes, I knew about violence, but it was a knowing that didn't really get to me. I was seeing it without seeing. Hearing it without hearing. I kept myself in a halfway state of awareness, a knowing stripped bare of its unsettling powers, a refusal to fully embrace the reality of it. I vividly recall how after the aforementioned bank robbery I even photographed the smashed car window and the bullet in the dashboard so as to offer myself proof that this really happened. Up until today, however, I keep telling people that the whole episode oddly remains "like a film" – I was in it, yet out of it.

My apparent capacity to shut out unbearable, unanswerable, or inassimilable dimensions of being corresponded with how locals reacted to instances of violence: they invest greatly in "not letting it get to them." Most people just did not want to hear that story about the bank robbery. They would say, "oh, really, did that happen to you?" in a way that made it crystal clear that this conversation topic was not to be pursued. Lucas's mother even reprimanded him for bringing it up when he visited her after the event: "Oh, is this the kind of story you are bringing into my home?"

Ruta Graveolens   119

There is, of course, a psychoanalytical vocabulary to describe such responses as defence mechanisms – referring to the mental work of negation, dissociation, denial, detachment. In Bahia, however, that's not the language people employ. They talk about "closing one's body" – fechar o corpo – which got me thinking about how bodies are involved in the existential project of not-letting-things-get-to-you.

"I understand what you said about it all feeling like a film," Lucas told me on camera, when I interviewed him for the film project, "and maybe that is how we manage to move on in a place like this. But I think my body passed through its own trauma."

The fact that I was making a *film*, a research practice which constantly forces one to think about "observables" – what should I be looking at? – greatly helped to keep the body centre stage. I kept pointing my camera at bodies as they were being treated and prepared to cope with a violent universe. I zoomed in on the many rituals performed on the body; sartorial practices through which bodies were covered and exposed, tied and loosened up; bodily adornments, including the highly popular thick silver chains, impenetrable sunglasses, and headphones. I became particularly interested in the human skin, the "outer covering of the body that both protects us from others and exposes us to them" (Cataldi, in Ahmed and Stacey 2001): a canvas that bears the marks of violent acts, scars and scratches, wounds and perforations; the site where the opening and closing of bodies – violence and healing – materializes in a most literal manner.

Somewhere along the line it had crossed my mind to make shots of a tattoo being inked on a body. Pondering the expressivities of the human skin I had become fascinated by the idea that a tattoo requires the opening of the skin, as well as its closing – a drawing drawn into the body rather than drawn onto it (cf. Benson 2000). Struck by the arruda tattooed on Lucas's chest, a plant used in various practices to close one's body, I sensed an interesting scene for the film.

Aberé: Opening One's Body to Close It

I left the tattoo shop in São Paulo with my lower left arm wrapped in plastic wrap and the instruction to thus keep the open wound of the tattoo protected for a couple of days. The fact that the drawing was an arruda, which supposedly would keep my body closed, was not commented upon. I was also told I had to rub the skin frequently with a special cream, so it would "scar nicely." The first days I noticed how my body seemed to be at work to expulse the ink before closing the upper layers of the epidermis. That at least is how I understood the

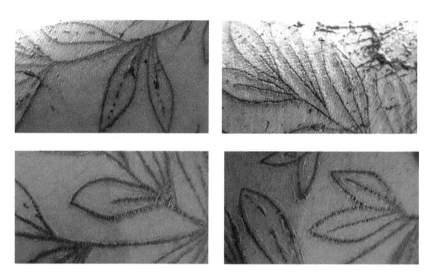

Figure 5.3. Arruda tattoo in different stages. Two images above, one day after the carving. The two images below, where dry crusts have begun to form, are some two weeks later.

fact that whenever I changed the wrap, drops of ink had formed on my skin. Later, when the wounds had healed, dry crusts started to form on the drawing. Although I would have thought that by now the drawing would be sealed in its final form, the ink kept spreading under my skin. The lines, which had not been very "fine" to begin with, started to blur.

"You might think of it as a watercolour," Lucas wrote me when, back in Bahia, I had send him a photo via Whatsapp. Undoubtedly he had figured I was distressed about where the tattoo was going, and wanted to kindly reassure me with a positive view. I responded by saying that this was something between my body and the tattoo, and that I would not trade this tattoo for any other in the world, however ugly it would become.

And that is indeed exactly how it feels. My immediate and total attachment to the tattoo was probably the most striking thing I learned from this experiment: that twig of arruda is me, just as I am that twig of arruda. The tattoo is as solidly a part of me as my nose and my earlobe and my index finger. I realize this has little to do with the image, or the special powers attributed to arruda. Sure, I like the arruda for aesthetic reasons, I'm glad it was drawn by a dear friend, and cherish its link with Bahian ideas of closing the body, which adds to the charm of the tattoo being a kind of souvenir. Yet it is the experience of having been tattooed itself – the drawing being carved in the flesh – which makes for this unwavering, strangely solid connection I feel towards it (to the point where even this phrasing sounds inadequate: just as I would not say I feel something "towards" my earlobe, which is already included in the "I," so it is with the tattoo). The sensation is probably best described what in a certain jargon would be called *hors discours*. I am acutely aware that none of my words can produce this experience for someone who has not been tattooed. I remember how previously, when Lucas had been saying similar things about his tattoos, I had been thinking, "yeah, sure, whatever" (and I am hyper-aware this may be exactly what many of my non-tattooed readers are now thinking). Apparently, it is the carving in the flesh – opening the body to let something in that is not of the body – and the subsequent experience of my body actually adopting this alien substance, that makes a difference.

"I love it that you now pertain to the tribe of the tattooed," Lucas exclaimed. And indeed, there is a striking parallel with initiation practices as I got to know them in candomblé. Time and again, people from candomblé told me that being initiated is in fact a way of closing one's body for *as mazelas do mundo* – the bad things of the world. Pai Pote, a well known priest in Santo Amaro, articulated it as follows:

> To close one's body in a *terreiro* (temple) is to prepare yourself for the life out there. In the terreiro it is about the spiritual life, but out there, there is another life. We are closing our bodies against our enemies, against negative influences, this is important in a terreiro. We work with the minds of people, and with the bodies of people. By committing oneself to candomblé, one is liberated of the things out there: freed from sex, freed from negative influences ... closing the body is to close the body against *as mazelas do mundo* (the evils of the world), the trouble we find out there, against racism, against religious intolerance, against the negative thoughts of people who are attacking our religion. Closing the body is defending our religion.

In order to arrive at this closure, however, the body is to be opened during initiation, in the literal sense of making incisions on the shoulders, the chest, the back, the tongue, the top of the head and the feet of the initiate. These wounds – called *kura* or *aberé* – are seen as openings in which "the orixá is planted," by smearing a herbal powder (*pemba)* onto them. As one priest explained it, pemba contains *axé*, the vital energy of the orixá, and by smearing it in the wounds, this energy becomes activated in both the physical and spiritual body of the initiate. Aberé often leave highly visible scars, "public signals" of one's initiation and one's commitment to the orixá, which is now enclosed in the body. The orixá's axé can be invoked to bring vitality, long life, health, and will protect the initiated against evil spells done through black magic.

"When an initiate has been eating something that was bewitched, it will not harm him. If he steps on something that was put in his path, it won't harm him. This is what we understand as 'closing the body,'" Pai Pote said.

The planting of the orixá is an irreversible act. In candomblé circles, many stories circulate of people who have been initiated to the wrong orixá, causing them many problems. Pai Ademir, another priest with whom I converse about such matters, explained:

> When a saint is made in the wrong way (*santo feito errado*), people usually go mad ... For example, you belong to [the orixá] Oxóssi, and you come to me to be initiated. But when I consult the oracle I see Ogum and initiate you to the latter. Clearly you will now carry negative energies because you were initiated to the wrong saint. This will cause you a lot of trouble in the future because you can only be initiated once. You cannot make a saint twice. That's impossible. Once done wrong, wrong for eternity, you know. ... One day you will have the pleasure of getting to know people here in my temple who, when they arrived, were completely mad. They were brought in from the madhouse. The problem? *Santo feito errado.* I take care of them. But all I can do is find the saint that ought to be in there and keep that saint close to that person. People do get better, but the wrong energy in their body remains.

Listening to Pai Ademir, I could not fail to notice the correspondence with stories about tattoo practices: tales of abandoned or disillusioned lovers who, in happier days, had tattooed the name of their loved one on their bodies, then to be left with the mark, long after the lover had disappeared.

As a non-initiate, I cannot be sure how much of a common ground the comparison between tattoo and aberé actually provides. Moreover, as an anthropologist, I have learned to be hesitant to assume pan-human experiences, which are universally understood. And yet, I'm intrigued that in both the tattoo and the aberé, the affordances of the sentient body have been put to work so that something that was external to the body became a part of it. I'd like to think that with the tattoo I have a new experiential ground on which to build understandings. Fact is that initiates talk about the relation with their orixá as being an indissoluble and irreversible bond, the way I now talk about my tattoo. Fact is also that this bond is forged in the process from cutting to healing, from

Ruta Graveolens 123

wound to scar. The orixá, and the image of the arruda, are thus, quite literally, *incorporated*.

Olhado, the Evil Eye

Back in Bahia, in the temple of Pai Ro, the tattoo met with enthusiastic responses from Rigne, the young guard. "Arruda!" Fingers ran over the scars to see if they had healed. And what had I paid? They immediately wanted to know. Shock and incredulity when I told them it had cost six hundred reais.

"Six hundred reais?" Rigne exclaimed, stressing every single syllable. "And it wasn't even coloured in!"

Embarrassed, I realized that six hundred reais is an awful lot of money in a poor neighbourhood in Santo Amaro. If they had already figured that I must have a big salary, going back and forth between Amsterdam and Santo Amaro, renting cars and hotel rooms, I had now shown myself to be a big spender, someone who could apparently afford such frivolous expenses.

In response I muttered that this was in São Paulo, where things are more expensive. And that the price had included a small tattoo that I had offered my friend Lucas for having drawn the arruda. They were unimpressed. In Santo Amaro I could have had the same tattoo for less than a third of the price. Full colour. And with a *fine* line. One of the initiates, Nito, bared his chest to show his lion-head tattoo. Fine lines indeed.

The practice of tattooing is widespread among Bahian youngsters. Frequently they pick religious imagery – crosses, rosaries, the Holy Virgin, saints, symbols or drawings of the orixás, Jesus figures, lines from the prayer of Saint Jorge, biblical texts. I'm not sure as to how their protective efficacy is judged. Was my body now considered to be "closed"?

"It is a first step," said old Dona França cautiously, a priestess who had been praying over me with arruda for the film project and had been quite intrigued that a gringo had tattooed an arruda on his arm.

As we talked about the powers of the plant, I told her about a series of misfortunes that had occurred the year before, when, in short time span, my rental car broke down, my wallet was stolen, and, worst of all, my camera short-circuited while filming and could not be brought back to life. All of this in a relative short time span.

"*Olhado*," she said decidedly. "I'll pray over you three times, and then, when I'm done, you'll take these herbs home and take a bath with them for three days in a row." The leaves with which she had been beating me were slightly hanging down from the branches, a clear sign,

Figure 5.4. Seu Dionísio, a vendor of herbs for ritual practices. Here he shows me the arruda.

Dona França told me, that I was "loaded" with evil dust. They were wrapped in newspaper after the session and then put in a plastic bag. I had to trample them with my feet. Unsatisfied with my half-hearted performance she urged me on.

"Trample, trample! You have to give yourself more!"

The bag was then thrown out of the house, onto the street. For Dona França, the faith healing session was never a mere shooting session for the film.

Olhado was also the diagnosis of many of my friends in Santo Amaro when I told them about the broken camera. What had I been thinking, they asked, that I could just walk around, flaunting my camera, my rental car, my money, and then not be the object of olhado?

"Why do you think I keep saying you ought to initiate?" Pai Ro asked me after having learned about the broken camera. "Olhado, my son. Of course people envy you. You walk around unprotected. You are way too open! You should initiate!"

Olhado is often translated as the evil eye. My Bahian friends kept explaining it to me as *inveja*, envy. People who have olhado – frequently without even knowing it – emanate an extremely harmful energy. Their touch can make a plant wither and die. Their gaze can kill infants. Their comments – "you have such beautiful hair" – can make your hair fall out. People who fare better than others, and therefore attract envy,

Ruta Graveolens 125

accumulate this negativity in their body, where it settles as "evil dust." It leaves people weak and without energy. Yet evil dust also operates beyond the body. It causes the energy that is necessary for movement and growing to be blocked, so projects one has embarked upon don't prosper. It is because of olhado that everything gets stuck: you opened a barber shop, building up a clientele, and then, all of a sudden, customers no longer show up. You did well selling beer and barbecued meat on skewers, but then nobody buys anymore. You were filming happily, and then, in the midst of a shoot, your camera breaks down. Of all the dangers people face, olhado was most frequently brought up when the concern to close one's body was discussed. If in the universe of candomblé the prospering of life is driven by the circulation of axé – the energy-to-get-things-done and *abrir os caminhos,* open the roads – then olhado is its evil counter-energy.

Clearly, olhado provides one of the motives why Pai Ro had been so insistent that I should initiate. A wealthy man, who blows six hundreds reais for a tattoo and has the audacity to talk about it in the open, has to take protective measures. And no better protection than to plant one's guardian angel – as the orixás are lovingly called – in one's body.

Patuá: Closing One's Body to Open Up to the World

Another recurrent story brought up around the topic of o corpo fechado was the idea that you could actually make the body invulnerable to physical violence and thus become fearless. Two old men, Julio and Luis, recalled how "in the old days," many young men would close their bodies for that purpose. Santo Amaro had an important sugar industry, which attracted great numbers of young labourers who lived in make-shift barracks. Julio, who had worked as a nurse in a medical post, spoke about a world where daggers, knives, and machetes were drawn at the slightest provocation, and where blood used to flow "like a river." Closing the body was done through special prayers, and with the amulets called patuá, obtained from candomblé priests. They would wear them on a necklace, or in their pockets, and their bodies would be impenetrable to anything made of metal – bullets, knives, machetes, daggers.

"These youngsters, they lost their fear. They would go anywhere, anytime. They were fearless. They would do it all," Luis said.

In capoeira, the Afro-Brazilian martial art, ideas such as these are still vivid. Not in the least because in songs and tales, memories are kept alive of the legendary Besouro Mangangá, a capoeira player from the early twentieth century who had his body closed with a particular strong magic (*mandinga*). Because of his temper and behaviour – and

126 Mattijs van de Port

a strong sense of the injustices black Bahians had to suffer – Besouro frequently got into trouble with state authorities, factory-owners, and the law, which earned him the reputation of being a *valente*, which my dictionary translates as a man who is "valiant, brave, stouthearted, intrepid, daring, dauntless." Here's the song Renato, a mestre in capoeira from Santo Amaro, sang in front of the camera:

Ei, Santo Amaro	Hey, Santo Amaro
Pelas bandas da bahia	On the fringes of the bay
Besouro era falado	Besoura was talked about
pela sua valentia	for his braveness
Besouro preto	Black Besouro
Forte como touro	Strong as a bull
Usava brinco de ouro	With his golden earing
E seu preso no pescoço	And his chain around his neck
Trazia su berimbau	He would bring his *berimbau*
E a navalha no bolso	And a stiletto in his pocket
Besouro preto	Black Besouro
Foi falado na Bahia	Talked about in all of Bahia
Vivido em Santo Amaro	Hailed in Santo Amaro
pela sua Valentia	for his braveness
Besorou ei! Besouro ah!	Besouro hey! Besouro ha!
Besouro preto,	Black Besouro,
Besouro do Mangangá, ei!	Besouro de Mangangá, hey!

The story about Besouro Mangangá contains many episodes in which the *capoeirista* stood up for the rights of the black sugarcane workers and turned out to be the winner in confrontations with those in power.

The gist of the story, however, concerns the *ponto fraco* of Besouro, his "weak spot," which led to his violent death. For all of the magic that may have been done to close a body, sexual relations with a woman – "or a man, or whatever," Renato added – leaves the body wide open. Knowing this to be Besouro's weak spot, a factory owner with whom he had a conflict set up a trap. A woman who worked at the factory was sent to seduce Besouro. In the morning, after a night of lovemaking, she stole his patuá, which he always kept in the pocket of his jacket. Fatally, Besouro did not check his pocket before leaving her house. In a banana plantation a young boy, contracted by the factory owner, had been waiting, and slashed him with a wooden knife. With his intestines hanging out of him (a detail that was never missed in the different versions I heard), Besouro was left in a ditch. He was found and brought to a hospital in Santo Amaro where he died.

"Dying wasn't easy for valentes who had their bodies closed," said Luis. "They would agonize and agonize! Sometimes a priest had to be called in to bless them, and break the magic, just for them to be able to die!"

Interestingly, the storyline of Besouro Mangangá is organized around the firm conviction that sexual relations open up a body that was closed and produce a ponto fraco. This resonates with a dilemma many of my Bahian friends brought up when discussing o corpo fechado: if a dangerous world asks for bodies to be closed, the best things in life require a body that is wide open. Pleasures such as sex, eating, drinking, singing a song from the heart, dancing, loving, perceiving beauty, receiving one's orixá, or keeping axé in circulation are at odds with o corpo fechado. Pai Aldemiro, from the village of Coqueiros, wholeheartedly agreed:

Indeed, indeed! In all of this we need to be open! When you talk about "opening the body," I understand this in terms of how the orixás penetrate us. Obviously, we always need to be prepared with a clean body, a purified body, because we do not know when the orixás will enter our bodies. We don't know when this energy will take over. We must always be prepared, with our arms wide open, our bodies open. So when I talked about o corpo fechado, I meant the protection we seek from God, from the orixás, so the evil that is out there [at which moment he points to the street on the other side of the window] doesn't get to us.

The open body, Pai Aldemiro seems to be saying, is vulnerable. It needs protection. But closing the body is not an attempt to turn it into a living fortress, sealed off from its hostile surroundings. To the contrary, in candomblé, the body is frequently being closed for it to safely open for the spirits, and the circulation of axé.

"Indeed, indeed!" Pai Aldemiro said. "We have to prepare the body for it to be able to receive the power of the orixá! We have to tie it!"

Thus, whereas much of the *talk* about o corpo fechado produces a dualism of bodies being either "open" or "closed" (and the totalitarian fantasies such talk triggers), candomblé *practices* seek to arrive at a balancing act in which bodies are closed in a certain way, yet open in another way.

Capoeira players were most explicit about this: closing your body makes you feel protected, and because you feel protected, you dare to take more risks. Elsewhere (Van de Port 2015, 92–3), I already quoted what my friend Adriana had to say about it. Given the relevance of her words for the topic under discussion, I will quote her again:

128   Mattijs van de Port

For me, this closing of the body is somewhat paradoxical. Because you close yourself to open yourself up. You protect yourself so as to be able to throw yourself ... with more security and less protection! For example, look at a group of capoeira players. The capoeirista who plays most daringly, who has the most beautiful performance, he certainly did a ritual to close his body. He knows that he need not be too concerned with the kicks of the other, and so he can put more into his own kicks. I am fascinated by this seeming contradiction because it is not a contradiction. When I do a ritual in a candomblé temple to close my body, then certainly I am not only closing my physical body. I am, above all, closing my ethereal body, my spiritual body. Knowing that I have a certain protection, the relation that my physical body has with the world can be looser (*seja mais solta*). And so I do not have to be so cautious, with the world, and with people. This is fantastic, don't you think? You close yourself to be able to open yourself up. You close something so that not everything can access you, but this enables you to throw yourself more easily into the world. So you are not invulnerable, simply because you did a ritual to close your body. These rituals don't make you invulnerable. They make you more daring.

For the young men in Santo Amaro, having their bodies closed so they dare to take a risk makes total sense. Unemployed and penniless, any advance in life asks for an openness to opportunities that might come their way. Indeed, *tem que se jogar*. As elsewhere in Brazil, these opportunities often take the form of the "fast money" that the drug trade offers. Or crime. Rigne, with whom I travelled a lot because he assisted me in my film endeavours, would become all excited whenever an armoured truck would pass by, on its way to deliver money to the bank. Beaming with enthusiasm over the fact that there is such a thing in the world as an armoured truck filled to the brim with banknotes, his body would literally start enacting the robbery, pointing his imaginary gun and screaming bang-bang-bang. When I pointed out his somewhat Pavlovian response to these armoured vehicles and told him to "forget about them," he would typically answer laughing, saying *"estou ligado"* ("I hear you"). Rigne is very keen to have his body closed. Having seen my tattoo, he immediately wanted one exactly like that, with an arruda. In fact, I worry that his participation in the making of my film, which made him listen to all the stories that go around about the prowess of closed bodies, only enhanced his desire. Weslei, another young man who appears in the film, took another stance. He told me:

Those who close their body have no fear. Walk in any place, go everywhere, do it all. For me, however, protection is to stay at home. That's

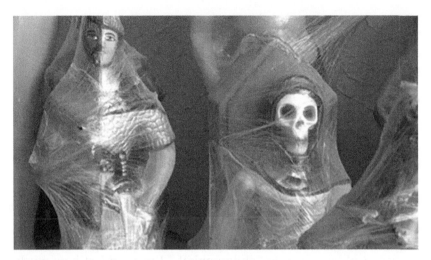

Figure 5.5. Xoroquê, half open – half closed.

where I am anyway. I do not go out. The problems are in the street. And of course, if I had no choice, and would have to go out and do these things, I would do it. But the difference would be that I would be afraid, always fearing some tragedy to happen. They have no such fears. But maybe, I'd be more alert.

People in Santo Amaro may fantasize about bodies that are fully closed, and therefore invulnerable, but in many instances, it is the open body that they want or need. On the shelves of the stores where people from candomblé buy their religious objects, one frequently encounters a statue which seems to be articulating this tension (see fig. 5). The spirit is called Xoroquê. The vendors of such statues couldn't tell me much more than that Xoroquê is half exu (the category of spirits to which Gira Mundo pertains), and half Ogum (which is an orixá). I cannot help thinking that the iconography of this figure speaks its own story about bodies in search of a balance between openness and closure. The half that is Ogum is the body of Saint Jorge (who in the candomblé of Rio de Janeiro, where these statuas are made, is associated with Ogum). He wears a helmet, a metal armour, and carries a huge sword. Interestingly, his one eye is blue, which in Santo Amaro first and foremost signals that he is not from Bahia. The other half is the naked body of an exu, red-fleshed, bare-headed, and brown-eyed. Exu spirits are frequently discussed as "tricksters," the ones who make a mess – spirits

130 Mattijs van de Port

like Gira Mundo, who tell a visiting anthropologist to "throw himself." The figure of Xoroquê, standing next to statues of wholly naked exus and statues of wholly armoured Ogums, underscores the contradictory demands that go into imagining the body in Santo Amaro.

Conclusion

The key to understanding religion, writes Michael Jackson in this volume, is not to transform its practices into "a systematic theology or metaphysics of existence," but to see how they are "a practical coping skill." Which is indeed what my current research project – which is ongoing, and far from closed – has been teaching me thus far.

Because of the research for this film, which focuses on violence and the vulnerability of the body, my previous discussions of candomblé religiosities highlighted their metaphysical underpinnings but took on the aspect of being overly "philosophical." I realized just how much my thinking – taking place in the setting of a Dutch university – had been catering to topics and issues that fellow academics might deem captivating and intellectually titillating. Thus, when I addressed the dynamics of "opening and closing" encountered in Bahia in a chapter in Michael Jackson's and Albert Piette's volume *What Is Existential Anthropology?* (2015), I pondered similar materials from Santo Amaro as those presented here to arrive at a critique of Bruno Latour's Actor Network Theory (which I admire for radically embracing the openness of Being, but critique for insufficiently addressing the human incapacity to live such openness). Or, to give another example, in my monograph on candomblé (Van de Port 2011), I had interpreted the important value of secrecy as an acknowledgment in candomblé that there are limits to verbal articulation; a reminder, common in mystical religiosities, that there is a knowing of the world beyond the grasp of language. On the streets of Santo Amaro, however, secrecy revealed itself as yet another form of closing one's body: the capacity to shut one's mouth, to not share information, to not reveal one's views and opinions, as these can always be used against you.

Clearly, the one understanding does not exclude the other. This is therefore not to say that my previous discussions of "philosophical" issues in the sayings and doings of my Bahian interlocutors were farfetched or irrelevant. Indeed, if there is one thing that keeps driving me back to Michael Jackson's existential anthropology, it is its recognition that all humans, because they participate in the world *as humans*, face similar issues and dilemmas in their lives: our dependence on language to make sense of ourselves and the world; our capacity to contemplate the finitude of our lives, to remember the past and imagine the future; our having bodies which do not necessarily comply with what we want to make out of them, producing unassimilable sensations and experiences – "alien feelings that are our own" as Alphonso Lingis (1994) called them. Such experiential domains produce "philosophies" wherever one goes, and although such "philosophies" may arrive at radically different understandings, they do provide a common ground for ongoing conversations between anthropologists and the people they study. Yet the thematic prism of o corpo fechado – and the lens of my camera – forced me to face the more immediate, concrete, and pressing concerns people in Santo Amaro have to deal with in their daily struggles. Violence in its manifold manifestations: physical violence, the violence of a ravaging disease, but also the violence of poverty, of inequality, of abuse. The maddening sense of being stuck, of finding all the avenues to progress being blocked. I am not sure where this awakening to what was always there, in my face, is going to take me, intellectually and artistically. At first sight, to go back to an understanding of religion as a "coping mechanism" feels like a flattening of discussions. But then again, the depth, subtlety, and theoretical complexity I fear losing out on might have to be produced in the descriptions and the depictions of the lives in which religion plays itself out. Back to the people. I guess I will have to throw myself again and see what comes. Good to know I can do so with an arruda tattooed on my arm.

WORKS CITED

Ahmed, Sara and Jackie Stacey, eds. 2001. *Thinking through the Skin*. London: Routledge.

Benson, Susan. 2000. "Inscriptions of the Self. Reflections on Tattooing and Piercing in Contemporary Euro-America." In *Written on the Body. The Tattoo in European and American History*, edited by Jane Caplan, 212–34. Princeton: Princeton University Press.

Jackson, Michael. 1983. "Knowledge of the Body." *Man* 18, no. 2: 327–45. https://doi.org/10.2307/2801438.

–. 1996. *Things as They Are. New Directions in Phenomenological Anthropology*. Bloomington: Indiana University Press.

Jackson, Michael, and Albert Piette, eds. 2015. *What Is Existential Anthropology?* London: Berghahn.

Lingis, Alphonso. 1994. *Foreign Bodies*. London: Routledge.

Port, Mattijs van de. 2011. *Ecstatic Encounters. Bahian Candomblé and the Quest for the Really Real*. Amsterdam: Amsterdam University Press.

–. 2015. "Reading Bruno Latour in Bahia. Or: How to Approach 'the Great, Blooming, Buzzing Confusion' without Going Mad." In *What Is Existential Anthropology?*, edited by Michael Jackson and Albert Piette, 84–104. London: Berghahn.

–. 2021. *The Body Won't Close. Bahian Tales of Danger and Vulnerability*. Royal Anthropological Institute. Film.

Taylor, Charles. 2007. *A Secular Age*. Harvard: Harvard University Press.

–. 2008. "Buffered and Porous Selves." The Immanent Frame. 2 September 2008. https://tif.ssrc.org/2008/09/02/buffered-and-porous-selves/.

6 Destiny as a Relationship and a Theory

SAMULI SCHIELKE

First Fragment: The Inevitable Hour of Death

At the end of June 2019, I travelled to Vienna, the hometown of my late wife Daniela Swarowsky. She had died in Berlin on the first morning of June after being sick with breast cancer for four and half years. I needed to sort out the furnished apartment that she had left behind in her hometown, but I ended up spending more of my time meeting her friends and family. Other friends in Vienna had recently lost close ones, too. Death was a frequent topic of discussion.

At a dinner with friends and relatives, somebody spoke about the illness and death of a close relative of hers, and then asserted that the date of death of each one of us is irrevocably fixed by the time of our birth. Others present expressed agreement with the idea. This was a gathering of a highly educated urban bourgeois, Catholic Christian to post-Christian, ethnic Austrian circle, that is, a place and people rather more associated with liberal values such as self-determination, individuality, and free choice. The same people who agreed about the predetermined hour of our death had just spoken at length about their choices of diet, expressed care for their bodily health and longevity, and acted as if they had a choice on such matters.

But this tension did not disturb people at the dinner. In fact, I have found that entertaining both ideas at the same time is quite widespread among people like me – highly educated white people from Europe. It is not a contradiction in need for a solution, but a fluctuating, ambiguous coexistence of different understandings about life and death.

It should come as no surprise that societies in which liberal values have currency are not consistently liberal (just as it should not surprise anybody that societies where Islamic values have currency are not consistently Islamic).[1] This echoes Michael Jackson's argument (in this

134   Samuli Schielke

volume) that it is an "illusion" to think that "forms of being correspond with forms of thought." On a conceptual plane, liberal political theory and ethics and various Christian and Muslim theologies may seem incommensurable. And yet diet choices for a longer life and faith in the predestined hour of one's death can easily coexist in one society, in one person's life, and in one dinner table conversation because both make specific sense as cultivated attitudes towards living. It makes sense to take care of one's health, the more so in a society and social class where advances in medicine and a high standard of living have made longevity a normal expectation. And it also make sense to understand death and its timing as something that is ultimately not in our hands, the more so in a world where we in spite of all advantages do not know how long we will live, what will eventually kill us, and when.

Such coexistence of different, at times conflicting values and ideas is quite unremarkable and often unproblematic. This might thus be the end of the story if it weren't for a drama that is remarkable indeed, and that does repeatedly generate problems that humans need to deal with in one way or another.

It is the drama of acting while being acted upon that was so pointedly described by Michael Jackson in his 2005 book *Existential Anthropology*. That drama stands at the heart of many moral dilemmas in which the monotheistic God of the Bible and the Qur'an is involved.[2] On the one hand, the monotheist God is omnipotent and already knows what we will do and what will happen to us. On the other hand, He holds us responsible for what we do and will reward and punish us according to our choices. Sunni Muslim theology has come up with an interesting and remarkably existentialist rendering of this drama (though definitely not on the atheistic terms of Sartre's existentialism), to which I will devote more detailed attention next. That rendering provides many people I know a compelling way to live the drama (which is not the same as solving it) – destiny.

Interlude in Place of an Introduction

Destiny is a relationship humans cultivate with superhuman actors and powers. At the same time, it is a theory of human action and its limits that may be true in an existential sense. To think about one's condition and trajectory in terms of destiny is to recognize that humans can have power over their condition only in accordance and alliance with powerful others. What kinds of power relations, or "relationship power," do humans and the superhuman authors of their destiny craft? What does the tension between responsibility and inevitability that destiny

Destiny as a Relationship and a Theory   135

thrives on teach us about the possibility of acting in the world? Much like our knowledge of our lives, my account in this essay is fragmentary. Instead of a straightforward argument that would lead from an introduction to a conclusion, I sketch four fragments (two of which are based on previous publications)[3] that draw upon my own biography, my fieldwork in Egypt and engagement with Sunni Muslim theologies, comparative anthropologies of destiny, and popular cultures.

The first fragment set the scene for the very ordinary yet compelling drama of acting and being acted upon that stories of destiny tell about. In the *second* and longest *fragment* that will now follow, I engage with lived Sunni Muslim theologies of destiny and argue that the intertwining of predestination and responsibility is a useful starting point for an existential anthropology that also has an eye for political economy and accounts for ecologies of livelihood and relations of power – importantly including power relations with God. By thinking of destiny as a relationship in the *third fragment*, I follow a lead offered by Robert Orsi (2005) to think of specific relationships between "heaven and earth," between humans and superhuman beings, rather than religion and religions (I have elaborated this thought in Schielke 2019). Relationships that humans build with God, gods, saints, and leaders are existential and political in the same instance. They are intimate relations of power that allow humans to deal with urgencies, find answers to problems that move them – and that at the same time impose upon humans certain solutions and answers rather than others. By relating destiny with the popular cultural genres of tragedy and happy endings in the *fourth fragment*, I suggest that destiny as a relationship and a theory thrives on an ambiguity that ought not to be resolved: it tells *both* about the "ethical negotiability in our relationship with life" evoked by Michael Jackson in this book, *as well* as life's non-negotiable hard limits: things over which we have no power, consequences that we cannot reverse, and the inevitable prospect of death.

Second Fragment: Did God Bring Down the Regime?

My first encounter with the Sunni Muslim theology of destiny took place almost thirty years ago, sometime in early December 1991. I was hitchhiking across Tunisia on a trip that would later inspire me to start studying Arabic and eventually to become an anthropologist. But I had no idea of that then. I was nineteen and enjoyed the first-world privilege of aimless travel for leisure and discovery. One day, I arrived in a village in central Tunisia, the name of which I no longer remember, and met two men of my age. They invited me to a drink in the car repair workshop of a friend of theirs. They brought beer and I had whisky in my backpack. Soon we were drunk. Before I realized, we were seated in an old half-broken car and were driving out of the village. My hosts had decided to take a joyride. The driver was so drunk that he had to stop the car to get out and vomit, while I loudly protested and demanded that somebody else should drive and that we should return to the village immediately. The others were not worried. "He's a good driver," they told me. When I continued protesting, one of them argued that as a Muslim, he has faith that the hour of our death is predestined by God, and we cannot change it. I found the claim badly out of place: "But your religion also forbids alcohol! Don't talk to me about Islam when we're all drunk." We did return safely to the village. The predestined hour had not yet come. I felt that I had been smarter than them, but in hindsight I feel rather embarrassed about the confident ignorance of my younger self.

Many years later I understood that destiny is religious in a rather different way than prayers, rituals, prohibitions, and ethical aims are. There was nothing strange at all about my hosts trusting in God while drinking and driving. Yes, most Muslims I know would agree that drinking is *haram*, prohibited. Yes, drinking and driving certainly is reckless and dangerous. And yes, this did not in any way lessen the anticipation that the hour of our death is indeed predetermined by God.

Luca Nevola (2015), who has written about ideas of destiny and choice in northern Yemen, argues that ethical and normative aspects of religious life are, in the terminology of Clifford Geertz (1973), "models for": they tell us how people ideally should be, and they may be considered as true also when nobody lives by them – or more likely, when many people live by them in a partial fashion (something I have written about in Schielke 2015). Destiny, in contrast, says Nevola, is a "model of," a theory of how the universe works for the faithful and the infidels, the righteous and the wrongdoers alike.

In Egypt, where I have spent many years of fieldwork, destiny is the most accessible theory to account for the uncertainty about the outcomes of an action. Various Christian and Islamic theories of destiny are current in Egypt, but for my purposes, I focus on one very influential Islamic theory. Sunni Muslim theologies of destiny (*qadar*; Shia Muslim theologies have a different take, see Nevola 2018) are grounded in the numerous Qur'anic assertions about God's omnipotence, all things in the universe happening through God's will and foresight, irrevocably written (*maktub*) by God at the beginning of time. At a first glance, destiny might seem to be not a theory of action at all, since it might be understood as attributing all power to God and none to humans.

Destiny as a Relationship and a Theory   137

However, the more specific vocabulary of destiny, the way people employ the notion in their lives, and the way it has been developed by Muslim theologians all tell a different story.

To start with, destiny has different aspects. There are absolute aspects, such as *qada'*, or "fate," the written hour of one's death, which one can neither know nor change. There are more pragmatic aspects like *nasib*, or "fortune," which one cannot plan but can and should make do with (*yitsarraf*) in order to make the best of it. More important, people I know speak about destiny but at the same time consider themselves and one another to be responsible agents who can and should be advised, helped, hindered, thanked, or blamed. Knowing that one's date of death is irrevocably written does not hinder one from searching out all possible medical and spiritual aid in the case of illness, for example. God willing, it may help. Knowing that God alone knows whether one's search for success and fortune is successful does not prevent one from searching – on the contrary, it can motivate one to search for success, to be prepared for surprises, and to pray for God's help while doing so (Gaibazzi 2015).

In principle, everything that happens is destiny written by God. But in practice people I know do not apply destiny consistently as a general rule but rather in a more specific manner and with a specific intention. It can mean praying that the will of God is on the side of one's plans. It can mean searching for one's fortune while acknowledging that God alone knows whether and where one will find it. It can mean taking risks, including reckless ones such as drinking and driving. It can mean encouraging people to accept a life of poverty and oppression as the will of God. It can mean insisting on a struggle for a better world because God has promised that it will be victorious.

The way destiny is used in everyday speech, it emerges as one of the two key elements of a partly explicit, partly implicit theory of action and consequences in which the notions of freedom (or human power) and destiny (or divine power) can be drawn upon for different uses and situations. Freedom is not the same as agency in this context; rather freedom and destiny are both parts of a wider notion of what for the lack of a better term can be called agency, in the sense of having the power to make a difference. Destiny implies that such power is God's, but it may be embodied and exerted by humans.[4] Destiny, therefore, does not exclude freedom. To speak of freedom, choice, responsibility, and human power is to say that decisions must be made, things changed, action taken. To speak about destiny, fortune, and the will of God is to say that greater powers are at play, that after one has done what one can, the further course of things is beyond one's power, or

138 Samuli Schielke

that contentedness with one's share is the proper attitude to cultivate. However, the evocation of destiny usually also involves taking action, often phrased with the word *yitsarraf*, "to make the best out of one's circumstances."

Most of the time, people I know refer to freedom and destiny separately, shifting seamlessly between one and the other, depending on what they want to emphasize. But occasionally, they take the time to sit down and debate how exactly the two come together. (Such conversations that I have been invited to join have been a key site of learning for me, much more in fact than interviews could ever be, providing a productive intersection of fieldwork-based anthropology and theoretical reflection by non-experts.)[5] Sometimes they do so in situations where the moral tension between one's own powers and greater powers becomes too troubling to overlook, and one has to reflect about their relation in more detail. Sometimes they also do so because of the pleasure involved in an intricate theological and philosophical debate. And sometimes they address the relationship of destiny and freedom with a political intention.

In the summer of 2011, when freedom was the talk of the day in Egypt, Safwat Hegazy, a leading figure in the Muslim Brotherhood, coined the slogan "God alone brought down the system." According to Hegazy, Egyptians went to the streets to protest not out of their own accord but by the power of God. The rhetorical intention of this slogan was that if the revolution was the will of God, then Egypt's political future must be Islamic (it was explained to me in exactly this way by an Islamist sympathizer at a demonstration on Tahrir Square in the autumn of 2011). Shady, an active supporter of continuing revolution from a village in the northern Nile Delta, socialist by conviction and a firm opponent of Islamist movements, unsurprisingly did not agree with Safwat Hegazy. But he could not simply ignore his claim, because he, too, believed that the revolution was the will of God. But he had a different theory.

Shady and I met in a café in Alexandria on 10 October 2011, one day after the massacre at Maspero during which the Egyptian army killed almost thirty mainly Christian protesters and then blamed them for attacking the army. Shady and I were in a gloomy mood, and Shady explained to me that, in his view, the revolution had failed, nothing good was to be expected from either the army or the Islamists, and the liberal and leftist revolutionary current was not able to contest the power of religious political discourse. Only when he started reminiscing about the first days of the revolution did his tone change. No matter how bleak the situation appeared to us then, those first days had been the happiest

Destiny as a Relationship and a Theory 139

moments of his life. He started to reminisce about some narrow escapes from death, injury, and arrest:

> I lived, and for me the fact that I lived means that I'm not done, that I have a mission [*risala*] to complete. The protests on January 25 began with a shared sentiment of us all being so upset that we were ready to die. When we decided to go to protest on the Twenty-fifth, each of us felt that we were alone. But we became hundreds, then thousands. After feeling powerless and alone, we felt a sense of power in the moment when we were able to do something together. The Muslim Brothers claim that God moved the revolutionaries in spite of themselves [*ghasban 'anhum*]. But that's not true. We did it ourselves, with the will of God [*bi-mashi'at Al-lah*]. From my religious belief, I believe that everything that happens to me is written. What happens to me is destiny determined by God. But it doesn't mean that I'm not free. It's like in the script of a film. When you watch a film, you don't think that the characters just do what is written in the script: you see them acting in freedom, making choices, turning left or right. God is the director, but the characters act their roles in freedom. I don't know what my destiny is. I fulfil it without knowing what it will be.

Shady did not invent this theory himself. It is a theory with a remarkable history that goes back to debates among early scholars of Islam about whether humans are capable of choice (*mukhayyar*) or are predestined (*musayyar*). The canonical sources of Islam do not offer a univocal answer. The Qur'an explicitly and repeatedly states that everything happens by the will of God, and God alone makes people believers and infidels. The Qur'an also explicitly and repeatedly addresses believers and infidels alike as agents who can make up their minds, decide and act accordingly, and are held accountable for their deeds. This coexistence of two contrary claims by God Himself about divine and human agency has invited different interpretations among Muslim specialists and non-specialists alike. The best-remembered (although in the end not victorious) party in this debate was the intellectual movement of the Mu'tazila (from the second to fourth century after Hijra), who favoured a rationalist approach, argued that predestination contradicts moral responsibility and divine justice, and came to the conclusion that humans were free and not predestined (Vasalou 2008). The Mu'tazila continue to inspire intellectuals who search for alternative formulations of an Islamic faith. But a different theory eventually became the standard view of freedom and destiny. It is associated with Imam Abu al-Hasan al-Ash'ari (d. 324 AH/CE 936) the founding figure of the Ash'arite school of theology, which marked a departure from the rationalist tendencies

140   Samuli Schielke

of earlier centuries (Griffel 2009, 124–8). According to al-Ash'ari, humans acquire (*kasb* is the theological concept) the deeds which God has created for them:

> Some have said: The meaning that the Creator creates is that the action took place with infinitely pre-existent power-to-act (*qudra qadima*), and only the Creator acts with infinitely pre-existent power-to-act. And the meaning of acquisition (*kasb*) is that the action takes place through a temporarily actualised power-to-act (*qudra muhdatha*). For who accomplishes an act with infinitely pre-existent power-to-act is a Creator-agent, and who accomplishes an act with temporarily actualised power is an acquirer (*muktasib*); and this is said by the people of truth. (al-Ash'ari 1980, 538–9)

In other words, humans are *both* capable of choice and predestined. We fulfil our written destiny in freedom. From a philosophical and logical point of view, it could be argued that while the Mu'tazilite theory is sound, the Ash'arite theory is unsound because it does not solve the paradox of reward and punishment in a world where one could not have acted otherwise. And yet the logical contradiction of the Ash'arite theory should not make us overlook its existential truth.

From an existential point of view, the contradiction at the heart of Ash'arite theology is a productive one because it describes what it means to act out of one's own accord in a world that is not of one's own making and in which one does not have the power to determine the premises and consequences of one's actions. From the worshipper's point of view, it therefore allows one to evoke the power of God in two different capacities at the same time. This was very pronounced in an interview Mukhtar Saad Shehata and I conducted in the autumn of 2011 with Hajja Z., a woman in her late fifties from a village in the northern Nile Delta. The topic of the interview was the recent revolution, which she had wholeheartedly supported. Her sympathies were with Islamist movements, but she also had misgivings about them, and she was angry about the many blatant injustices she was perceiving. She concluded her speech in a preaching tone:

> Z: So if I had the means to go to that square, or if it were close to me, or if somebody could take me there, I would have joined them, because I believe that our sublime and exalted Lord *does not change the condition of a people until they change what is in themselves.*[6] So if I [unclear]; what happens is that we escape from God's predestined decree to God's predestined decree (*min qada' illah li-qada' illah*) [meaning that an attempt to escape one's

Destiny as a Relationship and a Theory   141

destiny eventually results in the realization of one's destiny]. If I'm inside the house, it will also hit me. But I do something I can meet God with, that I can say to Him: I did, oh Lord. All I did was praying (*bad'i*) to Him, I was standing in front of them [meaning the demonstrators she saw on television]; changing and switching channels on television.

...

Mukhtar: Last word, Hajja. How do you see tomorrow?

Z: Tomorrow will be good, God willing (*in sha' Allah*), with the commandment of God (*bi-amr illah*) because He commands. Our sublime and exalted Lord, the hearts of the people are pure. You say: Oh Lord! It will not make you shy, Mukhtar. Our sublime and exalted Lord will not let anyone go to waste. ... I say to our Lord: Oh Lord, let everyone find their conscience and know that they stand in front of a Generous Lord, [the pitch of her voice increases and she raises her hand for emphasis] and they will be alone in the grave, and they will be questioned! There will be a day when they stand alone in isolation and darkness; nobody will stand by them, and no money and nothing else will work. And nobody will get more than is written (*maktub*) for them.

Hajja Z. did not try to elaborate how exactly predestination and responsibility go together. Instead, she evoked God as a constitutive third party of relations among humans in both capacities: as the Creator and the Protector who gives people only what He has written for them and protects them from being lost; and as the Judge and the Witness (all these are among the ninety-nine canonical names of God) who expects people to change themselves first and who will hold people accountable for their choices and judge them accordingly. Furthermore, her focus on justice, responsibility, and destiny reminds us that addressing God is usually not about establishing coherence (which it might be if she had tried to formulate a correct doctrinal understanding of what is and what is not justice, or how exactly responsibility and predestination come together), but about getting to the point, and firmly so.

In an earlier version of this fragment published in my book *Egypt in the Future Tense* (Schielke 2015, 220–3), I went on to propose that the Ash'arite theology of the power to act could also be made work without God; it can be formulated as a theory of acts and consequences, where every act is part of an immense chain of acts and consequences that may be called destiny. One does not have to believe that an omnipotent God has written our destiny for us to consider Ash'ari's proposition a useful existential theory of human action. In a materialistic reading of al-Ash'ari's theistic theory, destiny would be simply the sum of all consequences. We "acquire" the "temporarily actualised power to act" (to follow al-Ash'ari's terminology) while the reality from which our acts arise (and to which they contribute) is not our own creation.

But that would go against the grain of Hajja Z.'s point. The Ash'arite theology of the power to act is not about consequences; it is about God and humans. What makes it attractive is that God wants and plans it to happen, and yet He gives humans the freedom and responsibility to do it themselves, according to His plan. Egyptians who spoke to me about destiny were not just reflecting about inevitable consequences, but about God having written their life with a purpose and intention in His masterpiece. It is a masterpiece with some inevitable tragic turns but eventually, it shall have a happy end if you play well the role which God has written for you.

Predestination and responsibility are equally compelling ways to act and to judge the actions of oneself and others. Al-Ash'ari's theology of human and divine power to act is a complex intellectual justification for what Hajja Z. did in more straightforward terms: claiming both at once. Few people try to consistently think about the link between the two, however, because to do so is seldom helpful and potentially unsettling.

For some years, Shady was among those few. Around 2011, Shady was taking up the issue of destiny frequently and with various people. He had a political reason to do so. He insisted that we should be consistent about the unity of destiny and freedom: The revolution was the will of God, but so was the Mubarak regime. If we thank God for the fact that somebody is a Muslim, we should also thank God for the fact that somebody is a Christian or an atheist. We are taught to accept poverty and oppression as God-given destiny, but when we struggle to change those things, we do so with the will of God. Underlying Shady's insistence on consistency regarding destiny was, not surprisingly, a revolutionary politics of freedom – a politics that, according to Shady, was a mission, a destiny written for him.

Eventually, Shady's strive for consistency inspired him to think altogether differently about the relationship between humans and God. When I met him in Cairo in 2019, he was no longer interested in the topic of destiny. Years after the successful consolidation of a new military regime in Egypt, there was not much to say about revolution either. He had other worries. He was a successful graduate student of management in a public university now, but his progress was slowed down by a chronic and life-threatening illness that required regular and arduous treatment. Many people find in illness an urgent cause to engage with God and the afterworld, but Shady had done the opposite. "My paradise is here," he said, taking distance from dreams of migration to metaphorical paradises abroad as well as from the promise of Paradise

Destiny as a Relationship and a Theory   143

in life after death. We took a walk through an old quarter spotted with numerous Muslim pilgrimage sites where I had conducted my PhD fieldwork in the early 2000s. I was happy to see those places again after years of absence, but he was quite uninterested in the Islamic history of Egypt. He found Pharaonic history more authentic and inspiring. In a matter-of-fact tone he described the monotheist God as "a human artefact" and moved on to other topics of discussion.

Third Fragment: Was the Moment Structured That Way?

It is possible to imagine a destiny that is not a relationship but instead a deterministic causal chain that writes itself without intervention by powerful others. Kurt Vonnegut ([1969] 1979) did so in his novel *Slaughterhouse-Five* about the firebombing of Dresden, which he witnessed as a young prisoner of war. The protagonist, Billy Pilgrim, travels in time between World War II, a postwar American present, and a near future. At one occasion, aliens from Tralfamadore abduct him. Tralfamadorians do not experience time the way humans do. They know past, present, and future at once, and yet they feel no anxiety or futility about knowing, for example, that the entire universe will eventually be destroyed by one of their scientific experiments:

> "If you know this," said Billy, "isn't there some way you can prevent it? Can't you keep the pilot from pressing the button?"
> "He has always pressed it, and he always will. We always let him and we always will let him. The moment is structured that way." (Vonnegut [1969] 1979, 80)

The paradoxically comforting determinism of the novel does not, however, prevent Vonnegut (who appears as himself, the author, in the novel) from giving some very direct moral advice as if it were possible to choose:

> I have told my sons that they are not under any circumstances to take part in massacres, and that the news of massacres of enemies is not to fill them with satisfaction or glee. I have also told them not to work for companies which make massacre machinery, and to express contempt for people who think we need machinery like that. (Vonnegut [1969] 1979, 20)

Destiny tells us to accept that the course of important events is decided independently of what we want or choose. It also tells us that we need to act to make it happen, to inhabit that which will happen, and perhaps to manipulate or change it to our advantage. This "malleable fixity" (Menin and Elliot 2018) has made destiny an extraordinarily helpful idea for humans to find their way in a life that they live but do not own. But one rarely encounters people who express faith in a blind, meaningless destiny in the fashion of *Slaughterhouse-Five*. Humans around the world trust in God or gods, search for clues about their fate in divinatory techniques, and have faith in destiny-like historical forces such as progress, class struggle, or the market. Sometimes they insist that our own choices matter. The Tralfamadorians' recognition that "the moment is structured that way" is fundamentally less satisfying as an answer although I personally find it more likely to be true.

For most humans around the globe, destiny is not about a deterministic universe blindly stumbling along its inevitable path. It is about doing one's best in a relationship with greater powers.

This is evident in the articles of a recent collection of essays on ethnographies of destiny (Menin and Elliot 2018). In a contribution to the collection, Luca Nevola (2018) listens to Yemenis as they reflect about unfulfilled life plans. Destiny emerges as a "dialectical relationship between God's will and human intentional action." In the theological language of Zaydi Shiism, *qadar* (defined as potentiality)[7] and *nasib* (defined as destiny in hindsight) provide both a language of choice and a way to rationalize unhappy consequences. This characteristic dialectic gives destiny a political (or perhaps antipolitical) edge, which is even more explicit in Daniel Guinness's (2018) article in the same collection on Fijian rugby players and their aspirations. Three different destinies with different sources of power – ethnonationalist, professional, Christian – are at play there. For the rugby players, destiny in this constellation is not about limits of human power but, on the contrary, empowerment through alliance with divine power: "I can do anything through Christ who strengthens me" (Phillipians 4:13). But only few players become professionals. In her article on diviners and their clients in Taiwan, Stéphanie Homola (2018) sketches a non-monotheistic predestination where some knowledge and negotiation of one's fate is possible, even imperative. Such knowledge is comparably less accessible in monotheistic traditions. These three articles reveal an interesting contrast between the partially knowable and impersonal destiny of birth-hour signs and other non-monotheistic powers on the one hand, and the unknowable and personal destiny of the monotheist God on the other. The first type of destiny is a structure made of superhuman but comparably impersonal forces that humans may try to discover and manipulate in the best possible way. The latter kind of destiny involves a more personal relationship (often including a promise) that calls humans to submit to and trust an omnipotent, benevolent God. This is not a dualist alternative, of course: the traditions featured in the three articles all involve personal, intentional relationships as well as techniques to predict, facilitate, and perhaps also change fate. But they do so each with their own emphasis.

This is relational power not so much as in Michel Foucault's bio-power, but more as in contemporary English vernacular use of "relationships" as intimate bonds. Such bonds also link "heaven and earth," Robert Orsi suggests (2005). This kind of "relationship power" is effective by means of intimate, emotional bonds of friendship, enmity, love, fear, trust, help, guidance, and importantly, gratefulness.[8]

A power to which one can be grateful – this is crucial for the relationships humans build with the One God, gods of polytheist pantheons, saints, heroes, and leaders. But are clients of divinatory experts grateful to the stars, the spirits, or the divination sticks when they receive good advice that helps them make the right decision? Not in the same way, it seems. Different relationships of power are at play, and they make for different experiences of destiny.

The experience and narratives of destiny are evidently not limited to monotheist moral lives and dilemmas, although the monotheist relationship of power does add a heightened dramatic tension, further foregrounded by the Islamic focus of this essay. I suggest that destiny and destiny-like stories are a widespread and helpful theory that allows humans in different contexts and traditions to address the condition of acting and being acted upon. Their ontologies, conceptual languages, and ethical aims may be incommensurable; however, moments of incommensurability are already part and parcel of every ontological stance and ethical life I know of. Incommensurability is a common and practical complication; dealing with it is a major part of what anthropologists call ethics (Lambek 2015). It regularly results in problematic translations and ambiguous commitments, but it is not a fundamental obstacle to understanding and communication.

Destiny is an existential concept par excellence, a prime case of the productive tension between "being an actor and being acted upon" evoked by Michael Jackson (2005, 182). The issue of destiny usually arises in relation to urgent, compelling, or dangerous matters: livelihood and the risk of losing it; love and marriage; aspiration, success, and failure; health and illness; life and death. Contrary to twentieth century polemics against "fatalism," destiny in its different varieties is very much about risk-taking, initiative, and serendipity (D'Angelo 2015; Gaibazzi 2015; Hsu and Hwang 2016). This is not to deny that destiny also involves submission and waiting, but submission can be

146 Samuli Schielke

hard work that requires commitment and skill (Mahmood 2005), and waiting can be an active practice that requires energy and effort (Jeffrey 2010). Destiny is a religious concept in the widest sense of living in a meaningful world structured by greater powers which one needs to reckon with, which one may trust, which one can appeal to and search alliance with, and to which one may perhaps also be grateful. Specific experiences of destiny stand in traditions of moral and metaphysical reasoning which offer compelling ways to understand and deal with the urgencies humans face.

At the same time, those urgencies are structured by historically specific political economies and inter-human power relations. Destiny is also a relationship humans have with each other by mediation of nonhuman and superhuman powers. It empowers some humans over others. Experts specialized in reading signs of destiny profit from their skill – and yet, as Homola (2018) shows, this does not make them immune to failure and hardship. The politics of God and the Heavens often lean to the right: they encourage us to strive for improvement and success while accepting hierarchies and defeats as inevitable. Destiny is not always on the side of established hierarchies, and sometimes socialist revolutionaries find God on their side (like Shady did in the previous fragment). But destiny teaches us that free choice and individual autonomy are fictions – useful, inspirational fictions perhaps, but fictions all the same. And more often than not, destiny tells us that this is how it should be, that those who have power are destined to have it.

Radical, revolutionary movements in the past two centuries have often vehemently denied that such privileges are predestined. They have insisted that men are not naturally or by God's decree superior to women, that kings do not have a divine mandate to rule, that humans of European origin are not endowed with a civilizing mission to colonize the world, and that social hierarchies are neither necessary nor morally right. The attack on human inequality has occasionally involved an attack on the very idea of divine power (e.g., Bakunin [1882] 1907). But there is a twist to the story. These radical movements have often come up with destiny-like narratives of their own: Marxist socialists have come up with the inevitable progress of historical dialectics. Modernists from left and right have come up with the idea of an inevitable economic and scientific progress and (in liberal and social-democrat versions) human emancipation. Religious radicals have resorted to the power of God to counter human injustice (e.g., Qutb [1964] 1978). When such radical movements seize power, these new destinies become the metaphysical and moral foundations of new productive inequalities. The communist party tells workers what their true collective will must be and sends dissenters to concentration camps. Only those who are able to take destiny into their own hands in neoliberal markets are entitled to a good life in emancipation and comfort. Those who claim to overcome human rule for the sake of the rule of God become the new human rulers over others, in the name of God.

When Tralfamadorians abducted Billy Pilgrim in *Slaughterhouse-Five*, his first question was "Why me?" They explained to him that this is a typically Earthling question and unanswerable: "There is no why" (Vonnegut [1969] 1979, 56). Earthlings, however, do seem to prefer stories that tell them why. And this is what destiny as a narrative form does. It tells that there is a why. This is not simply the why of cause and effect. It is a why concerning the moral of the story, a moral and temporal why that calls for practical answers about how the past turned out the way it did, and what I should do now and in the future.

I will become a successful professional rugby player because my tradition, my genes, and my faith have elected me to be one, and in order to make that election true I have to train and pray hard (Guinness 2018). There was no *nasib* to realize my marriage plans, so I ought to look for another bride (Nevola 2018). My projects failed because I kept trying something that was not my fate: I should pay closer attention to the eight signs of my birth hour and avoid such disappointments again (Homola 2018). This moral quality of destiny (moral both in the sense of cultivation of what one understands to be good and right in a relationship, and in the sense of the moral to a story that makes it meaningful and helpful) is intimately linked with the way destiny works as "relationship power" between human and superhuman actors. Without the latter, there would be no moral to the story; the moment would simply be structured that way.

Greater powers to which we can relate, with whom we can communicate and create a relationship, are meaningful because they offer moral and practical guidance in a way that a blind deterministic destiny would not. In the face of overwhelming circumstances, destiny provides helpful allies or generous masters. As a moral relationship of power, destiny turns chance encounters into divine gifts and times of hardship into second chances. Equally, it also turns privilege into entitlement and force into legitimate authority.

Fourth Fragment: On Tragedy and Happy Endings

Destiny as a story that we tell of our lives thrives on contradictions and conflicts between hope and despair, responsibility and necessity, power

148   Samuli Schielke

and powerlessness. But while conflict is essential for drama, its characters and conventions do not stay the same.

A remarkable feature of Hollywood movies is the overwhelming dominance of happy endings. They proliferate also in other cinematic traditions, be it in Bollywood, Egyptian or other. This stands in a remarkable contrast to the historically widespread genre of tragedy. A happy ending – if well-written – is unlikely and against the odds of a story, yet possible and plausible. It follows after a near disaster, an almost final breakup, a difficult and dangerous confrontation. It might be read as the popular cinematic equivalent of liberal choice. In a world of Hollywood-style happy endings everything is possible as long as you take the right actions and say the right words at the right moment.

The Adjustment Bureau (Nolfi 2011), for example, is a safely entertaining Hollywood movie that takes up destiny explicitly and gives it a Hollywood twist: the hero and the heroine defy destiny (which is administrated by a bureaucratic crew of angels), and God sympathizes with their exercise of free will so much that He changes His plan and lets them have it their way. Happy ending!

Tragedy claims the opposite. The path of King Oedipus leads him towards the fulfilment of the prophecy that his parents wanted to avoid. Majnun's love for Layla, whom he was not meant to marry, results in madness and death. Macbeth's thirst for power drives him inevitably into his downfall. In tragedy humans challenge destiny, and destiny wins.

Perhaps happy endings of the Hollywood kind have become more popular in the wake of economic growth and ideas of individual fulfilment. If that has happened, the shift has been one of emphasis rather than substance. For happy endings were around long before liberal and progressive ideals of individual fulfilment. Happy endings are an established part of Islamic traditions and classical Arabic prose (Al-Tanukhi 1978). In the *Arabian Nights* they proliferate, often miraculous and unlikely, usually with the help of spirits and the supreme power of God. Abrahamic faiths promise happy endings of reunion and reward in a better life after death. They explicitly deny the possibility of tragedy as an ultimate outcome of eschatological history (al-Azm 1969, 74–5). Also among people in Egypt I know, the anticipation of destiny is more often than not accompanied by a fundamentally optimistic anticipation that everything will turn all right, or as the Qur'an says: "Surely with hardship comes ease" (94:5; see also Al-Tanukhi 1978, 59–60).

In life, tragedy is available in abundance. The only way to not lose those we love is to either love nobody or to die before them. Throughout most of human history, material well-being has been precarious at best for most, and a privilege bought with force and violence for the lucky few. The increasing wealth and freedom that many human inhabitants of the Earth today enjoy are based on accelerated growth – a tragic historical process if there ever has been one because it can impossibly continue for long, and will inevitably reach its limits with catastrophic consequences (Barnosky et al. 2012).

All religious traditions (in the widest sense) I know of promise ways to find ease in hardship. Some – not all – religious traditions also promise an ultimate happy ending in paradise in face of the tragic quality of life. That promise is very present and compelling in Egypt among Muslims and Christians alike. It structures life so deeply and intimately that most Egyptians I know find it hard to imagine how somebody would do the right thing and abstain from evil without the prospect of divine reward and punishment in the afterworld. Some fewer people I know ask heretical questions about the nature of evil. If God is omnipotent and Good, why is He committed to sending so many of His creatures to hellfire? Do we perhaps need Satan as a lead character in a meaningful drama of good and evil more urgently than we might want to acknowledge (al-Azm 1969, 55–87; Essakouti 2018)? And yet good and evil, hardship and ease, happy and tragic outcomes seem easier to deal with when we are not too consistent about them, and instead follow the lead of their constitutive, productive contradiction.

Destiny does not teach us to simply anticipate either tragedy or happy endings. Instead, it teaches us to structure our anticipation and hope along the dialectic tension between tragedy and happy endings, whereby either way has its good, inevitable moral of the story, and one may always turn out to be just the prequel to the other. The preliminary tragedy of death will be followed by the happy ending of paradise, say those with faith in God (and by saying so they express the trust that they are followers of the right faith because followers of other faiths will be deprived of that happy ending). The preliminary happy ending of progressive societal accomplishments will be followed by the tragedy of extinction, my friends versed in ecology will say (and at the same time, they fight to safeguard or advance some those progressive accomplishments).

Daniela was a Buddhist. She anticipated to be reincarnated as a new person in this same world, which is a story with less binary drama than is provided by Christian and Islamic eschatologies of salvation and damnation. In the teaching she followed, the principle of karma, the inevitable consequences of our freely chosen actions that follow us in our lives and from one reincarnation to the other, is connected with the promise of a gradual liberation from the dialectic of attachment and loss. During her final years, Daniela was keen to read Theravada Buddhist texts that teach us to calmly accept the inevitable decay of our bodies and to free ourselves from our attachment to them. Those readings strengthened her courage to face the situation as it was, to embrace life while knowing that there probably was little time left. She was not concerned with what comes after death. What appealed to her more was the Buddhist teaching to overcome attachment; yet at the same time, she was very attached to life and good things in it. She didn't go by the book, and she was not trying to.

After all, doing things by the book is not the point of either destiny or karma. Or it is a book we can never read. Instead, we can take destiny, karma, and others of their kind seriously as what they are: relationships and theories that do not tell a consistent truth but rather provide us a dramatic tension through which we may live our lives. That is also my personal view of that tension. I think that death came too early for Daniela, that she should have, could have lived longer. I also think that the moment was structured that way, that we did what we could with our temporarily actualized power to act; while a happy ending to our story was not available, it was as good as it could be. Both thoughts are true of me.

ACKNOWLEDGMENTS

Additionally to the people mentioned in this essay, thanks are due to Paola Abenante, Jamie Coates, Asmaa Essakouti, Alice Elliot, Paolo Gaibazzi, Laura Menin, Amira Mittermaier, Sadhu Panyasara, Devaka Premawardhana, and Don Seeman.

NOTES

1 I have dwelt on this theme in more detail in Schielke (2015).
2 Speaking of the monotheist God as the shared subject of worship in all Abrahamic traditions, I do not claim that He has a single reified set of characteristics. Rather, various (and mutually contested) ways to worship Him share important structuring tensions that compel worshippers to position themselves in one way or another; the tension between Divine omnipotence and omniscience on the one hand, and human choice and responsibility, on the other, is an especially prominent and productive one. Different positionings towards this tension have found their intellectual expressions, for example, in Arminian and Calvinist theologies of human freedom and divine

predestination, respectively, and in different configurations of the human and divine power to act among Sunni Muslims. The latter I discuss below.

3 The second fragment is a revised version of a passage of my book *Egypt in the Future Tense* (Schielke 2015, 220–3), except for the interview with Hajja Z. which is a shortened version of a passage published in my essay "The Power of God" (Schielke 2019, 7–8), and the opening story about the car ride Tunisia in 1991, which is previously unpublished. The third fragment is a revised and expanded version of my afterword (Schielke 2018) to the special section "Anthropologies of Destiny" (Menin and Elliot 2018). The first and fourth fragments are new.

4 The assumption of causal efficacy from the social scientist's point of view of human acts ("agency") as measured against a larger "structure" is not part of this theory. That assumption has been criticized by Laidlaw (2013, 185) whose fundamental misgivings about the concept of agency I share. The vernacular theory of human and divine power is not about acting against structure, and it leaves open the question who possesses the power of efficacy.

5 Existential anthropology has proven itself to be quite good at such conversations, taking as its guideline that "any interpretive synthesis one presents is the product of dialogue" (Jackson 1998, 5) while not being too heavily loaded by a discursive tunnel vision. Although Jackson's original sketch of existential anthropology of religion was rather opposed to the reliance on theological concepts, researchers inspired by the project (e.g., Premawardhana 2020; Seeman 2018) have engaged intensively with theologies as potentially good and true ways to understand the world *and* live in it.

6 This is a citation from the Qur'an, 13:11: *"inna llaha la yughayyiru bi-qawmin hatta yughayiru ma bi-anfusihim."*

7 The same word *qadar* has different uses in competing Muslim traditions, meaning divine predestination in the Sunni context, and potentiality that is up to human choice in Zaydi Shiism.

8 I have written more about the theme of relationship power and the triadic relationship between humans and God in Schielke (2019); I borrowed the notion of triadic relationship from Emanuel Schaeublin (2016).

WORKS CITED

Al-Ash'ari, 'Ali ibn Isma'il Abu al-Hasan. 1980 [died 324 AH/936 CE]. *Kitab maqalat al-islamiyin wa-khtilaf al-musallin* [The book of the professions of the Islamic people, and the disagreements among those who perform the prayer; in Arabic]. Edited by Helmut Ritter. 3rd ed. Wiesbaden: Harrassowitz.

152   Samuli Schielke

Al-Azm, Sadiq Jalal. 1969. *Naqd al-Fikr al-Dini* [The critique of religious thought; in Arabic]. Beirut: Dar al-Tali'a.

Al-Tanukhi, Al-Qadi Abu Ali al-Muhassan ibn Ali. 1978 [died 384 H/994 CE]. *Kitab al-faraj ba'd al-shidda*. [The book of happy endings after adversity; in Arabic] Edited by Abbud al-Shalji. Beirut: Dar Sadir.

Bakunin, Mikhail (Michel Bakounine). (1882) 1907. "Dieu et l'état." in *Oeuvres*, vol. 1, 5th ed., pp. 263–326. Paris: P.-V Stock. https://archive.org/details/oeuvresbs01bakuuoft/page/262/mode/2up.

Barnosky, Anthony D., et al. 2012. "Approaching a State Shift in Earth's Biosphere." *Nature* 486: 52–8. https://doi.org/10.1038/nature11018.

D'Angelo, Lorenzo. 2015. "'Diamond Mining Is a Chain.' Luck, Blessing, and Gambling in Sierra Leone's Artisanal Mines." *Critical African Studies* 7, no. 3: 243–61. https://doi.org/10.1080/21681392.2015.1077467.

Essakouti, Asmaa. 2018. "Fi l-haja al-jamaliya li-l-sharr wa-l-qubh min al-shaytan ila al-maskh." [On the aesthetic need for evil and ugliness from Satan to the monster; in Arabic]. Mominoun Without Borders. 9 May 2018. https://tinyurl.com/v6wuhse.

Gaibazzi, Paolo. 2015. "The Quest for Luck: Fate, Fortune, Work and the Unexpected among Gambian Soninke Hustlers." *Critical African Studies* 7, no. 3: 227–42. https://doi.org/10.1080/21681392.2015.1055534.

Geertz, Clifford. 1973. *The Interpretation of Cultures: Selected Essays*. New York: Basic Books.

Griffel, Frank. 2009. *Al-Ghazali's Philosophical Theology*. Oxford: Oxford University Press.

Guinness, Daniel. 2018. "Corporal Destinies: Faith, Ethno-nationalism, and Raw Talent in Fijian Professional Rugby Aspirations." *HAU: Journal of Ethnographic Theory* 8, no. 1–2: 314–28. https://doi.org/10.1086/698267.

Homola, Stéphanie. 2018. "Caught in the Language of Fate: The Quality of Destiny in Taiwan." *HAU: Journal of Ethnographic Theory* 8, no. 1–2: 329–42. https://doi.org/10.1086/698354.

Hsu, Hsin-Ping, and Kwang-Kuo Hwang. 2016. "Serendipity in Relationship: A Tentative Theory of the Cognitive Process of Yuanfen and Its Psychological Constructs in Chinese Cultural Societies." *Frontiers in Psychology* 7: 282. https://doi.org/10.3389/fpsyg.2016.00282.

Jackson, Michael. 1998. *Minima Ethnographica: Intersubjectivity and the Anthropological Project*. Chicago: University of Chicago Press.

–. 2005. *Existential Anthropology: Events, Exigencies and Effects*. Oxford: Berghahn Books.

Jeffrey, Craig. 2010. *Timepass: Youth, Class, and the Politics of Waiting in India*. Stanford: Standford University Press.

Laidlaw, James. 2013. *The Subject of Virtue: An Anthropology of Ethics and Freedom*. Cambridge: Cambridge University Press.

Lambek, Michael. 2015. "The Hermeneutics of Ethical Encounters: Between Traditions and Practice." *HAU: Journal of Ethnographic Theory* 5, no. 2: 227–50. https://doi.org/10.14318/hau5.2.014.

Mahmood, Saba. 2005. *Politics of Piety: The Islamic Revival and the Feminist Subject.* Princeton, NJ: Princeton University Press.

Menin, Laura, and Alice Elliot, eds. 2018. "Anthropologies of Destiny: Action, Temporality, Freedom." Special section. *HAU: Journal of Ethnographic Theory* 8, no. 1–2: 292–346. https://doi.org/10.1086/698223.

Nevola, Luca. 2015. "God Exists in Yemen, Part 2: The Moral Economy of Rizq." Allegra Lab. https://allegralaboratory.net/god-exists-in-yemen-part-2-the-moral-economy-of-rizq/.

–. 2018. "Destiny in Hindsight: Impotentiality and Intentional Action in Contemporary Yemen." *HAU: Journal of Ethnographic Theory* 8, no. 1–2: 300–13. https://doi.org/10.1086/698224.

Nolfi, George, dir. 2011. *The Adjustment Bureau.* United States: Universal Pictures.

Orsi, Robert A. 2005. *Between Heaven and Earth: The Religious Worlds People Make and the Scholars Who Study Them.* Princeton, NJ: Princeton University Press.

Premawardhana, Devaka. 2020. "In Praise of Ambiguity: Everyday Christianity through the Lens of Existential Anthropology." *Journal of World Christianity* 10, no. 1: 39–43. https://doi.org/10.5325/jworlchri.10.1.0039.

Qutb, Sayyid. (1964) 1978. *Milestones.* Beirut: Holy Koran Publishing House. http://www.kalamullah.com/Books/MILESTONES.pdf.

Schaeublin, Emanuel. 2016. *Zakat in Nablus (Palestine): Change and Continuity in Islamic Almsgiving.* PhD diss., University of Oxford.

Schielke, Samuli. 2015. *Egypt in the Future Tense: Hope, Frustration and Ambivalence, before and after 2011.* Bloomington: Indiana University Press.

–. 2018. "Destiny as a relationship ." *HAU: Journal of Ethnographic Theory* (afterword to thematic section "Anthropologies of Destiny") 8, no. 1–2: 343–6.

–. 2019. "The Power of God: Four Proposals for an Anthropological Engagement." *ZMO Programmatic Texts*, no. 13. http://d-nb.info/1175974781/34.

Seeman, Don. 2018. "Divinity Inhabits the Social: Ethnography in a Phenomenological Key." In *Theologically Engaged Anthropology*, edited by J. Derrick Lemons, pp. 336–54. Oxford: Oxford University Press.

The Adjustment Bureau. Vasalou, Sophia. 2008. *Moral Agents and Their Deserts: The Character of Mu'tazilite Ethics.* Princeton, NJ: Princeton University Press.

Vonnegut, Kurt. (1969) 1979. *Slaughterhouse-Five, or the Children's Crusade: A Duty-dance with Death.* London: Triad Grafton Books.

7 Worlds Colliding? Transnational Religion in Phenomenological Perspective

KIM E. KNIBBE

This chapter reflects on phenomenological and existential anthropology as a means of rethinking our approach to studying transnational religion. In my research since 2007, I have engaged with the expansion of a particular Nigerian-initiated Pentecostal church with a global presence, namely the Redeemed Christian Church of God (RCCG), building on the work of several colleagues who have studied the emergence and growth of this church in considerably more depth (see in particular Ukah 2005, 2008a, 2008b; Adogame 2008). This is a highly complex organization, and as I have argued elsewhere, should be seen as an agent in its own right. This would seem to contradict the warning of phenomenological anthropologist Michael Jackson against "reifying" religion. As an anthropologist and someone working in the field of religious studies with a "lived religion" approach, I am very much in sympathy with that caution. Nevertheless, I think it is crucial to also recognize that in particular cases, religion, or in this case, a particular type of Pentecostal Christianity, is reified into interlocking forms of practices, organizations, and networks that form a dynamic whole with some sort of agency. This agency, as many scholars of Pentecostalism have noted and debated, is singularly focused on calling into being a new reality on all levels: from that of the fate of the individual to the level of the spiritual fate of the whole world. Where Jackson draws our attention to events as the moments when something new is called into being (Jackson 2008), I would like to draw attention to the dynamics that emerge through an intentional focus on calling the new into being through church planting and "winning the whole world for Jesus."

How can we understand the ways a transnational religious actor such as the RCCG is able to mobilize individuals to participate in this enterprise, how does this enterprise gather power and intersect with the structures and processes of the contexts in which it tries to establish itself, and how can we relate this to the individual existential experience and orientation of migrants? These questions are important not only for debates in various sub-disciplines of anthropology, but also for the growing body of work developed under the rubric of "lived religion" in sociology and the study of religion. Research on transnational religion, both in anthropology and in the study of religion, rarely ventures beyond the religious setting itself, confining itself to the practices and narratives of the people who populate these settings (but see Premawardhana [2018] for an exception to this rule, also employing a phenomenological approach to Pentecostalism). Some research does bring into view the context in which these religious settings are created, but only incidentally. In this chapter, I propose that it is possible to be more systematic about looking into these questions by focusing on orientational dimensions, without either reifying religion or violating people's self-perceptions. Furthermore, this may also nuance the triumphalist narratives on the success of global Pentecostalism and transnational religion more generally (see Premawardhana [2018] and Freston [2010] for critiques of this narrative based on research in Mozambique and Europe respectively). Building on previous work, in the following I will think through these questions by drawing on phenomenological and existential anthropology, but also on some of the debate sparked by the ontological turn.

Transnational Religion as an Attempt at Worlding

Since the beginning of my research on the RCCG, my main fascination was with the ways in which this church was able to create vast transnationally stretched out worlds while also always being rooted firmly in local contexts. The first paper I wrote on this drew on Appadurai's notion of scapes, proposed in his influential collection of essays "modernity at large" (Appadurai 1996). Adding the suffix "-scape" (from landscape) to a particular phenomenon (e.g., ethnoscape, mediascape), Appadurai proposed a way of apprehending dimensions of global cultural flows that take into account the position of the observer, the irregularity of these flows, and their dimensions, but also their factuality: people must negotiate these overlapping and interlocking scapes. Thus, they are "perspectival constructs" (Appadurai 1996, 33).

The notion of scape, while often critiqued as too vague, helped me to conceptualize something that puzzled me from the beginning of my research: how could a phenomenon that was so big, powerful, and numerically impressive as the growth of Pentecostal churches in Nigeria and other parts of the world be simultaneously invisible, or when visible be dismissed as marginal, unimportant, a temporary "reaction" against modernization that would soon be overcome by many of the people in my own social and academic environment? "Scape" then, enabled me to conceptualize how two people travelling in the same tram in Amsterdam, to the same location in the south-east of Amsterdam, but with two different final destinations (for example, one Ikea, one the RCCG parish, located within a block of each other), could be in completely different worlds that are not aware of each other's existence (see Knibbe 2009 for an exploration of these themes).

As useful as this notion is, however, it does not help to understand how the "scape" of a secular Dutch Ikea-shopper relates to the "scape" of the RCCG, especially in terms of the constraints one would be able to impose on the other. Related terms, such as transnational social fields and networks (Levitt and Schiller 2004), are more precise in indicating what constitutes these "scapes" (social relationships, the circulation of goods and people). For the purposes of this chapter, however, I would like to borrow the term "worlding" from what has come to be called the ontological turn. Although not entirely in agreement with some of the agendas and propositions of this "turn," I am in sympathy with the attempt to more deeply engage with "radical alterity": the questioning of the reductionism that may follow from the assumption that people and their lifeworlds everywhere deep down are "just like us," and that we, as anthropologists, simply serve as translators of this difference to arrive at an insight into sameness. This questioning of reductionism and the underlying assumption of sameness is, as I have argued elsewhere (Knibbe 2020) very much in line with the initial impetus of phenomenological anthropology and existential anthropology.

In using the term "worlding" I refer in particular to an article by Mario Blaser in which he discusses the political implications of the ontological turn in relation to the proposition that anthropology should not depart from the assumption that the world consists of a "universe" differently perceived by different peoples, but could be perceived as a pluriverse, allowing for the possibility of different ways of "worlding." In Blaser's words:

> ontology is a way of worlding, a form of enacting a reality. ... What does this mean? (a) That we avoid the assumption that reality is "out there" and that "in here" (the mind), we have more or less accurate cultural representations of it; and (b) that reality is always in the making through the dynamic relations of hybrid assemblages that only after the fact are purified by moderns as pertaining to either nature or culture. (Blaser 2013, 551–2)

158   Kim E. Knibbe

Interestingly, this understanding of worlding is very close to or perhaps even identical to phenomenological understandings of "lifeworlds," in particular in the refusal to re-enact the distinction between nature (what is real) and "culture" (what is interpretation, imagination, etc.). In dealing with lifeworlds that include beings and agencies that are not conventionally recognized by Euro-American secular science, this suggests a radically different and non-reductive approach similar to the approaches developed in phenomenological and existential anthropology. Building on the understandings developed in the work of Michael Jackson and others, I have argued against the premise that the ontological turn goes "beyond epistemology." Rather, perceiving the world and enacting it cannot be seen as separate from each other (Knibbe 2020, 258). This means that the "worlds" that collide or live side by side in the case of Nigerian Pentecostals in the Netherlands each exist based on taken for granted ways of being in the world, knowing the world, and acting in it that individuals themselves do not necessarily question unless severely challenged.

By using the term worlding rather than lifeworlds, I also aim to stress the emergent and evolving character of the "reality in the making," leaving open the question of how successful this worlding is and how the "realities in the making" of, in this case, Nigerian Pentecostals interact with other "worlds." Furthermore, by using the term worlding as proposed by Blaser, there is an explicit recognition that the lifeworlds created through the activities of Nigerian Pentecostal missionaries may be "totalizing" in their aims but also always fail to be total.

In trying to gain an understanding of the Nigerian-initiated Pentecostal networks in Europe, the question is always "what" do we actually study? It may be clear "who" we study, namely those people who identify as Pentecostal, Nigerian, and are in Europe, but it is not clear *what* we study, since the lifeworlds and contexts in which they are situated and that are relevant keep shifting (Knibbe 2019, 135). For example, they shift in scale, from a local neighbourhood in Amsterdam, to global imaginaries and networks of Pentecostals variously based in the US, South Korea, Australia, and South Africa). But they also shift in terms of the particular sociopolitical arrangements that may be relevant or become irrelevant: from city ordinances affecting the availability of spaces to worship, to national policies affecting who can come in legally, and who is "illegal." These complexities are not necessarily new or unique to the phenomenon of Nigerian missionaries in Europe, but the particular local/global nexus and the ambitions of this church as an institution and a collection of individuals make them particularly visible. The term "worlding" thus encompasses both the ambition of this institution and the individuals engaged in church planting, the activities that create these worlds. But it also draws attention to the worldings created by the actors active in the same geographical location, such as policymakers, legislators, volunteers, academics.

So how can we observe and think about the ways different worldings, that is, the worlding of Nigerian Pentecostals and those of the actors in the contexts in which they are planting churches, interact and relate to each other (cf. Blaser 2013, 552)? I suggest that this can be done through a focus on what I call "orientational dimensions," in terms of time, space, embodiment, movement, materiality, relationality, as well as the "forces of otherness" to which everyone must find a way to relate existentially (Jackson 1998, 19). Following such orientational dimensions links the emphasis on the experiential and existential orientation of individuals as developed in Jackson's work, with the agency and worlding enacted through an institutional actor like the RCCG, allowing us to see how its narratives and practices orient, existentially engage, and become embodied in individuals, drawing them in to become missionaries and church planters. Crucially, a focus on orientational dimensions involves the recognition that individuals are often part of and affected by different worldings, with different narratives and practices enacting different notions of time, space, materiality, etc. simultaneously. While institutions often aim for singularity, transparency, and uniformity, a task for anthropologists and scholars of lived religion is to understand how these institutional actors, their practices, and mobilizations relate to the inevitability of contemporary life that one's life unfolds in settings that are affected by different worldings interacting with each other.

As Jackson has pointed out, commenting on the scholarship on transnational social fields, but also the work of Bayart and others, the perspective from which globalization and transnationalism are commented on is that of policymakers, never that of migrants themselves (Jackson 2013). Yet, those perspectives do also affect people existentially. The very designation of "migrant," "refugee," "undocumented person," or "expat" powerfully orients and materially affects the people to whom such categories are applied in quite different ways. In addition, part of the migration experience is often the loss of the "naturalness" of the ways of orienting oneself in the world that one normally, habitually, relies on, and much of the literature focuses on the loss of agency and "empowerment" that results from this process. The literature on "migrant churches" has often described these as a "home away from home," a safe haven in a hostile or indifferent environment, where people can briefly share the naturalness of having similar language, gestures, food preferences, and

160   Kim E. Knibbe

understandings of the world (Ukah 2005; Koning 2009). While this role may certainly be important to many of the congregants populating the parishes of the RCCG, it is in particular the enormous "worldbuilding" energy that accompanies the activities of a mega church such as the RCCG that draws the attention.

This worldbuilding energy contradicts the migration experience in that it is not predicated on a sense of loss of power. Rather, it force-fully poses the opposite: the notion that with God, anything is possible, church planting is necessary, and must therefore be tried against all odds. How does this worlding orient those individuals that are designated to become leaders and church planters in the context of secular Europe? Potentially, anyone belonging to this church can become a leader and church planter, since churches have a policy of immediately assigning a task to anyone who attends the services. At the same time, leaders often complain about the lack of capacity they encounter in their European congregations: while in Nigeria, there are always many people to choose from in assigning tasks and projects, in Europe congregations are much more unstable, often populated by students who are here only for a year, or expats. To offset this high turnover and lack of experience, older and more experienced missionaries are transferred to Europe, and there is a programme of very active cultivation of leadership among expats and those students who end up staying and finding a job in their host country.

Despite many challenges, in terms of church planting the RCCG is very successful: when I started my research in 2007, there were ten parishes in the Netherlands (Burgess, Knibbe, and Quaas 2010), while in 2020 there were over forty. In the UK and the US, their presence and power have grown in ways that are impossible to keep track of fully. They have a presence in almost all nation states of the world. How is this energy generated and sustained in people, how does it impact the world? How is this energy sustained in contexts that are hostile or indifferent to the world-making efforts of this institutional actor? How do the worldings thus generated interact with, intermingle, and become undone by other worldings in the context of Europe, the Netherlands, and Amsterdam as postcolonial frontier zones (Meyer 2018)? And how does this affect the existential trajectories of church planters? Below, I will sketch some of the dimensions through which these questions can be traced, following the trajectory of one particular interlocutor. I will focus in particular on the dimensions of space and time, noting that materiality, embodiment, and relation to the domain of things beyond human control may be other interesting dimensions to explore (see e.g., Smit [2009] for an exploration in terms of materiality). Before I do this, however, I will sketch the ways the RCCG as a religious actor has been interpreted as responding to existential dilemmas arising from life in postcolonial Nigeria.

Existential Dilemmas and the Question of Sovereignty

In her seminal book on Nigerian Pentecostalism, Ruth Marshall asks: if Jesus is the answer, then what was the question (Marshall 2009, 17)? Guided by this dilemma, she navigates the different explanations that had been offered thus far for the rise of Pentecostalism, and before that prophetic Christian churches collectively labelled African Indigenous churches, Zionist churches, or, in Nigeria, Aladura churches. Often, authors implicitly or explicitly interpreted these movements as a response to capitalist globalization. In contrast (although many of those cited here would argue that this contrast is exaggerated), Marshall emphasizes that we must understand the popularity and appeal of the answers offered by Pentecostal churches in terms of the histories of problematics and distinctions that have emerged out of the colonial and postcolonial developments of Nigeria (Marshall 2009). As she shows, one of the major problems addressed by Pentecostalism is that of sovereignty, in a context of occult economies (see also Comaroff and Comaroff 1999; Geschiere 1997; Meyer 1998b; Moore and Sanders 2001; Enwerem 2002). In other words, the Pentecostal revolution provided workable ways of dealing with the question of where power (and wealth, success, etc.) comes from. In the context of Nigeria and many other regions in sub-Saharan Africa, power is often assumed to have a supernatural source (Ellis and Ter Haar 2004). The Pentecostal revolution rephrased this question as a binary: does it come from God or from the Devil? This immediately suggests a way forward as well: align oneself with God and others who have aligned themselves with God.

Like other scholars of Pentecostalism (Meyer 1998a), Marshall points to the dialectical relationship between Pentecostalism and discourses on witchcraft, sorcery, and cults (2009). Where educated elites of postcolonial Nigeria expected that modernization combined with a revival of African culture would bring prosperity and progress, political reality soon dashed these hopes (See for example the memoir of Soyinka [2000] spanning the years 1946–65). The political turmoil and quickly exacerbating inequalities in Nigerian society, combined with the austerity measures imposed in the 1980s, created a situation where the question of sovereignty became existential: possibilities for advancement at the individual level were unpredictable, and the future seemed to hold decline rather than progress. A good education and hard

162   Kim E. Knibbe

work were no guarantee for success. Corrupt people became rich; honest and hardworking people were victimized. The suspicion that the rich and powerful gained their wealth through witchcraft and occultism periodically led to violence and riots (Enwerem 2002; Smith 2001).

In this situation, Pentecostal churches offered a way out, particularly through the combination of holiness and prosperity. The notion that "God wants you to be rich" offers a way to be both godly and successful. Thus, to be "born-again" became the existential portal through which many passed (sometimes several times!) (Maxwell 1998; Meyer 2007).

To become born-again, furthermore, immediately entails the participation and extension in what Coleman has called the economy of the charismatic gift (Coleman 2004). The practices fostered by prosperity teachings collapse the distinction between the financial and the spiritual: through giving generously to the church, Christians aim to claim back their right to a prosperous and healthy life from the ministry of the Devil. Furthermore, it generates an impetus to expansion since it is only through encouraging others to give their lives to Christ that prosperity for societies as a whole can be elevated.

The successful implementation of modern church growth and church planting models inspired by other Pentecostal movements across the world (in the US, South Korea, and South America) created new contexts for success and upward mobility for highly educated urban professionals in Nigeria. Through special trips and exclusive clubs and networks, new elites consisting of a mix of politicians and businessmen were created that centred on the pressing need to expand, pass on the charismatic gift (Coleman 2004), bring more people to Christ, and fulfil the covenant between God and the RCCG that is part of the founding narrative of this church (Ukah 2008b).

In short, the "worlding" that emerged from the Pentecostal revolution is impressive, expansive, and powerful in what it has accomplished (Adogame 2010). By reaching far into the existential dilemmas people face in making their way in society and combining this with gathering power socially and politically, they have changed the power dynamics of Nigerian society. It is significant to note that this worlding turns many of the historically grown hierarchies and orientations upside down: rather than the periphery, Nigerian Pentecostals put their own location, Nigeria, as the centre of a new global Christianity. By drawing on the notion of charismatic gifts and the covenant church, a source of sovereignty at the individual and the institutional level is proposed that simultaneously draws on and reverses many of the hierarchies of power that have emerged through colonial and postcolonial history.

Transnational Religion in Phenomenological Perspective   163

Furthermore, as Coleman and Maier have shown, it creates new spaces and continuums along which people and goods travel (2013).

In the context of Europe, however, this worlding intersects with national and municipal contexts that do not have the categories to recognize this religious actor and the individuals linked to it as powerful, expansive, ambitious, and global. Missionaries, even when paid by the RCCG or working for powerful transnational organizations and companies such as Shell or the International Criminal Court in the Hague, are primarily viewed as migrants, leaders of groups that are marginalized in Dutch societies, and thus spokespersons and potential brokers between these groups and local policymakers (Knibbe 2009; Knibbe and Van der Meulen 2009; Van der Meulen 2009; Maier and Coleman 2011).

As Jackson argues, these views of individuals as part of a classification (migrants, displaced, dispossessed, marginal, poor) does not do any kind of justice to the ways people see themselves (Jackson 2013). Yet, these classifications and the attendant practices do affect people as individuals, as well as the worldbuilding energy of institutional actors such as the RCCG. This becomes visible particularly through a focus on spatial dimensions and practices, such as mapping.

The Power of Maps

> But the way we imagine space has effects. … Conceiving of space as in the voyages of discovery, as something to be crossed and maybe conquered, has particular ramifications. (Massey 2005, 4)

As an institution, the RCCG maps the world in terms of the density of local congregations established. This is evident in the mission statement that has been guiding the expansion of this church for a long time (see fig. 7.1):[1]

One could argue that this is not a text, but a map. And, as cultural geographers such as Massey (2005) teach us, maps mobilize and incite to action. This particular banner hangs in the main hall of the parish of the RCCG located in Amsterdam. Amsterdam as a location is a particularly provocative place for missionary ambitions because of its international reputation as the place for sex, drugs, and rock 'n' roll. The red-light district, its tolerant and pragmatic policy towards drug use, the annual gay parades: in everything Amsterdam seems to be the antithesis of the world that a church such as the RCCG is aiming to bring into being. Furthermore, historically Amsterdam is one of the centres of European capitalist expansion, and thus one of the prominent geographical landmarks in many different global imaginaries.

164 Kim E. Knibbe

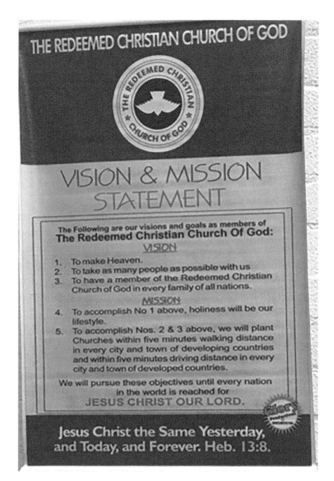

Figure 7.1. Vision and Mission Statement, Jesus House Amsterdam. Picture taken by author

This particular parish was planted by Ibrahim Abarshi, a missionary who was funded by a rich network of parishes based in Lagos, Nigeria and London, UK (the Apapa network). This network emerged in the 1990s and has brought forth several other notable church planters, most prominently the leader of Jesus House London, one of the biggest and most influential parishes outside of Nigeria. Crucial in solidifying the calling of the pastor who established Jesus House Amsterdam was Abarshi's participation in the annual pilgrimage to Israel with the

Transnational Religion in Phenomenological Perspective   165

general overseer of the Church. During this pilgrimage, he felt that God called him to plant a church in Amsterdam. At first, he resisted this call: he had a good career as a banker in Lagos, and his London-born wife preferred to go to the UK if they must relocate. Yet, after a business visit to Amsterdam he was certain: he had to go to Amsterdam. It took several years to wrap up his business in Lagos and find a way to go to the Netherlands, where he first entered as an MA student in the Hague School for Social Sciences.

Starting up a parish in Amsterdam, he came face to face with two challenges: the people who came to worship were marginalized, and he himself was addressed as part of this marginalized group despite his high educational level and previous professional accomplishments. Resisting this classification and the implications that he and his parishioners needed "help," he mobilized the finances to buy a large building in the south-east of Amsterdam, expecting it to soon be filled with worshippers. Church growth was slower than expected. In addition, he had to recognize that indeed, the people who came to worship were marginalized in Dutch society, often without documents, sometimes on the verge of criminality. Rather than leading a parish of wealthy and upwardly mobile Christians, as he had in Lagos, he now found himself organizing Dutch classes and courses in basic skills for the Dutch labour market, as well as helping people sort out their legal situation in the Netherlands. This was his situation when I first met him in 2007. Nevertheless, during this first interview, he firmly positioned himself and the church he is part of as different from other "migrant churches" in Amsterdam, in fact as not a migrant church at all: "we did not come here as tenants, but as landlords" (which became the title of the first article I published on this research [Knibbe 2009]).

Through my fieldwork with other Nigerian-initiated and African-dominated churches I learned that among fellow church leaders in Amsterdam, the RCCG pastors are known for going their own way, not depending on support from the local government. This work has paid off: ten years after my initial interview with him, Abarshi pointed toward the parking lot full of gleaming cars on a Sunday, evidence that many of his parishioners are now in a much better place and most are now legalized. The latter he attributes to their active prayer life. From 2003–6, the Netherlands had a minister of migration who was famously strict, named Rita Verdonk. In Abarshi's words "we prayed Verdonk away." This freed up the process towards a one-time legalization of many undocumented migrants who were members of this parish (general pardon of 2007).

166 Kim E. Knibbe

In sum, the mapping of the RCCG – as embodied in their mission statement – focused on church planting and created a worlding that enabled people who participated in it to flourish through the finances, organizational formats, practical support, and spiritual practices that this mapping mobilized. Yet, in order to do this Abarshi and other missionaries had to counter, resist, and ignore the undoing influences of other types of worldings, in which they were positioned as migrants, undocumented people, and even as criminals. While Abarshi did not explicitly reference processes of criminalization, this tendency was evident in the mapping of the police and the media of this part of Amsterdam as a hotbed of criminal activity, specifically of Nigerian (sometimes modified to West-African) criminal networks involved in advance fee crime. Churches such as this one were suspected of laundering money for these criminal networks (Knibbe 2009). The combination of location, skin colour, and inferred nationality thus became enough to arrest people as criminal suspects as happened in a raid during the performance of the popular Nigerian artist Nkem Owoh, at which at least one Pentecostal pastor was present. Specifically, the suspicion of criminal activity became a pretext for asking everyone who attended this performance to present their papers. While those who were white and did not have their papers on them were let go, black and people of colour were detained and in some cases deported. This event was written up by Amnesty International as an example of the criminalization of irregular migrants (Amnesty International 2008, 32).

While the banner in the main hall of Jesus House reminds the congregants to view themselves as part of a global church that is carrying out a covenant with God to enable everyone to reach heaven, the world in which this is true has to be created, maintained, and defended against other ways of mapping the world. Through those efforts, ways of orienting oneself towards a God with whom all things are possible were developed that were both spiritual and practical, as is evident in the language classes, legal help and courses set up. In this way, the realities of powerful rival worldings were fended off and managed, whether they were nation states establishing the reality of borders, the police and public seeing Nigerians as potential criminals and money-launderers, or municipal do-gooders wanting to help marginalized groups.

Hierarchies of Time

> We argue that institutions *mediate* divergent representations, techniques, and rhythms of human and non-human time. Time thickens with ethical problems, impossible dilemmas, and difficult orchestrations. (Bear 2014, 6)

Another orientational dimension along which to examine how different types of worldings intersect, interact, and counter each other is the dimension of time. In her work, Bear builds on the notion of the chronotype developed by Bakhtin: materialized representations of time and their links to forms of agency (Bear 2014). One has to be able to orient oneself in terms of past and future to come to a coherent understanding of what one should be doing in the present. This orientation is important from the granular level of our understandings of simple cause and effects relationships, to the interrelational level (what kind of past and future do I have with this person), to the level of social imaginaries (what kind of past and future do I have with this place, Amsterdam, this nation, the Netherlands, this region, Europe). As individuals, we all engage with different chronotopes simultaneously: for example, those of our workplace, of popular culture, our religious practice, the rhythms of family life, and daily routines.

As an institutional actor, the RCCG produces various chronotopes simultaneously, for different levels and different purposes. Like the spatial practices described above, these chronotopes mobilize, synchronize, and coordinate people in ways that produce tangible results. At the level of the self-understanding of the RCCG as an institutional actor, the chronotope produced by the RCCG can be described by the notion of modern time, a time of progress at the personal level linked to a lifestyle that is materially wealthy. This is exemplified by the themes of many of the sermons and special programmes, suggested prayer points etc., which emphasize personal success, health, and wealth as an inevitable result of obedience and dedication to God. Similarly, in many of the narratives around the founding of the RCCG and the emergence of the current leader, Adeboye, a premodern "Africa" is contrasted with the brightness of the current global empire that the RCCG has built, fulfilling God's promise to the founder of the RCCG to bring his church to "the ends of the earth" and the brilliant personal and professional future that awaits those who become born-again (Knibbe 2011b).

This modernity, however, is linked to the horizon of the end times, as seen in the mission statement, which is expected to be coming soon. The focus on church planting is a preparation for these end times: by ensuring that there is a parish within walking distance or driving distance everywhere in the world, this creates the opportunity for everyone to give their life to Christ when the end times come.

This notion of modern time thus creates a lens through which Europe is viewed as "not yet born-again," as well as one of the biggest battlefields between the forces of God and the Devil that is expected to take place soon. The rise of Islam in Europe is seen as a sign that this battle is

168   Kim E. Knibbe

coming or already here. Through events such as the biennial Eurocon, gathering Pentecostals from all over Europe, attendants are mobilized to become "soldiers" in the army of God. While this notion of history counters Eurocentric notions of history and modernity (while still employing a stadial consciousness), the question is whether it is also able to counter the power of these Eurocentric notions of time. Or, more generally, how do the chronotopes produced by the RCCG intersect with Eurocentric chronotopes of modernity?

Interestingly, the rhetoric employing the call to action in preparation for the end times embeds within it the ways that the sense of agency that it calls for may be undone by other forces, for example in a sermon preached by a prominent exponent of the RCCG's successful mission strategy, Agu Irukwu. Irukwu embodies the success that is possible "in the supernatural." He has developed one of the most powerful and successful hubs of RCCG activities outside of Nigeria, radiating outward from the Jesus House London parish. It has several services each Sunday in several languages, a flourishing array of ministries for all age groups, and charity activities and drop-in centres for youth; it also organizes well-visited conferences and has hosted prominent political figures such as Boris Johnson and David Cameron. Yet, for many of those attending the European Convention of the RCCG in Amsterdam at which he was invited to preach, this kind of success was still a mirage: many, while identifying as missionaries, worked menial day jobs, most likely a substantial number of them were undocumented and / or working in menial jobs. Recognizing this reality, Irukwu exclaimed: "This is the army that God has chosen. But, look around you, seriously? In the natural, we are fooling ourselves. But in the supernatural, it is possible" (Agu Irukwu, speaking at Eurocon 2017).

Thus, while Irukwu's message was focused on a horizon of time linked to a chronotope that involves wholesale destruction of the world as we know it, as a person he embodies the kind of success that those attending Eurocon are asked to strive for as missionaries and church planters. The persistent rhetoric of the prosperity teaching pervading the religious activities is focused on getting ahead, breaking through to the next level, and the promise of God that you will succeed once you dedicate your life to Christ.

In contrast, most Dutch notions of modern time are markedly secularist: there is the pervasive assumption that secularization is inevitable. Thus, as "migrants," Nigerian Pentecostals are assumed to eventually shed their religious "baggage" (Knibbe 2011b, 2018). This word baggage, or sometimes "backpack," is often used in the rhetoric of municipal policymakers. Interestingly, the use of this word is often a marker of the willingness to be inclusive and respectful, signalling that for the time being, the speaker is prepared to accommodate the religious diversity that migrants bring, and is even reflecting on how this accommodation may be "useful" for the successful implementation of policies. However, it is assumed to be a temporary accommodation, a stage in the process of the "integration" of migrants (see e.g., Fleischmann and Phalet 2012). Also in more recent research from an "anthropology of the secular" perspective, this plot of secularization as an inevitable precondition of a modern, enlightened citizen of the Netherlands is projected onto incoming migrants particularly around issues of gender and sexuality. The chronotope of integration in the Netherlands thus assumes that time progresses from a religious past to a secularized present and future (Balkenhol, Mepschen, and Duyvendak 2016; Wiering 2020; Bartelink and Wiering 2020).

So how do these chronotopes intersect? In the time that I have been following the RCCG, my observation has been that they mostly do not intersect; rather they exist side by side. Whereas the RCCG chronotopes orient and mobilize people, they do not affect the secularist understandings of the direction of history as increasingly secular espoused by many Dutch when the two are confronted with each other. Nevertheless, as an exponent of the more general phenomenon of Global Christianity and the expansive dynamic of Pentecostalism, the RCCG does challenge the implicit assumptions embedded in the chronotopes of policymakers, opinion leaders, researchers, and ordinary citizens in the Netherlands: apparently, the rest of the world is not following the example of north-western Europe in secularizing, but is forging different historical trajectories. As such, for a particular class of intellectuals, the presence of Nigerian-initiated and other Pentecostal and evangelical churches becomes evidence for the dawn of a post-secular epoch. In this post-secular society, the assumption that those who are religious are lagging behind is abandoned, and religious as well as secular actors may learn from each other. However, observing the interaction of Dutch political and policymaking actors with religious actors, particularly those with a migration background, shows that they overwhelmingly orientate themselves with the help of the secularization narrative. This is most visible in relation to Islam, as many scholars have pointed out (Bracke 2011; Mepschen, Duyvendak, and Tonkens 2010; Balkenhol, Mepschen, and Duyvendak 2016), with Christianity seen as relatively harmless. However, in specific cases, such as a media storm around healing practices in Pentecostal churches in Amsterdam which arose during my fieldwork there, secularist perspectives were applied rather

170   Kim E. Knibbe

forcefully as well, condemning such practices as premodern "folklore" that should be eradicated (Knibbe 2018, 20).

The Power of Pentecostal Worldings and Existential Orientations

As noted, the religious agency the RCCG has developed overturns many of the established ways that Europeans orient themselves in the world: the RCCG conceptualizes Europe as "the dark continent" and views Nigeria as the centre from which salvation will be spread. Furthermore, church members resist the designation common in north-western Europe that they are somehow less "modern" because they are "still" religious. By drawing on the notion of charismatic gifts and the covenant church, a source of sovereignty at the individual and the institutional level is proposed that both draws on and reverses many of the hierarchies of geography and time that have emerged through colonial and postcolonial history. This is of existential importance not only at the level of the individual but in fact brings into being a world in which people are existentially oriented in ways that contribute to their flourishing rather than block and diminish them both in Nigeria, where this church originated, and across Europe.

Does this worlding then "undo" the other worldings, such as those of Dutch policymakers and politicians, it encounters? In the context of Europe, the answer is "no," or a cautious "not yet." Developments in the UK show that there is an aligning of the agendas of megachurches such as the RCCG with conservative political agendas which may fit in a trend worldwide of an aligning of conservative Pentecostal and evangelical networks with populist and conservative agendas, leading them to promote "religion" as an antidote to what they perceive to be the evils plaguing contemporary societies. Following the orientational dimensions of space, it becomes clear that while the mapping of the RCCG projected onto Amsterdam powerfully brings new realities into being for marginalized migrants, the mapping of the police and policymakers positions the same people as potential criminals. Following the orientational dimension of time, the notion of modernity espoused by Dutch policymakers in many instances is blind to the forward trajectory into a better future born-again Pentecostals see themselves as following through their obedience to God.

Furthermore, as my colleague Joram Tarusarira argues in the many conversations we had on this topic, the notion of modernity espoused by the RCCG is, like other notions of modernity, infused with coloniality: it draws on and reworks the civilizational hierarchies formed through the imperial encounters of Europeans and their "discovery" of the rest of the world (e.g., Grosfoguel 2011; Mignolo 2012; Ndlovu-Gat-sheni 2013; Tarusarira 2020). Within the hierarchies produced by the RCCG, the distinction between those who are modern and not yet modern is linked to the distinction between those who are born-again and not yet born-again. The world is mapped in terms of areas ruled by darkness, and areas where prayer warriors are holding the line against the ministry of the Devil, places already covered by networks of parishes and blank spots on the map of the world.

Finally, and not insignificantly, while very successful in church planting, the RCCG is not very successful in terms of one of the criteria they set for themselves: drawing in the "Dutch Dutch" (i.e., white Dutch, they do draw in some Dutch of Caribbean descent). This is similar to what many other researchers found for African-initiated churches in north-western Europe: they remain enclaves despite their efforts at outward projection (Ukah 2005; Freston 2010; Koning 2009; Knibbe 2011a).

In Conclusion

How do worldings gather power in relation to other (sometimes more powerful) ways of worlding and how can we understand this process in relation to people's individual being in the world? That is the question this chapter has sought to address based on the insights gained from research on a Nigerian-initiated Pentecostal church, the RCCG.

In this chapter I have proposed that the complex relationships between the worlding of global Pentecostalism and the local and national contexts they encounter can be approached by following the "orientational dimensions" produced by transnational religious actors such as the RCCG and by examining how these work to orient people individually and as groups. With the term orientational dimension I refer to the phenomenological and existential ways that people orient themselves and are oriented by the structures around them in relation to time, space, materiality, embodiment, life projects, and the "forces of otherness" that affect everyone's lives (Jackson 1998, 2008). Through an emphasis on orientational dimensions, it becomes possible to see both the ways individuals are positioned within multiple worlds simultaneously, and to examine how these worlds relate to each other and require individual and institutional adjustment. Thus, as we saw in the story of Abarshi, he adjusted to the reality of ministering to a congregation that was very different from the successful "model parish" populated by young, upwardly mobile professionals in Lagos he ministered to previously. At the same time, by drawing on the rhetoric and mapping of the mission of the RCCG

172   Kim E. Knibbe

as a powerful and rapidly expanding church preparing for the end times he continued resisting the categorizations of policymakers, police, and fellow pastors of himself and his church as marginal, in need of help, and a potential site of criminal activities.

Jackson may be correct to note that, at the level of individuals, "religion" is neither an actor nor a system of beliefs and practices. Yet, we have to recognize that as a transnational institution, the RCCG and other institutions like it are able to mobilize and sustain agency at the individual level through the different formats for orienting oneself in the world that the institution of the RCCG spreads. As shown here and in other publications, the religious agency that this church has developed overturns Eurocentric mappings, presenting Nigeria as the centre from which salvation will be spread, and it assumes that "modernity" is gained through becoming born-again rather than through losing one's religion. Through orienting "migrants" as missionaries and potential church planters, it also invites individuals to view themselves as part of an "army of God" placed in Europe to save the continent during the end times battles coming near, to shed the ways they are designated as marginal, powerless migrants "in the natural," and to recognize that "in the supernatural" they are part of God's plan for the world. And crucially, to keep returning to this way of orienting oneself even in the face of the racism, criminalization, and marginalization one may encounter. A focus on orientational dimensions as an entry-point for enquiry and analysis of the ways global Pentecostalism interacts with the contexts in which it becomes established recognizes both the multiplicity of the "fixed," reified societal structures and forms to which people relate, contribute, are enclosed and constrained by, as well as the flux and flow of religious (and other) ways of being enacted, created, and embodied (cf. Premawardhana 2018). Thus, this focus serves to examine the ways people are oriented both individually and as groups, develop agency and intentionality, and encounter the agency and intentionality of other actors.

ACKNOWLEDGMENTS

I would like to thank all those missionaries in various churches across the world who have given their time to talk to me and extended their hospitality in letting me attend services, special programs, and conferences over the years. Further, I would like to thank in particular pastor Ibrahim Abarshi, professor and special assistant to the general overseer of the RCCG Dele Olowu, and his wife, pastor Bukky Olowu, for their help in understanding the history of the establishment and expansion of the RCCG in the Netherlands and across Europe. Furthemore, I would like to thank my colleague, Joram Tarusarira, for the many discussions on modernity and coloniality we have had. Gratitude also to the editors of this volume, Devakaka Premawardhana and Don Seeman.

NOTE

1 Please note that "to make heaven" means "to reach heaven," not to establish heaven on earth. Only those who are saved (born again) can reach heaven.

WORKS CITED

Adogame, Afe. 2008. "Up, Up Jesus! Down, Down Satan! African Religiosity in the Former Soviet Bloc the Embassy of the Blessed Kingdom of God for All Nations." *Exchange* 37, no. 3: 310–36. https://doi.org /10.1163/157254308X312009.
–. 2010. "How God Became a Nigerian: Religious Impulse and the Unfolding of a Nation." Journal of Contemporary African Studies 28, no. 4: 479–98. https://doi.org/10.1080/02589001.2010.512742.
Amnesty International. 2008. "The Netherlands: The Detention of Irregular Migrants and Asylum-Seekers." 27 June 2008. https://www.amnesty.org /en/documents/eur35/002/2008/en/.
Appadurai, Arjun. 1996. *Modernity at Large: Cultural Dimensions of Globalization*. Minneapolis: University of Minnesota Press.
Balkenhol, Markus, Paul Mepschen, and Jan Willem Duyvendak. 2016. "The Nativist Triangle: Sexuality, Race and Religion in the Netherlands." In *The Culturalization of Citizenship*, edited by Jan Willem Duyvendak, Peter Geschiere, and Evelien Tonkens, 97–112. London: Palgrave Macmillan. http://link.springer.com/chapter/10.1057/978-1-137 -53410-1_5.
Bartelink, Brenda, and Jelle Oscar Wiering. 2020. "Speaking the Body: Examining the Intersections of Sexuality, Secularity and Religion in Dutch Sexuality Education." In *Embodying Religion, Gender and Sexuality*, edited by Sarah-Jane Page and Katy Pilcher, 39–56. London: Routledge.
Bear, Laura. 2014. "Doubt, Conflict, Mediation: The Anthropology of Modern Time." *Journal of the Royal Anthropological Institute* 20, no. S1 (April): 3–30. https://doi.org/10.1111/1467-9655.12091.
Blaser, Mario. 2013. "Ontological Conflicts and the Stories of Peoples in Spite of Europe." *Current Anthropology* 54, no. 5: 547–68. https://doi .org/10.1086/672270.

174 Kim E. Knibbe

Bracke, Sarah. 2011. "Subjects of Debate: Secular and Sexual Exceptionalism, and Muslim Women in the Netherlands." *Feminist Review* 98, no. 1: 28–46. https://doi.org/10.1057/fr.2011.5.

Burgess, Richard, Kim Knibbe, and Anna Quaas. 2010. "Nigerian-Initiated Pentecostal Churches as a Social Force in Europe: The Case of the Redeemed Christian Church of God." *PentecoStudies: An Interdisciplinary Journal for Research on the Pentecostal and Charismatic Movements* 9, no. 1: 97–121. https://doi.org/10.1558/ptcs.v9i1.97.

Coleman, Simon. 2004. "The Charismatic Gift." *Journal of the Royal Anthropological Institute* 10, no. 2 (June): 421–42. https://doi.org/10.1111/j.1467-9655.2004.00196.x.

Coleman, Simon, and Katrin Maier. 2013. "Redeeming the City: Creating and Traversing 'London-Lagos.'" *Religion* 43, no. 3: 353–64. https://doi.org/10.1080/0048721X.2013.798161.

Comaroff, Jean, and John L. Comaroff. 1999. "Occult Economies and the Violence of Abstraction: Notes from the South African Postcolony." *American Ethnologist* 26, no. 2 (May): 279–303. https://doi.org/10.1525/ae.1999.26.2.279.

Ellis, Stephen, and Gerrie Ter Haar. 2004. *Worlds of Power: Religious Thought and Political Practice in Africa*. Vol. 1. New York: Oxford University Press.

Enwerem, Iheanyi M. 2002. "'Money-Magic' and Ritual Killing in Contemporary Nigeria." In *Money Struggles and City Life: Devaluation in Ibadan and Other Urban Centers in Southern Nigeria, 1986–1996*, edited by Jane I. Guyer, LaRay Denzer, and Adigun Agbaje, 189–205. Portsmouth, NH: Heinemann.

Fleischmann, Fenella, and Karen Phalet. 2012. "Integration and Religiosity among the Turkish Second Generation in Europe: A Comparative Analysis across Four Capital Cities." *Ethnic and Racial Studies* 35, no. 2: 320–41. https://doi.org/10.1080/01419870.2011.579138.

Freston, Paul. 2010. "Reverse Mission: A Discourse in Search of Reality?" *PentecoStudies: An Interdisciplinary Journal for Research on the Pentecostal and Charismatic Movements* 9, no. 2: 153–74. https://doi.org/10.1558/ptcs.v9.i2.8948.

Geschiere, Peter. 1997. *The Modernity of Witchcraft: Politics and the Occult in Postcolonial Africa*. Charlottesville, VA: University of Virginia Press.

Grosfoguel, Ramón. 2011. "Transmodernity, Border Thinking, and Global Coloniality: Decolonizing Political Economy and Postcolonial Studies." *Transmodernity: Journal of Peripheral Cultural Production of the Luso-Hispanic World* 1, no. 1. https://doi.org/10.5070/T411000004.

Jackson, Michael. 1998. *Minima Ethnographica: Intersubjectivity and the Anthropological Project*. Chicago: University of Chicago Press.

–. 2008. *Existential Anthropology: Events, Exigencies and Effects*. Oxford: Berghahn Books.

–. 2013. *The Wherewithal of Life: Ethics, Migration, and the Question of Well-Being*. Berkeley: University of California Press.

Knibbe, Kim. 2009. "'We Did Not Come Here as Tenants, but as Landlords': Nigerian Pentecostals and the Power of Maps." *African Diaspora* 2, no. 2: 133–58. https://doi.org/10.1163/187254509X12477244375058.

–. 2011a. "'How to Deal with the Dutch': The Local and the Global in the Habitus of the Saved Soul." In *Encounters of Body and Soul in Contemporary Religious Practices. Anthropological Reflections*, edited by Anna Fedele and Ruy Blanes, 91–109. Oxford: Berghahn Books.

–. 2011b. "Nigerian Missionaries in Europe: History Repeating Itself or a Meeting of Modernities?" *Journal of Religion in Europe* 4, no. 3: 471–87. https://doi.org/10.1163/187489211X592085.

–. 2018. "Secularist Understandings of Pentecostal Healing Practices in Amsterdam: Developing an Intersectional and Post-Secularist Sociology of Religion." *Social Compass* 65, no. 5: 650–66. https://doi.org/10.1177/0037768618800418.

–. 2019. "Conflicting Futures, Entangled Pasts." *PentecoStudies* 18, no. 2 (November): 133–54. https://doi.org/10.1558/pent.37795.

–. 2020. "Is Critique Possible in the Study of Lived Religion? Anthropological and Feminist Reflections." *Journal of Contemporary Religion* 35, no. 2: 251–68. https://doi.org/10.1080/13537903.2020.1759904.

Knibbe, Kim, and Marten van der Meulen. 2009. "The Role of Spatial Practices and Locality in the Constituting of the Christian African Diaspora." *African Diaspora* 2, no. 2 (September): 125–30. https://doi.org/10.1163/1872545 09X12477244375012.

Koning, Danielle. 2009. "Place, Space, and Authority. The Mission and Reversed Mission of the Ghanaian Seventh-Day Adventist Church in Amsterdam." *African Diaspora* 2, no. 2: 203–26. https://doi.org/10.1163/187 254509X12477244375175.

Levitt, Peggy, and Nina Glick Schiller. 2004. "Conceptualizing Simultaneity: A Transnational Social Field Perspective on Society." *International Migration Review* 38, no. 3: 1002–39. https://doi.org/10.1111/j.1747-7379.2004. tb00227.x.

Maier, Katrin, and Simon Coleman. 2011. "Who Will Tend the Vine? Pentecostalism, Parenting and the Role of the State in 'London-Lagos.'" *Journal of Religion in Europe* 4, no. 3: 450–70. https://doi.org/10.1163 /187489211X594146.

Marshall, Ruth. 2009. *Political Spiritualities: The Pentecostal Revolution in Nigeria*. Chicago: University of Chicago Press.

Massey, Doreen B. 2005. *For Space*. Thousand Oaks: Sage.

Maxwell, David. 1998. "'Delivered from the Spirit of Poverty?': Pentecostalism, Prosperity and Modernity in Zimbabwe." *Journal of Religion in Africa* 28, no. 3 (August): 350–73. https://doi.org/10.2307/1581574.

Mepschen, Paul, Jan Willem Duyvendak, and Evelien H. Tonkens. 2010. "Sexual Politics, Orientalism and Multicultural Citizenship in The Netherlands." *Sociology* 44, no. 5: 962–79. https://doi.org/10.1177/0038038510375740.

Meyer, Birgit. 1998a. "'Make a Complete Break with the Past.' Memory and Post-Colonial Modernity in Ghanaian Pentecostalist Discourse." *Journal of Religion in Africa* 28, no. 3: 316–49. https://doi.org/10.1163/157006698X00044.

–. 1998b. "The Power of Money: Politics, Occult Forces, and Pentecostalism in Ghana." *African Studies Review* 41, no. 3 (December): 15–37. https://doi.org/10.2307/525352.

–. 2007. "Pentecostalism and Neo-Liberal Capitalism: Faith, Prosperity and Vision in African Pentecostal-Charismatic Churches." *Journal for the Study of Religion* 20, no. 2: 5–28. https://www.jstor.org/stable/24764190.

–. 2018. "Frontier Zones and the Study of Religion." *Journal for the Study of Religion* 31, no. 2: 57–78. https://www.jstor.org/stable/26778575.

Mignolo, Walter. 2012. *Local Histories/Global Designs: Coloniality, Subaltern Knowledges, and Border Thinking.* Princeton, NJ: Princeton University Press.

Moore, Henrietta L., and Todd Sanders. 2001. *Magical Interpretations, Material Realities: Modernity, Witchcraft and the Occult in Postcolonial Africa.* London: Routledge.

Ndlovu-Gatsheni, Sabelo. 2013. "The Entrapment of Africa within the Global Colonial Matrices of Power: Eurocentrism, Coloniality, and Deimperialization in the Twenty-First Century." *Journal of Developing Societies* 29, no. 4: 331–53. https://doi.org/10.1177/0169796X13503195.

Premawardhana, Devaka. 2018. *Faith in Flux: Pentecostalism and Mobility in Rural Mozambique.* Philadelphia: University of Pennsylvania Press.

Smit, Regien. 2009. "The Church Building: A Sanctuary or a Consecrated Place? Conflicting Views between Angolan Pentecostals and European Presbyterians." *African Diaspora* 2, no. 2: 182–202. https://doi.org/10.1163/187254509X12477244375139.

Smith, Daniel Jordan. 2001. "Ritual Killing, 419, and Fast Wealth: Inequality and the Popular Imagination in Southeastern Nigeria." *American Ethnologist* 28, no. 4: 803–26. https://doi.org/10.1525/ae.2001.28.4.803.

Soyinka, Wole. 2000. *Ibadan: The Penkelemes Years: A Memoir, 1946–1965.* London: Methuum.

Tarusarira, Joram. 2020. "Religion and Coloniality in Diplomacy." Transatlantic Policy Network on Religion and Diplomacy. 10 February 2020.

https://religionanddiplomacy.org/wp-content/uploads/2020/02/TPNRD-Tarusarira-Religion-and-Coloniality.pdf.

Ukah, Asonzeh. 2005. "Reverse Mission or Asylum Christianity." In *Africans and the Politics of Popular Culture,* edited by Toyin Falola and Augustine Agwuele, 104–32. Cambridge: Cambridge University Press.

–. 2008a. "Roadside Pentecostalism: Religious Advertising in Nigeria and the Marketing of Charisma." *Critical Interventions: Journal of African Art and Visual Culture* 2, no. 1–2: 125–41. https://doi.org/10.1080/19301944.2008.10781334.

–. 2008b. *A New Paradigm of Pentecostal Power: A Study of the Redeemed Christian Church of God in Nigeria.* Trenton: Africa World Press.

Van der Meulen, Marten. 2009. "The Continuing Importance of the Local. African Churches and the Search for Worship Space in Amsterdam." *African Diaspora* 2, no. 2: 159–81. https://doi.org/10.1163/187254509X12477244375094.

Wiering, Jelle O. 2020. "Secular Practices: The Production of Religious Difference in the Dutch Field of Sexual Health." PhD diss. Groningen University.

8 The Plain Sense of Things: Time, History, and the Dream

ADITYA MALIK

The Fortress

An impenetrable, sprawling fortress atop a remote flat hill surrounded by barren, dry land, speckled with thorny green shrubs, thickets of tall yellow-green grass, and the occasional precious shimmering, shallow lake. Who built it? How many kings and queens occupied it? When? Do we know anything about it? Perhaps we know so much that we cannot confidently place it in space or time even though it is visible to us, and we can touch its thick stone walls, walk on the uneven cobbled pathways meandering up to its giant, wooden gates armed with menacing iron spikes to keep out rushing enemy elephants and their riders. The fortress of *Ranthambore* in material form apparently *is there*, and yet it hangs suspended in the sky tethered like a balloon to imagination … to unending stories of valour and betrayal … victory and defeat … sacrifice and loyalty. A history so concrete that it dissolves at midday like a wall of winter mist along its towering, sheer ramparts. Its origins remain unknown despite the best efforts of discerning historians committed to its *real and true story*.

Wahid Mohammed who worked as a tour guide for tourists and pilgrims visiting the fortress for over two decades told me:

Wahid Mohammed: There is no history whatsoever of this fort! [We don't know] who made it.

Me: Really? There is no history?

Wahid Mohammed: There is no history of its construction. There is no history regarding who constructed it until today.

Then where did it appear from? Why claim we do not know who constructed it? What do we know about it? One idea that recurs in different narratives is that of a series of pairings or twinnings are associated with its founding. As another tour guide whose name is Manohar Lal Mina

180   Aditya Malik

pointed out, two individuals named Ravana and Basava from the tribal community of the Bhils who live in large swathes of western and central India sacrificed themselves to build the fortress. They stopped the king who was trying to build it from slaying himself claiming,

"Rao Jeyat [the king], the fort is emphatically ours, although you have nominal title to it. You are but our guest. The fort is emphatically ours. It behoves you, therefore, to cut off our heads and raise the wall upon them." Ravana said, "Only look after my son Bhoj." The brave Bhils were beheaded, their heads placed as foundation-stones, and the wall built thereon became as firm and lasting as a rock." (Bandyopádhyáya 1879)

The pair of the two tribal men, Ravana and Basava, are mirrored in two princes who, according to the guide Manohar Lal Mina, first found the location upon which the fortress is built:

Manohar Lal: Sages used to meditate here … right on this hill. Two princes came by here while they were playing and so they met the sages. After speaking to the sages they realized [that the hills were special]. Otherwise they never knew that hills like these existed. They had not travelled around much. So they did not know about these hills. So the sages told them that there are such hills and that there are no other hills anywhere else. They told them everything. Ever since then the princes started thinking about constructing the fort here. It began from there."
     Me: Who were these princes of the past … was it not Hammīra [who built the fortress]?"
     Manohar Lal: No, no … this was far, far earlier. This incident took place before the fifth century. The princes names aren't mentioned. It just says two princes. It's from here that we believe – they didn't construct it – but that is from here that it all started. The princes spoke about this and later on discussions continued. Kings discussed it and later on the foundation of the fortress was laid."

Much later in another story, Hammīra, the Rajput king of the fortress in the fourteenth century, and his arch enemy, Alā' al-Dīn Khaljī, the Mongol-Turk sultan of Delhi, are born from the body of one the sages who meditated at the place where the fortress stands now. The sage's name was Padam:

The austere penances of the Sage Padam greatly frightened Indra. His throne shook. In fear he sent Cupid to allure the sage … The apsaras danced, and Kinnaras sang … The forest became full of flowers and bees, cuckoos and peacocks … But the soul of the sage could not be moved …

The Plain Sense of Things   181

it remained firm as a rock ... Spring failed ... Summer failed ... The rainy season failed ... Then came with fury the severe winter ... Then came with pride the season of dew and bowed before Cupid ... He [Padam] saw the nymph and became greatly delighted ... and felt a fever of love ... but the nymph vanished, triumphant at her success. Stung by separation he breathed his last in the month of Magh in Samvat 1140, the moon being in the sign of Adra. *The body of Ala-uddin was made of his head, that of Hamir of his breast, and those of Muhammad Shah and Mir Gabru of his hands.* (Bandyopádhyáya 1879, emphasis added)

The King's Body

The symbolism of both 'Alā' al-Dīn and Hammīra as well as the rebel general Muhammed Shāh and his brother Mir Gabru[1] being born or having their origin in the same body is one that indicates profound belonging through the image of organic unity. The image is reminiscent of the idea of the cosmic man, Purusa, through whom various regions of space and social body emerge subsequent to him being sacrificed by the gods. The sage's body dies to its identity as the Sage Padam from which, however, the historical figures of Mongol/Turk and Rajput leaders and rulers emerge. The emergence of each individual from different parts of the sage's body – 'Alā' al-Dīn from his head, Hammīra from his breast or torso, and the former's general Muhammed Shāh and his brother, Mir Gabru, from his hands or arms – may also indicate a hierarchy of importance and sovereign strength with the head representing the most significant part of the human body, while the torso and hands or arms represent physical strength, bravery, and warrior-like qualities. The imagery is, however, deeply powerful in that it does not indicate separation or conflict but rather unity and a common source of origin – almost like referring to children of the same parent. This idea in itself emphatically counters the notion of an essentialized, historically "true" "Hindu-Muslim" enmity based on religious grounds. Although a conflict does develop between 'Alā' al-Dīn and Hammīra in a subsequent time, this clash can, on the basis of this "origin story," just as well be legitimately viewed as a confrontation between family members related through close kinship ties.

This pairing is continued in Wahid Mohammed's narrative concerning a Hindu deity whose shrine inside the fortress is visited by hundreds and thousands of devotees and a Muslim saint:

Wahid Mohammed: Then there is the famous temple of Lord Ganeśa that is visited by hundreds of thousands of devotees each year. Beneath the

182   Aditya Malik

shrine of Lord Ganeśa, however, is original sacred site of Gajānand Pīr, a Sufi saint, who was there and is still there – though hidden from the view of most devotees – underneath the visible image of Lord Ganeśa.

The Sufi saint is named Gajānand Pīr – Gajānand being another name for Ganeśa coupled here with the Sufi honorific Pīr denoting an "elder," mentor, guide, or master (often translated into "saint"). The Sufi "elder" or saint with the name Gajānand is transformed, so to speak, into Ganeśa. But this is a kind of esoteric knowledge that is known only to a select few, including the senior and now aged priests of the temple of Lord Ganeśa. How did Gajānand Pīr appear? He appeared or manifested himself or was self-generated, so to speak. This idea is similar to the creation stories of many Hindu deities who manifest on their own without human impulse. This act of self-generation is pristine and causeless except for an inner motion. But later, according to the narrator, who is Muslim, "people of Hindu faith" began believing in him (i.e., Gajānand Pīr), and they installed an image of Trinetra ("the one with three eyes"). This image was worshipped as Gajānand or Ganeśa for whom a huge *melā* (fair) with hundreds of thousands of devotees is celebrated in the month of September.

Wahid Mohammed: There is a Ganeśa temple and it is believed that Lord Ganeśa had appeared here.

Me: Oh … on his own?

Wahid Mohammed: Yes, on his own … so the public started believing in him. Now the real idol is beneath and is known by the name Gajānand Pīr.

Me: Oh Gajānand Pīr!

Wahid Mohammed: Yes, Gajānand Pīr. The Madohi priests [residing there], Shuklaji and Madhubaniji can tell you what it really is. Today there has been a proliferation of many smaller priests, the new youngsters have turned into priests. However, the ones who were there earlier are still here. There is a small temple where they sit. They are both very aged now. This is famous by the name Gajānand Pīr. It is beneath the temple, they know it is a Dargāh.

Me: Oh, it is below.

Wahid Mohammed: Yes, it is below … There is a vault in which there is a Dargāh.

Me: It is a Dargāh?

Wahid Mohammed: Yes, it is known as Gajānand Pīr. People having Hindu faith started believing in him, so they established an idol and they began worshipping him as the Trinetra. And this region came to be called as Ranbhom (battle-ground) due to the battles that took place here.

The Plain Sense of Things   183

Me: So when did he … How did Gajānand Pīr come here?

Wahid Mohammed: He appeared on his own. So he is known as Ga-jānand Pīr. A fair is organized in the month of September and people in lakhs pay a visit to this temple. A fair is organized, and food is offered to the people. People are served and the place is equipped with police and doctors and other things.

The Dream

There is one more important thing we know about the fortress Ran-thambore: it was the site of a great battle between Hammīra, the Rajput king of the fortress, and Alā' al-Dīn Khaljī, the powerful sultan of Delhi in the fourteenth century. But even this historical event, like the stories told earlier, does not seem to match up to the standards laid down by serious historians because it is narrated in a dream. The dream I am talking about here is one that Nayachand Suri, a poet and scholar from the fifteenth century, had of the warrior king Hammīra and his dra-matic, heroic death. The dream is like a seed, a vision, or perhaps an urge planted in the subconscious that bubbles over into a cascading poem. The poet's dream sets off reverberations and ripples in space and time once it has been birthed in material form as written language. What sorts of spirals and whorls of meaning emanate from an ephem-eral dream? Can history begin in a dream? What does it mean to write a history – an account of *factuality* – from a seed planted in a dream? Why does the poet who is setting out to write a history turn to the dream and not to the usual avenues of "hard" evidence?

The whorls of meaning are literary and historical accounts of the events the poet wrote about elaborately in his poem that have found their way into different languages – Persian, Rajasthani, Hindi, and even English – in different genres – ballads, royal chronicles, transla-tions, scholarly essays, and the voices of tour guides across vast regions of space and of time. How does the inception of region, history, and literature flow from the poet's dream? It is not uncommon for poets and writers to be inspired by the things that they are going to write about. The poet in question is no exception, except that the warrior king that he will write about appears to him – like apparitions sometimes do in people's dreams – with a request, perhaps a directive. A directive that lodges an unusual but urgent desire, possibly a demand in the poet's mind: to compose a poem about the warrior king, a poem that recounts his ancestors' deeds, his own birth, his reign as a king in the remote fortress of Ranthambore. The warrior king directs the poet to write a poem: not just any poem, but a poem that runs over a thousand and five hundred verses in the most complex and difficult Sanskrit, embellished with all forms of alliteration, rhythm, metre, and grammatical twist for knowledgeable readers of high culture to decipher and relish. The warrior king commands the poet to write a story, a compilation of facts put to wonderful verse about how the stubborn and strong king gave refuge to enemy generals who had mutinied from the army of their commander-in-chief, the sultan of Delhi Alā' al-Dīn Khaljī, and how after defeating the sultan's armies, the warrior king's fortress was besieged by the sultan himself for months, even years. Some say that the siege lasted so long that mango kernels the sultan's soldiers had thrown away grew into shady fruit-bearing trees themselves.

In the end, the warrior king was deceived by his own trusted generals and only the mutineer generals who sought refuge by him remained close. The warrior king's wife, daughter, and all the other noble women of the fortress dressed in their finest, flowing garments and bedazzling jewelry before burning themselves alive in a flaming pit. Then the king and a handful of remaining loyal friends rode out of the fortress to confront the camping sultan's army only to die in flamboyantly heroic ways – the warrior king, struck by a hundred arrows, severed his own head lest he be taken captive.

Some may want to argue that the dream is symbolic, merely representing a form of legitimization. The poet does not claim that he is the source of his creative act; rather it is the historical character of Hammīra who is "dictating" the sequence of verse. In other words, perhaps the author is trying to say that the poem – precisely because it has been revealed in a dream by the hero Hammīra – is not a product of imagination but is true. The dream, in this case, states precisely the opposite of what "we" as modern readers would understand it to be, an entity belonging to the larger realms of imagination, fiction, day-dreaming, subtle disclosures of the unconscious, symbols of simulation. The dream legitimizes by belonging not to the realm of the imagination as a function of fickle thought but as being the presence of the concrete, of the real. Thus, the real is not limited to or solely defined by the material: it lies in that which cannot always be comprehended through the senses or through labels and linguistic terminology. It lies at "the threshold between what can and what cannot be entirely grasped – intellectually, linguistically or practically" (Jackson 2009, x). The poet in this case derives strength from the dream which itself lies, to follow Michael Jackson's phrase, in the penumbral region – "an area in which something exists to a lesser or uncertain degree" (2009, x).

The dream can only legitimize if it is not a representation or accumulation of fictitious scenarios. But in order for this latter argument,

The Plain Sense of Things   185

namely, that the dream is being used by the author to legitimize, to carry weight, it must indeed coincide with the idea that the dream belongs to the realm of the imagination, or that it is a portal, an opening to truths that are more real than those that appear to be real through our everyday experience of a reality that is presented to us through our five senses. The dream does not belong to the experience given to us through the senses. And, yet, while it is made of sensory elements, it transports us or rather the poet into the past in a manner that is concrete, palpable, and in some ways indestructible as the narrative continues to exist through future centuries in a manner that is not available to actual events that last only for the moment in which they come into existence, disappearing or mutating into something else once the singular moment has gone by:

> The dream, or any of its analogues, offers a way back. It is a subtle and ambiguous state, often encoded. It is, however, an "earlier" form of consciousness than awakening, which is given to externalized and objectified fixations. In this sense, one does not actually "wake up" to enlightenment, or even to relatively less profound forms of truth; one is more likely to move toward insight by releasing oneself into dream. The dream, generally, acts like memory – a memory lost and restored. Its basic direction is backward, toward a beginning. It expands identity, on the one hand, by literally dis-closing its rupture with earlier lives and forgotten experience, but also loosening the tight grasping of present identity boundaries, on the other. It seems to fill up the porous and forgetful mind as food fills the hungry body or rain fills the fields. (Shulman 1999, 59)

The poet's dream is thus a way of bringing into consciousness something that has been forgotten or perhaps only vaguely remembered; events whose contours are worn, dusty, like shapes of distant dilapidated huts on the edge of a sandy desert settlement. The dream resurfaces a buried knowledge that now demands attention by appearing in the central field of vision of the poet, but not only of the poet. The poet's consciousness of the past, made present through the dream, now becomes present to readers and listeners across swathes of time and space reaching outside the pinpoint of its beginning in a formidable fortress in Rajasthan. The poet's dream with its seeming interiority occupies ever-widening external realms of historical knowledge, poetry, literature, historiography, and nationalism. The dream as an element of the imagination as a faculty that propels creation into physical, concrete shape becomes, to cite the title of David Shulman's deeply insightful work on the imagination, *More than Real* (2012). The dream was never and

186 Aditya Malik

certainly is no longer a subjective, individualized experience lacking "objective" corroboration and validity as "personal" experience tends to be criticized for. The dream, in fact, protects the poet from claims of a subjective assessment of historical events. It retrieves the poem from the murky waters of fantasy and fiction, of diluted facts. The poem is real because it has been dreamt.

Nayachand Suri's dream represents "a near-universal experience of dreaming as communication, a more or less enigmatic presentation of meaningful messages to the self (and *from* the self, or from some profound dimension of reality, or from God) ... The basic pattern ... is well represented in Indian literature. The dream is an objective 'fact' that can be found or recovered in the outer world, and that makes itself present in consciousness through mechanisms, say, of karmic memory or inter-subjective sensitivity ... In this sense ... the dream speaks a powerful truth" (Shulman and Stroumsa 1999, 7–8).

The dream world may be a partial or complete simulacrum of partial or complete configurations found in the real world, but then, once created, the dream world becomes an impetus for an intervention into the real world. The real world begins to alter and shift its contours through the emergence of intentionality originating in the dream world. The dream world pressed upon the real world and vice versa. Dream world and real world are conjoined like a Mobius strip that has a single contiguous surface broken, if at all, for the sake of convenience, only by arbitrary points of commencement and departure. Inside and outside can become outside and inside at any given moment or through a change in perspective. The viewer determines whether he or she is in dream state or waking state and that too remains – even with the "sign" that signifies the "real" – uncertain and ambivalent.

The Real World

(the) desire for the imaginary, the possible, must contest with the imperative of the real, the actual. (White 1980)

History can broadly and perhaps without much controversy be defined as the study of the past. But while history concerns itself with the past, it is also obvious that not all statements about the past are considered to be history. It is only when the past is presented to us – "constructed" one could say – in a particular manner that it becomes "history." Not every statement or perspective of the past therefore qualifies as history. But how exactly does history get constructed? What

The Plain Sense of Things   187

indeed does it mean to state that history can be defined as a particular articulation of the past? To expand on this definition one could say that history as a "study" of the past involves thinking about the past in a particular manner. Before one can identify what this particular mode of thinking, abstraction, and articulation involves one must ask: What does it mean *to think* about the past? Where does thinking about the past arise? Where is this thinking about the past located? Where indeed is thinking located and what is thinking?

Can there be any thought without past, present, and future? Put another way can there be any thought without time? Put in yet another way: does time (past, present, and future) come into existence when there is thought and *vice versa*, does thought come into existence when there is time? In other words, can we say that thought and time *arise* together not as cause and effect but as co-dependent entities? In a sense, thought engenders time and time engenders thought. It becomes impossible to conceive of the one without the other. In order for time to arise with thought the latter must be linked to memory which is composed of images, multi-sensory experiences, and narratives that collectively could be said to constitute thought. These images, experiences, narratives and so on from the past (what has happened) are further distinguished from what is happening (the present) or what could happen (the future) by means of negation, resemblance, similarity, and projection. Thought itself is thus made up of images, multi-sensory experiences, and narratives. But it is more than that, or rather it occurs in something that encompasses it. Not only encompasses it but actually represents the conditions for the possibility of thought. This is language. Thought, with its apparatus of multi-sensory experience which is made up not only of our memory of the past but also our recollection of the present and remembrance of the future, occurs in language that may have to do with words, but also sounds, images, and olfactory and kinaesthetic experience. To go one step further one can now state that thought, time, and language all arise simultaneously. When there is language there is also the possibility of thought that gives rise to the possibility of time. Time, language, and thought together allow for the possibility of *Being* to be known as being-in-the-world. Without time, language, and thought the possibility of *Being* as a being-in-the-world ceases. In other words, the possibility of *Being* as existence and non-existence occurs with the arising of language, thought, and time.

History like thought and time arises when there is language. Without thought there is no time; there is no becoming aware of what is no longer present and what is about to become present. All there is the present moment of now. When thought ceases so does the existence of time and its occurrence as a pulling in and releasing out of objects and events. However, apart from the present moment, our experience of past and future is conceptual, embedded in narratives, stories, a putting and piecing together of what has happened or will happen in some sequence that purportedly makes sense to us and to the people we join hands with in agreement or even disagreement. This making sense is contingent. It is not absolute. It is contingent on many things: community, Zeitgeist, culture, prejudices and judgments that do not show up as prejudices and judgments but rather as "facts" and the "truth," and language itself as the compass that we use to describe and orient ourselves in the world. However, language is a constraint: it represents a set of distinctions through which we know the world and "create" the world as something, but which we have limited access to. It limits our access to world in its expression as a conceptual apparatus that labels, defines, and contains experience and possibility, although the latter emerges in language. Language in its deepest senses involves both creation or "bringing forth" but also interpreting and narrating. As Michael Jackson in the preface to *The Palm at the End of the Mind* perceptively states:

> I decided to turn myself to those situations in life where we come up against the limits of language, the limits of our strength, the limits of our knowledge, yet are sometimes thrown open to new ways of understanding our being-in-the-world, new ways of connecting with others ... the meanings of all human experience remain ambiguous, containing within it both the seeds of its own comprehensibility *and* nuances and shadings that go beyond what be comprehensively thought or said. (Jackson 2009, x)

While it seems that history clearly lives in and is skilled at producing interpretation and narration, it is not clear to what extent history can or does participate in the act of bringing forth or creating new possibilities. As an act of interpretation and a discipline that is committed to fostering narratives that sustain interpretation, history must always be one step removed from experience:

> as ultimate codified "truth" (History) ... must always present itself as story. Since History exists in language, its strange task becomes the giving of an unavoidably spectral half-life to events which no longer exist in experience, only in words. (White 1980)

Although history deals, sometimes almost exclusively, with written texts (as though all reality and experience is encoded in writing), that

The Plain Sense of Things 189

is, with words in a particular configuration or order that is intended to make sense, the meaning behind those words and the context (author, society, political and religious milieus, patronage, cultural and temporal region, language as it used in a particular province of the past and so on) must all be (re-)imagined. In other words our access to texts that are often considered to be prime bearers of language, truth, and meaning is again through the language and words we use now and their situational significance. There seems to be no escape from the covering and layers of language, words, and concepts not only to perceive and understand events of the past but also texts that describe events or ideas that have their origin in the past. Still those events and texts come into existence within and from the intentionality of the present moment that hauls back that which is no longer present into being present through memory, language, and narrative. The past as event(s) and as text(s) and non-event(s) and non-text(s) exists solely in the present moment together with scholarly or other texts that function as commentaries that also exist in the present moment. In other words, there is nothing that exists or does not exist outside the present moment which can be experienced, but known only in a second order as concept, interpretation and story. In short it can be known only as a model, likeness, image, and representation, that is, as a simulacrum.

Into the Forest

The dream-like character of the fortress continues in Wahid Mohammed's narration of its more recent history:

> Wahid Mohammed: My name is Wahid Mohammed. I am from Sawai Madhopur. In the Ranthambhore [area], Sawai Manpur was named after King Sawai Man Singh. He was the king of Jaipur. So possibly, it was named after him. Ranthambhore is thirteen kilometres from the railway station. In between, you will see Amaresar, Misaldara, Keshdhar. From then on, the forest entry gate starts. When you enter into the forest, you will find yourself in Misaldara. Misaldara was earlier known as Gomukh and there you will see statue of a cow with water flowing through its mouth. Gomukh means where water comes from the mouth of cow. Beyond that there is the forest. And that's the area from where our Ranthambhore national park starts. Ahead of that the area is known as Bahadurpur. So, there was a guard named Bahadur. The area was named after him. At that time, all the animals, be it tigers, bears, and so on knew him by the smell of his body. He used to call out to them once, and they would come to him immediately. He was a *harijan* and was known as *Maliya Baghel*.

190   Aditya Malik

Me: When was this?

Wahid Mohammed: I am talking about 1982.

Me: It's fairly recent, then.

Wahid Mohammed: So, he was guard and he used to roam around to check security [in the forest]. He was the only guard in the jungle, and no one was there with him. Animals loved him so much that they would always roam with him. There were trees everywhere and he used to prepare his cot near some trees. The animals used to guard him. He used to feed them and if any of them got injured, he used to take care of that animal. For example, if a thorn pierced an animal's paw, he used to pluck it out and take care of it. He loved them like his own pets just as we love our pets and cattle, and the animals loved him as well. So, [that location] was named as Bahadurpur.

In this conversation Wahid Mohammed situates the fortress of Ranthambore, which is the location for the heroic deeds of Hammīra, in a narrative regarding the forest and lakes that surround it. The journey into the fortress begins so to speak with the large and dense forest at the foot of the hill upon which the fort has been built. The forest is populated with tigers and crocodiles inhabit the lake that is on the forest's edge. The description suggests that this is a kind of magical forest in which animals, including dangerous predators, and the forest guard who works there are able to communicate and care for each other. The description of the forest then moves on to describing in succession the various gates, deities, shrines, mosques, and *dargāhs* (usually the tomb of a Sufi saint) that saturate the inner and outer features of the fortress with historical, religious, and ritual significance. Each material or architectural detail is amplified through a story or anecdote, each gathering together to offer us an interlocking sequence of the "present-past" that comes into existence when it is spoken and narrated. In this passage there is also a longer autobiographical portion that vividly reveals the intersection between the "personal" and the "historical" and how these two seemingly distinct discourses begin to merge and flow into one another in the arena of the "everyday" that is defined by struggle, hardship, aspiration, and also success.

The fortress transforms into the potent site of a pilgrimage, reinforcing the idea that its compounds and ramparts are an auspicious location whose sacredness is engendered not only through the presence of shrines, temples, and *dargāhs* but also through the fact that it is a battlefield (*raṇbhūmi*) and tantric field (*kṣetra*). After losing the battle to Alā' al-Dīn Khaljī through acts of treachery on the part of his own generals and the overseer of the royal granaries, Hammīra, according

The Plain Sense of Things 191

to this account and others retold at the fortress, severs his own head in an offering to Lord Śiva. But because he is such a staunch devotee of Lord Śiva his head is rejoined to his torso again and again until at the seventh and final attempt it falls away from his body and lands next to the *Śivaliṅgam* that he has continuously worshipped. There after this image is called Hammīr-Śiva. The narrative journeys through different gates and important locations of the fortress before finally turning into a biographical account in which the narrator interweaves his own experience as a guide and as someone who has worked for the Archaeological Survey of India into the remnants of the historical narrative he has been recounting.[2] These personal details give us an insight into the more recent history of the fortress and the gradual development of the forest into a tiger reserve and important tourist attraction. The account also moves from more "legendary" and "mythical" tropes to concrete transactional descriptions involving payments for services in rupees and the transportation of goods such as sugar, wheat, and so on in the present time. Thus, the narrative retelling of historical memory is based on a "composite" construction or amalgam of different and differently recognizable registers of historical meaning derived from a temporal palette of events and actions reaching back several centuries until a few decades ago each with variable degrees of substance (Cf. Narayana Rao, Shulman, and Subrahmanyam 2002).

Me: So you worked as a guide here earlier?

Wahid Mohammed: I used to work as a guide. I told you that I have been here since 1985. As I worked as the agent of the bus, I came here. Then I got into the taxi business. I left that as well and got into the work related to parking. It was contractual work. I used to go from here and if, in between, there were no passengers, I used try something else. If it was two o'clock and the gates were closed, and if anybody came, I used to show him the place. They used to come telling me that they didn't want to hear anything. They just wanted to see things. Gradually I started telling them the stories as well so somebody used to give me Rs 20 or Rs 10 sometimes. It kept on going like this ... then it rose to Rs 60, then Rs 150. After that I left this too. My home is at a distance of twenty-two kilometres from there, so I used to go on a bicycle.

Me: Oh my god…

Wahid Mohammed: Although I use to run too. I have rode bicycle for twenty-two years but all those working with the bus and Jeep used to ask me not use the bicycle. They asked me to go comfortably. That's how I used to go. Now the times have changes and the place remains crowded and the goods and items for the shops are also transferred there. Ten to

192   Aditya Malik

twelve people also stay there in groups. After I stopped going, there was a Gujjar milkman who used to go there to supply milk from the village. He used to carry the dung on top. He used to supply milk. Slowly he learnt what I used to do. So all these [guides] are the ones who started this [job] after me … He goes there often to supply milk and used to take Rs 10 commission each time. He used to carry the load of the wheat sacks, *makhāna* sacks, sugar sacks, gram flour sacks each weight fifty kilograms. He used to carry that load initially and he used to earn Rs 1.50 per kilogram load. He used to make Rs 20 for each sack he used to carry up there. The distance up the hill distance was 1.5 kilometres. It was none other than me who got the price increased from Rs 1.50 per kilogram to Rs 2 per kilogram by asking the shopkeeper. The shopkeeper now gives Rs 100 for a sack of fifty kilograms. He used give Rs 5 for a canister so now it was raised to Rs 10 for a canister. Later on from Rs 10 I got it increased to Rs 15 and then Rs 20. Today a 15 kg canister pays Rs 20. Therefore people there know me, and I have also done all the work there [is to do]. Gradually, I came here and left everything. Then I got entangled in the case. I worked from 2002 to 2007 in the Archaeological Survey of India. I have been the one to get the digging of all the buildings done here by the labourers. All the sections you see here were once ruins. There were big trees growing in them, the buildings had sunk. The officers used to come from Delhi, and I used to get the visits coordinated. I used to send a message to them that they will find a boy who will show them everything. The building that was getting broken used to get surveyed first, and from there the budget used to get approved. I used to write that such things were happening. It is in danger as there are so many guests coming from outside, and this is the situation here. It is good, since the place of deity is there, etc. So I have wrote to them on multiple occasions. So from there the budget was approved. The officers used to live in Delhi. …

It is very good. Doesn't matter what you may think, but I am a Muslim and I have earned a lot of money through the blessings of Ganeśjī situated in the fortress. In fact, my house was constructed using that money.

Me: Very nice!

Wahid Mohammed: I am there since 1985. I remained there till 2007. I have also worked in it.

Me: In the temple?

Wahid Mohammed: No, in the Archaeological Survey Department. I had also joined the course. I just did not pay attention at that time and today even my [legal] case is ongoing in the Archaeological Survey Department.

Me: What?!

Wahid Mohammed: That's how it is. All the dates [for court cases] have come and gone. I have a knowledge of each and everything including

The Plain Sense of Things 193

which officer was there and who is there now. Even if I go there today, the permanent staff of that department will treat me with a lot of respect ...

The several narrations that Wahid Mohammed provides are deeply expressive, one could say, of an "ecology of relatedness" in which past and present, wilderness and settlement, distinctive religious traditions, humans and non-humans, and the personal and the historical interweave in an effortless arc of convergence, into interdependent, intertwined identities that acknowledge and thrive through each other's existence. The descriptions of the fortress and its surroundings, and the stories of their manifold inhabitants, live in and speak for an increasingly elusive possibility of intimacy alongside a more antagonizing and fragmented view of the social and political world that seeks to erode and interrupt the experience of profound connectedness illustrated above, especially among religious communities in contemporary India.

The Plain Sense of Things

After the leaves have fallen, we return
To a plain sense of things. It is as if
We had come to the end of the imagination,
Inanimate in an inert savoir.
It is difficult even to choose the adjective
For this blank cold, this sadness without a cause.
The great structure has become a minor house.
No turban walks across the lessened floors.
The greenhouse never so badly needed paint.
The chimney is fifty years old and slants to one side.
A fantastic effort has failed, a repetition
In a repetitiousness of men and flies.
Yet the absence of the imagination had
Itself to be imagined. The great pond,
The plain sense of it, without reflections, leaves,
Mud, water like dirty glass expressing silence
Of a sort, silence of a rat come out to see,
The great pond and its waste of the lilies, all this
Had to be imagined as an inevitable knowledge,
Required, as necessity requires. (Stevens 1972, 382–3)

The seemingly simple and straightforward temporalities of past, present, and future with which we are all familiar are entangled with one another. Past, present, and future are imbroglios of one another. We cannot talk about the past without invoking the present and the future. This insight requires no great effort of intelligence. Yet, as historians and social scientists we must ask in what manner these temporalities are entangled. What are the ramifications of these imbroglios? If past, present, and future all exist in the "now," then what are the implications for a study of the past? Not only the past but also the present and future are steeped in memory and imagination. Not only is the past as a present that is longer present a function of reimagining what took place, but the present too as it unfolds itself before us is recognized based on our imagining of the past. The future too as the present that is yet to become present is inhabited by our imagination that almost completely originates in our knowledge of the past. The future as the present that has not yet come to be present does not occur to us as the empty space of potential or as a clearing for possibility, but as a room that is occupied with aspirations, fears, anxieties, and dreams somehow curbed by good sense and reasonableness; it occurs to us as the location not for unlimited expansion, opening, and creativity but for limited action and movement forward. Yet all this has to be imagined. Time is otherwise empty. It takes on form and meaning only when anchored by our imagination of events that have arisen and disappeared from our view or events that lie beyond the horizon of our view, that are about to occur and show themselves to us such that they become part of who we are, through which our own being acquires a shape and form. Past and Future are thus empty spaces that require imagination in order to come into existence. The Present too is imagined inasmuch that we recognize it and treat it as something that we know, that we somehow remember as resembling what we have already experienced. Yet the Present is the location for *"this" "now."* It too is empty as a signifier for *what is*; for what cannot be thought of, for what cannot and need not be imagined. The Present *is*. In order for it to become something it too must be imagined.

As Stevens's poem says, even the absence of imagination had to be imagined. The absence of imagination leaves us not with despair and ruin, rather it catapults us into the suchness of the present moment, stripped of pretention, fame, effort, and meaning: *to a plain sense of things as they are and as they are not*. It is above and inside this plain sense of things that time hovers, spiralling out like a swarm of bees or locusts that cloud this plain sense; presence and non-presence, concealment and unconcealment. Imagination is the source of the swarm that adopts an ever twisting and turning phantasmagoria of events, people, feelings, actions, memories, dreams, stories, and more in an unending mixture. If imagination is the swarm of images without which there is no past or future, without which there is no history, then what does it mean to think about the past that is the purpose of history? Thinking as in a turning towards that which has already withdrawn itself from human being?[3] Can there be an engagement with the past that involves thinking in the sense we have been discussing it? Or must history as a study of the past that is deeply anchored in imagination be relegated to a second level of thinking that endorses and valorises the phantasmagoria of the dream, of the simulacrum that is detached from the real, that has become the desert, racing away from which is worthy of thinking? Speeding away from the question of *Being*? Does history promote alienation? Alienation and detachment from what is, from a plain sense of things?

NOTES

1 *Gabru* is a Punjabi and Hindi word for boy or youth.
2 The narrator also states how he has – even though he is a Muslim – benefited from Lord Ganeśa (or Gajānand Pīr) by bringing devotees to the deity's shrine in the fortress. This again represents, in a sense, an "inter" or "co-mingling" of religious identities at a heritage site that, as we have seen, historically encouraged the bonds of friendship, loyalty, and mutual respect across religious and ethnic boundaries.
3 "dass, wir noch nicht denken, liegt keineswegs nur daran, dass der Mensch sich noch nicht dem genuegend zuwendet, was von Haus aus bedacht sein moechte ... Dass wir noch nicht denken, kommt viel mehr daher, dass dieses zu-Denkende selbst sich von Menschen abwendet, langher schon abgewendet hat.

     ... das, was uns eigentlich zu denken gibt, hat sich nicht zu einer historisch datierbaren Zeit vom Menschen abgewendet, sondern: das eingentliche zu-Denkende haelt sich von einsther in solcher Abwendung." (Heidegger 1954, 4).

WORKS CITED

Bandyopádhyáya, Brajanátha. 1879. "Hamír Rásá or a History of Hamír, Prince of Ranthambor." *The Journal of the Asiatic Society of Bengal* 48, 186–252.
Heidegger, Martin. 1954. *Was heisst Denken?* Tuebingen: Max Niemeyer.
Jackson, Michael. 2009. *The Palm at the End of the Mind: Relatedness, Religiosity and the Real.* Durham: Duke University Press.
Narayana Rao, Velcheru, David Shulman, and Sanjay Subrahmanyam. 2002. *Textures of Time: Writing History in South India, 1600–1800.* New York: Other Press.

Malik, Aditya. 2021. *Hammīra. Chapters in Imagination, Time, History*. Berlin: De Gruyter.

Shulman, David. 1999. "Dreaming the Self in South India." In *Dream Cultures: Explorations in the Comparative History of Dreaming*, edited by David Shulman and Guy Stroumsa. New York: Oxford University Press.

–. 2012. *More than Real. A History of the Imagination in South India*. Cambridge: Harvard University Press.

Shulman, David, and Guy Stroumsa, eds. 1999. *Dream Cultures: Explorations in the Comparative History of Dreaming*. New York: Oxford University Press.

Stevens, Wallace 1972. *The Palm at the End of the Mind. Selected Poems and a Play*. New York: Vintage Books.

White, Hayden. 1980. "The Value of Narrativity in the Representation of Reality." *Critical Inquiry* 7, no. 1: 5–27. https://doi.org/10.1086/448086.

9 Boundary Situations: An Existential Account of Wounded Healing

SÓNIA SILVA

In Northwest Zambia, those who show disrespect towards the living and the dead may be afflicted by their ancestors manifested as *mahamba*. A renowned example of these mahamba runs in the families of basket diviners and goes by the name of Kayongo. Kayongo is the spiritual manifestation of a distraught male ancestor who was a basket diviner during his lifetime. When a man falls prey to Kayongo, he feels pain in his chest, strong headaches, and moments of mental confusion. Fearing the worst, his relatives take the case to a practising basket diviner, who identifies Kayongo as the source of suffering. The situation is concerning but not hopeless. If the patient refuses to join the divining profession, as his ancestor wishes, he will die. No one escapes Kayongo's wrath. If, however, the patient shows respect towards his precursor by complying with his wishes and demands, then he will become a reputable healer, a wealthy man, and a highly respected member of his community. Sakutemba and Sangombe, two professional basket diviners whom I met in Northwest Zambia during ethnographic fieldwork in 2002, explained this quandary to me:

> Sakutemba: I had a very high fever and this heaviness in my chest, this feeling I had been crushed by a heavy load. We went to consult a diviner, who said to us, "It's the oracle of your forebear; you must receive it." So, we summoned diviner Litwayi who brought out the drums, and we purchased a new divination basket, a billy goat, and a rooster to sing for Kayongo [i.e., conducted a night-long ceremony]. After receiving the oracle and undergoing the ritual ordeals, I felt well and began divining.
>
> Sangombe: Kayongo gives wealth, but at the same time he is a very unfeeling *lihamba* [singular form of mahamba]. If he catches someone, and no ceremony is promptly conducted, he gets angry. That person will go insane and drown in the river. His relatives must hurry. Kayongo does not

forgive. Some throw themselves into the river and are eaten by crocodiles; others get hold of a knife and stab themselves ... Kayongo is fierce. But if you receive the oracle, he becomes very docile and brings you riches. He who defies him by not observing the taboos will surely die, and others will say, "His oracle killed him." Many are dying in this way.

I owe my understanding of this existential theme of suffering and renewal to Sakutemba and Sangombe. Unless otherwise stated, all quotations in this chapter were excerpted from separate conversations with both diviners. I recorded these conversations inside my mud-brick dwelling in Chavuma District to protect us from the Kalahari sands blown by the winds of April. Sakutemba and Sangombe spoke about their relationship with Kayongo, engaging with a theme that runs through the ritual and religious life of Central and Southern Africa. While your ancestors may catch you and make you suffer, they also give you the precious gift of ritual expertise.

In this chapter, I draw on concepts and ideas from existential anthropology in an attempt to comprehend and do justice to the accounts offered by Sakutemba and Sangombe. Researchers of religion are familiar with the archetypical figure of the wounded healer and Turner's idea of rituals of affliction. These concepts begin to explain the figure of the basket diviner who can heal because he has endured suffering. That said, these concepts do not fully capture critical dimensions of the basket diviners' accounts. I therefore suggest that we turn to existential anthropology, a tactical, theoretical approach that prioritizes human existence over reified theoretical concepts. While reifications thrive on lines of separation, the concept of existence shifts our attention to the place of ambiguity, nuance, and oscillation in human life. In Michael Jackson's words, existential anthropology helps us "recover a lost sense of the immediate, active, ambiguous 'plenum of existence' in which all ideas and intellectual constructions are grounded" (Jackson 1989, 3; Jackson and Piette 2015, 7). To elucidate the accounts of Sangombe and Sakutemba, I also draw inspiration from the work of other existential thinkers, namely Hubert Dreyfus and Karl Jaspers.

This chapter is divided into four parts. In part one, I return to the relation between suffering and ritual expertise in Northwest Zambia through the lens of the two classic concepts mentioned above: the archetype of the wounded healer and the concept of rituals of affliction. In part two, I give the floor to Sangombe and Sakutemba, allowing these diviners to speak in their own words and on their own terms. All of their quotations from elsewhere in this chapter appear in part two in order to convey some the flow and integrity of their accounts as recorded. In part three, I seek to do justice to the basket diviners' accounts by showing that ritual expertise enables them to cope with the suffering inflicted by two distinctive, yet existentially homologous sources: *lihamba* Kayongo and the political and economic conditions of life in Northwest Zambia at the turn of the millennium. While the archetypical figure of the wounded healer and Turner's concept of rituals of affliction help illuminate the transformation of the afflicted into healers, they preclude the serious consideration under the same light of both "religious" and "mundane" causes of suffering. In Northwest Zambia, if not elsewhere, religious expertise is well described as a set of coping skills, to borrow a concept from Hubert Dreyfus (2014), and the basket diviners are well portrayed as experts in the existential art of skilful coping. Finally, in part four, I revisit the main existential themes and antinomies that run through the accounts of Sakutemba and Sangombe, seeing them now through the lens of a concept developed by the German thinker Karl Jaspers (1994): boundary situations (*Grenzsituationen*). In these critical situations, the basket diviners find themselves oscillating between two opposing tendencies that are at once closely intertwined and irreducible to one another.

Rituals of Affliction and Wounded Healers

In *Schism and Continuity*, first published in 1957, Turner writes, "What I have called cults of affliction are performed for individuals, who are said by Ndembu to have been 'caught' (*ku-kwata*) by the spirits of deceased relatives whom they have forgotten to honour with small gifts of crops and beer, or whom they have offended by omitting to mention their names when prayers are made at the village *nyiyombo* (sing. *muyombo*) tree-shrines" (Turner [1957] 1972, 292).

This idea of being caught could have been rendered as possession, a concept highly disseminated in anthropology and religious studies by the 1950s (Prince 1977, xi). Turner, however, preferred the notion of affliction for good reasons. Not only does this notion speak to the Ndembu experience of suffering, but it also places the Ndembu rituals in a broader comparative field.

Equally important to Turner's argument, as well as my own, is that the notion of affliction is key to understanding the relation between suffering and religious expertise in Northwest Zambia. A structural functionalist by training, young Turner explained the cults of affliction by relating them to the Ndembu political structure as he studied it in Mwinilunga District in the 1950s. In a society without a centralized

200 Sónia Silva

political system, those cults brought the Ndembu together, performing, as he put it, "a politically integrative function" (Turner [1957] 1972, 288–317).[1]

Yet Turner did not simply relate ritual to politics; he also identified an important theme that ran through Ndembu religious and ritual life.

Turner mentioned a spirit that afflicted a woman who could not conceive, only to make her fertile and give her the power to heal as a doctor (1967, 294). Similarly, in the case of Muchona, Turner's main source on ritual topics, his deceased mother helped him become a religious expert by afflicting him with disease (1967, 134). Knowing that her slave status prevented Muchona from rising to prominence in secular Ndembu society, she gave her son the gift of religious expertise so he could gain respect and recognition. In both cases, I am reminded of an ancient piece of Ndembu wisdom: "through punishment, bane may become a blessing" (1967, 139). Elsewhere Turner writes: "affliction is potentially a boon, not merely a present pain, for it is the royal road to ritual eminence in a cult" (1957, 303).

As I discovered in my ethnographic study of basket divination among the Luvale and related others residing in Chavuma District, some 230 miles southwest of Mwinilunga, the same idea that affliction leads to religious expertise informs all rituals associated with Kayongo. In affliction rituals of the kind described by Turner (night-long rituals that transform a patient into a doctor), ailing men who fell prey to Kayongo are once again afflicted by Kayongo in order to heal and become healers. Not only are these sick men splashed with herbal potions from dusk to dawn, but they are driven into a trance and expected to kill a sacrificial rooster with their bare teeth. The following day, drained and fatigued, they are asked to divine the location of hidden objects in front of a large crowd, a public confirmation of their ability to divine and readiness to join the divining profession. They comply with the wishes because they fear the wrath of Kayongo. They also hope that the divining profession will grow on them.

This dynamic between affliction and ritual expertise is an important religious theme in Central and Southern Africa. In this vast region, the rituals of affliction are oftentimes known as *ngoma*, meaning drum, the central musical instrument played at those events. Hence Turner's book title *The Drums of Affliction* (1968), and, more recently, John Janzen's *Ngoma* (1992), an ambitious project in which the author takes as his object of study the complex and multimedia institution of rituals of affliction from Central to Southern Africa. Janzen lists an impressive number of similarities among *ngoma* performances in this vast region, noting that "the single most characteristic feature of *ngoma* is [the]

An Existential Account of Wounded Healing   201

transformation of the negative, disintegrating affliction into positive, integrative wholeness" (Janzen 1992, 105). The lyrics of *ngoma* songs echo this core feature. In a song from ancient Lemba on the Kongo coast, we hear: "That which was a stitch of pain has become the path to priesthood" (Janzen 1992, 1). On the Western Cape, we hear, "Let darkness turn to light" (Janzen 1992, 105).

Considering the extraordinary importance of these ritual events across Central and Southern Africa, as well as Turner's devoted attention to the topic beginning with his fieldwork among the Ndembu in the 1950s, it should not come as a surprise to find the "rituals of affliction" represented in the work of other researchers of religion. This concept appears, for example, in the ritual classification proposed by Catharine Bell, next to rites of passage; calendrical and commemorative rites; rites of exchange and communion; rites of feasting, fasting, and festivals; and political rites (Bell 1997, 94). For typological reasons, Bell broadened the scope of these rituals from their original concern with ancestral affliction to a plethora of cases which, in Bell's words, "attempt to rectify a state of affairs that has been disturbed or disordered" (1997, 115). This broad category stretches from those afflictions that one brings on oneself (sin and Karma) to recurring afflictions such as pollution from menstruation, childbearing, and death (1997, 115). Although Bell's taxonomic concerns inevitably weaken the relation between her "rituals of affliction" and the rich religious life of Northwest Zambia, Bell does not fail to acknowledge that those rituals speak loud to the human determination to "redress wrongs, alleviate suffering and ensure well-being" (1997, 119). In her words, these rituals serve as a reminder of "the all too human" side of religion (1997, 119–20).

Turner's idea of religious experts who can heal because they have "themselves known the suffering the candidates are experiencing," as he put it (Turner 1957, 302), is reminiscent of another concept with a different genealogy: the Jungian archetype of the wounded healer. I should mention here that Carl Jung did not coin the term "wounded healer" or even describe it as an archetype, by which he meant a typical figure that is built into the structure of the human unconscious and recurs through time (Jung 1951, 124). Jung did, however, refer to the equivalent idea of the "wounded physician." In his words, "It is [the doctor's] own hurt that gives the measure of his power to heal. This, and nothing else, is the meaning of the Greek myth of the wounded physician" (Jung 1951, 116). Not unlike Chiron, the wise and kind Centaur who became a wounded healer in ancient Greek mythology, Jungian psychologists, basket diviners, shamans, and many others are able to heal because they have suffered and continue to suffer.

202   Sónia Silva

Considering the similarities between the mahamba doctors of Northwest Zambia and the so-called wounded healers who appear not only in the Greek myth but also in contemporary shamanic practices reported in Siberia, Central Asia, and North America (Eliade 1964, 4–5), it is perhaps not surprising that Bell's category of "rituals of affliction" encompasses both mahamba rituals from Northwest Zambia and the *mansin* or *mudang* shamans from Korea (Bell 1995, 116). Notwithstanding the real differences between these religious experts, they are both aptly described as wounded healers.

That said, from the standpoint of existential anthropology, to restrict the conversation to ritual types and archetypes would be a lost opportunity to engage with those individuals whose lifeworlds, activities, and accounts become our research projects. It would also be short-sighted. How might Sakutemba and Sangombe enrich our understanding of the relation between suffering and expertise?

Sakutemba and Sangombe

Sakutemba: I had a very high fever and this heaviness in my chest, this feeling I had been crushed by a heavy load. We went to consult a diviner, who said to us, "It's the oracle of your forebear; you must receive it." So, we summoned diviner Litwayi who brought out the drums and we purchased a new divination basket, a Billy goat, and a rooster to sing for Kayongo. After receiving the oracle and going through the ritual, I felt well and began divining.

...

To the sound of drumming your heart feels restless, you tremble, that's it, you start jerking [i.e., you go into trance] ... Your heart has changed and your head has changed, too. You say, "Sakutemba?" but I do not respond. My wife runs to the oracle and brings the *lilembu* medicine container. I sniff it a few times before she places it on top of my head. The jerking subsides. I go, *hya, hya* [sigh of relief]. I *feel nyeka nyeka nyeka* [lowering or sagging]. You say, Sakutemba?" Yes, my friend," I reply. You say, "What's going on, my friend, why are you so calm?" I say, "the *lihamba* has entered my heart."

...

It is like I have left and Kayongo, he is in command of my heart. My head has no wisdom, I have lost my own mind. When my heart calms down you hear me saying, "I am Sakutemba, I am Sakutemba." By then my heart has calmed down and Kayongo has departed.

...

As I am today, Kayongo is not with me. I am Sakutemba and no one else because Kayongo has gone elsewhere. He's far away. When he crushes me, as happened yesterday when you went to visit me and I didn't come out to greet you, I feel my heart tightening, I feel like dying.

…

Sometimes I feel that my heart is restless, so I say, this is Kayongo. I start trembling, so I say, this is Kayongo. My heart goes *luku luku luku luku* [the sound of pounding], so I say, this is Kayongo, this is not a disease. That is when I take my *lilembu* medicine and sniff it a few times. That's it, *hee* [a sigh of relief].

Sangombe: Women's mahamba are Khula, Tembwa, Lwangu, Kamavya, Kahembi, and Kakuka – these are women's mahamba. Men have Unyanga, Kayongo, Ngungu, and Kazanga. Kayongo, however, is the strongest lihamba of all. Kayongo brings you out of your mind, drives you insane, and kills you. He blocks your path and kills you.

Sakutemba: I was not happy with the news. I said to myself, "I'm still young, what will happen when I receive that oracle? It's better I die." My father said, "No, don't say that, you must receive the oracle to get well." So I received the oracle and got well. Later I told him, "I cannot divine," but he replied, "no, don't say that. When they rub *jisozo* medicine on your eyes, you'll be able to divine." And so it was. They applied *jisozo* on my eyes and I began divining the cause of death and illness. I felt strong. And I rejoiced in my heart.

…

Because we diviners know well that Kayongo brings wealth. Kayongo may catch you, but once you sing for the oracle and receive it, you will find wealth.

…

Before Kayongo caught me, I was a simple farmer and fisherman like any other man. Now, I am making money … When others see it, they like me. I buy my friends relish, I buy them beer to drink, and they rejoice … My wife, is happy, too. She dresses and eats well. She feels good and says, "If we were still living as before, I would have gone back to my relatives."

…

Yes, Kayongo is a bad *lihamba*: he gives you both wealth and pain (*apwa lihamba wamupi wakuhana luheto kaha wakukenyuka*).

Sangombe: Kayongo gives wealth, but at the same time he is a very unfeeling *lihamba*. If he catches someone, and no ceremony is promptly conducted to sing for him, he gets angry. That man will go insane and drown in the river. His relatives must hurry. Kayongo does not forgive. Some men throw themselves into the river and are eaten by crocodiles; others get hold of a knife and stab themselves … Kayongo is fierce. But if you receive the oracle, he becomes very docile and brings you riches. He

204 Sónia Silva

who defies him by not observing the taboos will surely die, and others will say, "His oracle killed him." Many are dying in this way.

Religious Expertise as Skilful Coping

When those who are afflicted by Kayongo join the profession of basket divination, their suffering does not end. Indeed, like the centaur Chiron in Greek mythology, the basket diviners of Northwest Zambia come to accept the existential link between the sensation of pain and the rewards of expertise.

Suffering under Kayongo

This rejoining of suffering and expertise recurs throughout the ritual universe associated with Kayongo. In the night-long ceremony that transforms patients into doctors, they go through trials and ordeals that intensify the suffering inflicted by Kayongo. As previously mentioned, they must stay awake all night while they are splashed with an herbal potion; they fear the experience of trance, from the feeling of chest pain and breathing difficulties to other, more unpredictable concerns (what if they fall into the large open fire burning in the middle of the ritual yard? What if they run into the forest in the pitch of dark and get lost?). As mentioned, the afflicted also worry about the litmus test that takes place on the following morning, when they are asked to divine the location of several small objects hidden by the ritual participants, a public test they must pass to join the divining profession.

And this is only the beginning of a long journey of pain and expertise. During divination, diviners feel a piercing pain in their hearts. This pain, however, is not deprived of meaning and value. Pain is the means through which Kayongo lets the diviners know that truthful configurations of small symbolic pieces have emerged on top of the pile.

It is also true that the diviners' sense of control swiftly wanes when they break a taboo. A few examples will suffice. Diviners ought not to eat cassava leaves lest they talk nonsense while divining; they ought not to eat the soft roselle leaves lest they "slip" and become apathetic; and they ought not to eat the single-striped mouse (*ngendamusana*, or walker-by-day) lest their oracles "miss" the right answers. Moreover, should diviners engage in sexual intercourse during the daytime, they will fall seriously ill and be carried back home on a stretcher, as some diviners like to say. The diviners' long list of prescriptions and proscriptions serves as a constant reminder of the thin line that separates

An Existential Account of Wounded Healing   205

their confidence and pride as religious experts from their feeling of smallness at the hands of Kayongo.

To convey the real impact of their numerous religious obligations on their personal and social life, diviners might bring up the topic of their relationship with their wives. The diviner's wife (or his first wife in the case of a polygamous marriage) is customarily given the prestigious ritual status of Nyaminenge. In this capacity, her role is to ensure her husband's well-being by protecting his oracle in the safety of their home. She is also expected to bring out his *lilembu* healing medicine when Kayongo strikes; never give her husband prohibited foods to eat; and abstain from engaging in sexual intercourse during the daytime. This being said, some diviners become distrustful of their wives on these vital matters. Tired of worrying for his well-being each time his wife left for the cassava fields at the crack of dawn, Sakutemba made the difficult decision of depriving his wife of her religious status. Taking the matter to another level, Sangombe denied his wife the opportunity to become his Nyaminenge. In place of her, he created a surrogate Nyaminenge by tying a woman's *chitenge* wrapping cloth around the trunk of a *musole* tree in the forest. As he explained, "I made a tree in the forest Nyaminenge because you cannot place your oracle in the hands of someone else. If your wife does not observe the taboos, the oracle will kill you."

It goes without saying that these men, like the rest of us, have their moments of weakness. They might forget or ignore their obligations and engage in sexual intercourse before sunset, for example, enraging Kayongo. When their heart accelerates and their chest tightens, they know that Kayongo is near.

It should be noted that all these ritual activities are associated with a particular set of sensorial markers imputed to Kayongo. Sometimes diviners report fears of going insane and unknowingly committing suicide. More typically, though, they describe a sensation of growing pressure in the chest and an increasingly faster and louder heartbeat, as if their heart was being pushed towards the head. Kayongo causes the heart and head to "change." His arrival is both felt and identified as a movement from the heart towards the head and an increased heartbeat. His departure is described as a movement in the opposite direction. To vividly convey these sensations, diviners employ ideophones: *luku luku luku luku luku* (the sound of pounding); *lu lu lu lu lu* (a fast heart beat); *mba mba mba mba* (a heavy thump); *palakanyi* (the feeling of pressure); *heee* (a sigh of relief); *nyeka nyeka nyeka* (lowering or sagging).[2]

Diviners also report a strong sense of inescapability. Sangombe often referred to his oracle as his *lukano*, a metal bracelet that mature men and women wear on their wrists as a token of their lasting relationship with close ancestors. In his words:

> The life I have lived for a long time and continue to live at the moment is the life of Kayongo. I am still alive, and I continue to look after my oracle with my child [meaning his classificatory grown-up son who joined the divining profession and shook his father's basket]. I have not let go of my oracle, how could I, it is my *lukano*.

Back in the late nineties, while we were going over the details of a rarely performed Kayongo ritual whose purpose is to transform an ordinary woven basket into a potent oracle, Sangombe said:

> When a diviner feels tired, the oracle moves on to another diviner. When this diviner feels tired, it will move on to someone else. Diviners will pass on their oracle to others until they are all dead, they have all disappeared. Then, it's the end. He who denies his obligation will be crushed by Kayongo. His close relatives will take his case to a practicing basket diviner, who will warn them that the oracle will kill their sick relative. Then they go home and sing for Kayongo. They will sing for Kayongo in fear. Otherwise, their relative will die, and others will bury his body. We are keeping the oracle for someone else.

For this reason, Sangombe often referred to Kayongo as an obstacle blocking his path. Other diviners, including Sakutemba, preferred the metaphor of a crushing load, more commonly heard among diviners.

In sum, suffering is not in any way restricted to the early symptoms of Kayongo affliction that force an ordinary man to join the divining profession. As Sakutemba and Sangombe reported, Kayongo continues to torment his descendants and cause similar symptoms in a variety of ritual settings, from divination seances to the less public occasions when diviners do not follow their ritual obligations. In a real sense, all these events are well described as rituals of affliction.

According to Sakutemba and Sangombe, however, this portrayal is incomplete. While the diviners report that their suffering has no end, they also say that ritual expertise enables them to cope with suffering. Their first step towards their physical relief and renewal is to answer their predecessors' call by joining the divining profession. As novices, they apprentice themselves to senior diviners who teach them invaluable practical skills, from mastering the technique of shaking the divining basket in a vertical motion to learning the symbolism of the thirty or so symbolic pieces contained in the basket, both individually and in complex configurations. To alleviate suffering and ensure the veracity of their divinatory statements, senior diviners also tell their students to always remember to sniff their *lilembu* container when Kayongo strikes and rub *jisozo* medicine on their forehead and eyelids at the beginning of each séance. By sharpening the diviners' vision, *jisozo* enables them to see Kayongo's truth when it emerges in the oracle.

Religious expertise is therefore a form of skilful coping, as Dreyfus puts it, a form of coping that relies on bodily skills and techniques (Wrathall 2014, 3). Diviners do not move from their initial state of affliction to a life of expertise free of suffering; they continue to suffer in order to divine, and to rely on specialized knowledge and techniques in order to cope.

Suffering from Hunger

The idea of religious expertise as a form of skilful coping is important for another reason. In addition to helping the diviners cope with the suffering wrought by Kayongo, a cruel ancestral manifestation, religious expertise helps them cope with the suffering caused by a different, yet existentially homologous, source: poverty and dispossession. Let us revisit the words of Sakutemba and Sangombe on this vital matter.

> Sangombe: Kayongo gives wealth, but at the same time is a very unfeeling *lihamba*. If he catches someone, and no ceremony is promptly conducted, he gets angry. That person will go insane and drown in the river. His relatives must hurry. Kayongo does not forgive. Some throw themselves into the river and are eaten by crocodiles; others get hold of a knife and stab themselves ... Kayongo is fierce. But if you receive the oracle, he becomes very docile and brings you riches. He who defies Kayongo by not observing the taboos will surely die, and others will say, "His oracle killed him." Many are dying in this way.
>
> Sakutemba: I was not happy with the news. I said to myself, "I'm still young, what will happen when I receive that oracle? It's better I die." My father said, "No, don't say that, you must receive the oracle to get well." So I received the oracle and got well. Later I told my father, "I cannot divine," but he replied, "no, don't say that. Once they rub *jisozo* medicine on your eyes, you'll be able to divine." And so it was. They applied *jisozo* on my eyes and I began divining the cause of death and illness. I felt strong. And I rejoiced in my heart.
>
> ...

Because we diviners know well that Kayongo brings wealth. Kayongo may catch you, but once you sing for the oracle and receive it, you will find wealth.

...

Before Kayongo caught me I was a simple farmer and fisherman like any other man ... Now, I am making money ... When others see it, they like me. I buy my friends relish, I buy them beer to drink, and they rejoice ... My wife, is happy, too. She dresses well, she eats well, so she feels good. She says, "Were we still living as before, I would have already gone back to my relatives."

How can we do justice to the accounts of Sakutemba and Sangombe without overlooking their insistence that suffering brings wealth? It is not a coincidence that Muchona, Turner's Ndembu informant and fellow philosopher, said to the anthropologist: "What hurts you, once discovered and propitiated, helps you" (Turner 1967, 133). Turner's point that ritual expertise among the Ndembu is achieved through affliction is well known to researchers of religion. Muchona's dictum, however, differs from Turner's main point in one important respect. While Turner tied the concept of affliction to ritual expertise tout court, Muchona related affliction to a broader set of advantages and opportunities that he aptly condensed in the term "help." This notion of "help" echoes Sakutemba and Sangombe's preoccupations at the end of the millennium, particularly their allusions to "wealth." These and other diviners continue to make good use of their religious expertise as a means to help themselves as well as those who are under their care and responsibility. For these diviners, their religious expertise is as legitimate a way to earn a living as any other.

Writing from an existential and phenomenological perspective, Dreyfus asks whether philosophers can "successfully describe the conceptual upper floors of the edifice of knowledge while ignoring the embodied coping going on the ground floor" (Dreyfus 2014, 105). Writing from the same perspective, I ask whether we can adequately describe ritual expertise while ignoring the skilful coping going on the ground.

At this point of my argument, some scholars might see no value in extending the analytical scope of "religion" to the travails of daily survival. Meanwhile, other scholars may recognize some value in this approach but worry that it might further decrease the already low standing of divination and other too often marginalized practices in religious studies (Silva 2018). While studying the practice of Ifá divination among the wealthy and powerful of Chicago seems apposite and even critical in the current global moment, the humble explication

An Existential Account of Wounded Healing 209

of basket divination by correlating it with the daily travails of survival seems superfluous and irrelevant. Yet this is the conceptual challenge that we must face in our commitment to seriously acknowledge and address the implications of Sakutemba and Sangombe's accounts.

With this in mind, I start with the reminder that perceiving ritual as work is not uncommon. In Jewish contexts going back to the Hebrew Bible "work" is the standard word for divine service, including sacrificial rite and prayer.[3] In many present and past societies, from the ancient Hindu and the pre-Christian Greeks to the present Ndembu, Luvale, and others, in Africa and elsewhere, ritualization is described as work (Turner 1982, 30–1).

This view of ritual as work helps explain why ritual experts may sometimes receive remuneration. Across Africa, the idea that ritual experts (as well as accomplished performers such as singers and drummers) deserve compensation for their work is never disputed. In Northwest Zambia and neighbouring countries, basket diviners are well known for their high earnings in kind or cash. While some Christians and non-Christians alike may look down on the basket diviners for exploiting their clients at their weakest moments, others will recognize that becoming an accomplished basket diviner requires years of training and a life of suffering. The work of divining also generates something new time and again, from an activity such as a séance to the verbal translation of an ancestral truth. For those who reach out to diviners in times of need, the benefits of divination outweigh its cost.

Basket diviners, however, do not explain their work in one single way. In addition to speaking the language of remuneration, they also describe their work as a means to grow stronger and satisfy their hunger pangs, an idea that is perfectly encapsulated in the Luvale term for the divinatory payment – *chikoli*. This term derives from the verb *kukola*, or to become strong. It evokes bodily and emotional connotations that are absent in the equivalent English terms of payment or fee.

It is worth sharing here an old song recorded among the Ovimbundu people of Angola in the 1930s. The Ovimbundu are culturally related to the Luvale, Ndembu, and others from Northwest Zambia (Tucker 1940, 178).

I didn't say, "Come and get me,"
You were the one who was ill.
Oh, my fellow diviners,
Hunger hurts.

This reliance on basket divination to help satiate one's hunger pangs becomes all the more important during times of scarcity and upheaval.

210　Sónia Silva

Before the end of the Angolan Civil War in 2002, several basket diviners crossed the international border and made their way to Chavuma District in Northwest Zambia. Like so many other Angolan refugees, they attempted to rebuild their lives by tilling the land, selling *tukeya* fish at the local markets, and thatching house roofs, to mention a few common activities. By the time we first met in the mid-1990s, however, their lives had changed. It was clear that their ritual expertise had given them a noticeable advantage in the formidable task of remaking their life in exile. Basket divination helped these men become strong in at least two related senses: the sense of bodily strength and contentment and the existential sense of bringing overwhelming circumstances under some degree of control.

In his seminal book *The Logic of Practice*, Pierre Bourdieu captures the idea of the vital importance of "wealth" in a religious context. In his words, "magical or religious actions are fundamentally 'this-worldly' (*diesseitig*), as Weber puts it; being entirely dominated by the concern to ensure the success of production and reproduction, in a word, survival, they are oriented towards the most dramatically practical, vital and urgent ends" (Bourdieu 1990, 95). Sakutemba and Sangombe similarly recognize the vital importance of "wealth" in a religious context. In their view, to separate the work of ritual from the work of making a livelihood is to misunderstand it.

Acting and Being Acted Upon

In the study of religion, existential anthropology is often associated with ethnographic research methods for a good reason. This methodology yields valuable thick descriptions, rich verbal accounts, and experiential knowledge, all of which deepen our understanding of the myriad ways in which religion is lived and explained. However, this close attention given to minutia should not be read as a return to a pristine world preceding the arrival of theoretical concepts. As this volume illustrates, existential anthropologists rely on theoretical concepts to do their work. The value of existential anthropology lies not in the dismissal of all academic concepts but in the insistence on giving priority to the viewpoints, activities, and concerns shared with the researcher. No theoretical concept, however rooted in the history of religious studies, should justify the dismissal of lived religiosity. Similar to archival sources and foundational tomes, ethnographic research generates new insights that challenge old assumptions and rejuvenate the science of religion.

An Existential Account of Wounded Healing   211

How then did my conversations with Sakutemba and Sangombe help me better understand the idea that suffering leads to religious expertise?

I knew that the archetype of the wounded healer and the concept of rituals of affliction would be helpful in the task at hand. After all, these concepts capture the affliction-religious expertise dynamic with great simplicity and conciseness. That said, thanks to Sakutemba and Sangombe, I came to realize that those important concepts in the study of religion lead the researcher to reduce the idea of expertise to the liminal spaces of the affliction ritual or the Jungian clinical office. In other words, those reified concepts lead one to favour certain segments of Sakutemba and Sangombe's accounts over others and to imagine lines of separation between domains of life and action where the basket diviners see ambiguity and oscillation. Religious matters are not always unequivocally clear.

At this point in my argument, it is important to revisit the concept of liminality that we inherited from Arnold van Gennep (1960) and Victor Turner (1967). This seminal concept derives from the Latin *limen*, or threshold, a term once used to refer to the wooden frame that physically separates the rooms from the corridor. In van Gennep's architectural portrayal of liminality, one is either separated in a secular room that one shares with others in one's social group, or located in the liminal and ritualized space of the corridor. In line with this portrayal, van Gennep speaks of a "great incompatibility between the profane and the sacred worlds" (van Gennep 1960 1).

Yet Sakutemba and Sangombe challenge us to reimagine a concept of the liminal that differentiates between the sacred and the mundane without reifying this distinction. Basket diviners explained to me how, during Kayongo rituals, they become "set apart," or *kujila*, to become separated. This statement, however, does not imply an impervious line of difference and separation. As a basket diviner once put it, diviners have many responsibilities towards others. They have a long series of responsibilities towards the living, including their relatives, neighbours, and business partners, to name a few. They also have another set of responsibilities towards Kayongo, an ancestral manifestation, from honouring their forbearers by continuing the divining profession to following a long series of ritual observances. No one in the know would deny the differences between these two sets of responsibilities. At the same time, he asked, why would anyone challenge the idea that all those different obligations belong in the same bag of one's responsibilities? As Sakutemba and Sangombe saw it, diviners and their clients are

212   Sónia Silva

both sufferers (Silva 2011, 80). Religious expertise is a way of helping others and helping oneself in the same gesture.

Determined to highlight the existential ambiguity between the sacred and the profane, I interpreted ritual expertise as skilful coping, a concept I borrowed from Dreyfus (2014). Thanks to this helpful concept, it became possible to acknowledge the classic idea of ritual expertise in a liminal setting while doing justice to Sakutemba and Sangombe's words. For these diviners, "being apart" does not mean inhabiting a religious realm where bodily needs, social obligations, and money have no place. It means to oscillate, as they do, between experiencing ritual expertise as something liminal and something mundane. The realm of the sacred remains connected with the everyday without, however, being reducible to it.

Jaspers's concept of boundary situations (also known as limit, border, or ultimate situations) captures this dynamic well. Although Jaspers sees the boundary as a threshold, similarly to Turner and van Gennep, his model does not rely on the spatial imagery of rooms and corridors. Instead, he proposes an existential framing of the boundary in the context of boundary situations. According to this philosopher, boundary situations occur when we are caught in a moment of crisis – when we feel that the ground has been pulled out under our feet, as he puts it (Jaspers 1970, 281). In these situations, we face a contraction between opposing tendencies, or antinomies, which cannot be resolved or overcome.[4]

In the Zambian religious universe of mahamba spirits, this existential theme of oscillation is perfectly illustrated by the affliction-expertise dynamic. Here we see diviners alternate between suffering at the hand of others, spiritual and human (Jaspers would speak here of destruction and foundering, meaning failure), and other moments in which the same diviners see their boundary situation as a turning point, welcoming basket divination into their lives as a practical coping skill (Jaspers would speak here of creativity).[5] At its most encompassing, the dynamic speaks to the diviners' oscillation between a sense of themselves as being actors and being acted upon. This is the struggle for being, which Jackson describes as "a continual if frequently unreflective quest for some sense of balance between being an actor and being acted upon – negotiating a 'fair' trade-off between the need to decide our own lives and the need to come to terms with the forces against which we cannot prevail" (Jackson 2005, 182). In the lifeworld of basket divination, success cannot be simply measured by the total number of clients received over the years. The most successful diviners are those who willingly surrender control in the existential sense of empowerment to increase

An Existential Account of Wounded Healing   213

their expertise and grow their reputation. These diviners understand that there is no expertise without suffering, that the road to fame and success is not to veer in one or the other direction, but to "steer a course between" (Jackson 1998, 18).

This chapter would be incomplete if I omitted the aspect of my conversations with Sakutemba and Sangombe that most moved and impressed me. I noted above that Sangombe often referred to Kayongo as an obstacle blocking his path, and Sakutemba spoke of a crushing load. Despite their prolonged suffering, Sakutemba and Sangombe never wished that Kayongo had never caught them. When asked whether they had considered the possibility of severing their relationship with Kayongo if they could, they replied that they had no reason to worry as long as they followed their taboos. Sangombe said that those taboos were very few and light anyway and that most of the ritual observances were to their advantage, since they ensured the truthfulness of their divining statements, therefore growing their reputation and increasing their earnings. How could they complain when the divinatory profession had made them wealthy? Basket diviners may be under Kayongo's rule, but their spirit is not broken. As anyone who has had the good fortune of meeting a basket diviner in person will be able to confirm, these wise men exude professional pride and self-confidence. These men are determined to turn their bane into an opportunity, to increase their influence and affluence despite the forces that weigh heavily on them.

Referring to this existential theme, Jackson reminds us of "[the] stubborn human refusal to take life lying down, to resist subjugation, to struggle against being seen as a mere instantiation of transpersonal forces, a playing thing of faith, driven by circumstances that one can neither comprehend nor control" (Jackson 2005, 182). He also describes the question of being as "a relationship between the forces that act upon us and our capacity for bringing the new into being" (Jackson 2005, xi), an idea that Hannah Arendt encapsulates in her concept of natality (Arendt 1958, 176–7).

In *The Palm at the End of the Mind*, Jackson reminds us that the theme of creative destruction is an ancient one, appearing everywhere, from the Egyptian and Greek myth of the Phoenix and the Hindu figure of Siva to the Christian idea of the resurrection (2008, 37).[6] This theme of creative destruction also appears in countless contemporary ritualized settings, from the affliction rituals of Northwest Zambia to Jungian clinical practices located in Zambia and elsewhere.

To help his readers identify a universal theme in the Zambian insight that suffering leads to religious expertise, Turner liberally translated it

214   Sónia Silva

in the form of an English proverb: "suffering is a blessing in disguise."
I end this chapter in the same spirit by listing a handful of other translations of the Ndembu saying which could be offered:

Spanish
No hay mal que por bien no venga. (There is no bad that brings no
   good.)
Turkish
Her şerde bir hayır vardır. (There is goodness in every evil.)
Zulu
Isibusiso sokufihla (A blessing in disguise)
Aramaic
leit nehora ella de-nafik migo hashokha (There is no light but that which
   comes out of darkness.)
Chinese
sài wēng shī mǎ, yān zhī fēi fú (The old man lost his horse, but it all
   turned out for the best.)

NOTES

1 Turner also offered a sophisticated analysis of the symbolism of affliction
   rituals, for example in "Chihamba the White Spirit" (1975). For a critique
   of the reduction of ritual to culture and symbolism informed by the idea
   of lived religion and intersubjectivity, see Don Seeman's "Otherwise than
   Meaning" (2004).
2 On the important role of the senses in basket divination, see Silva (2021).
3 Don Seeman, personal communication.
4 Building on Jasper's idea of limit situations, as well as "the encompassing,"
   Jackson proposes his concept of limitrofe (Jackson 2008, 37).
5 Jaspers's concept of boundary situations brings to mind Turner's
   work on rites of passage, particularly his description of the liminal
   stage as a transitional period full of ambiguity and paradox, and, for
   that very reason, "a realm of pure possibility" (1967, 97). In Turner's
   work, however, this ambiguity is resolved and overcome in the final
   phase of incorporation back into society. For another existentially
   driven critique of Turner's concept of liminality, see Premawardhana
   (2018, 73–93).
6 In a recent article, Sean Winter (2020) describes how Paul of Tarsus
   moved from affliction (*thlipsis*) to consolation (*parakle͞sis*), as described in
   2 Corinthians 1:8–11. A key concept in Winter's argument is the "suffering-
   consolation dynamic."

WORKS CITED

Arendt, Hannah. 1958. *The Human Condition*. Chicago: University of Chicago Press.

Bell, Catherine. 1997. *Ritual Perspectives and Dimensions*. Oxford: Oxford University Press.

Bourdieu, Pierre. 1990. *The Logic of Practice*. Translated by Richard Nice. Stanford: Stanford University Press.

Dreyfus, Hubert. 2014. "Overcoming the Myth of the Mental." In *Skillful Coping: Essays on the Phenomenology of Everyday Perception and Action*, edited by Mark A. Wrathall, 105. Oxford: Oxford University Press.

Eliade, Mircea. 1964. *Shamanism: Archaic Techniques of Ecstasy*. Translated from French by Willard A. Trask. Princeton: Princeton University Press.

Jackson, Michael. 1996. "Introduction." In *Things as They Are: New Direction in Phenomenological Anthropology*, edited by Michael Jackson, 1–50. Bloomington: Indiana University Press.

Jackson, Michael. 1989. *Paths Toward a Clearing: Radical Empiricism and Ethnographic Inquiry*. Bloomington: Indiana University Press.

–. 1996. "Introduction." In *Things as They Are: New Direction in Phenomenological Anthropology*, edited by Michael Jackson, 1–50. Bloomington: Indiana University Press.

–. 1998. *Minima Ethnographica: Intersubjectivity and the Anthropological Project*. Chicago: The University of Chicago Press.

–. 2005. *Existential Anthropology: Events, Exigencies, and Effects*. New York: Berghahn.

–. 2008. *The Palm at the End of the Mind*. Durham: Duke University Press.

Jackson, Michael, and Albert Piette. 2015. "Anthropology and the Existential Turn." In *What Is Existential Anthropology?*, edited by Michael Jackson and Albert Piette, 1–10. New York: Berghahn.

Janzen, John M. 1992. *Ngoma: Discourses of Healing in Central and Southern Africa*. Berkeley: University of California Press.

Jaspers, Karl. 1970. *Philosophy 2*. Translated by E.B. Aston. Chicago: University of Chicago Press.

–. 1994. *Psychology der Weltanschauungen*. Munich: Piper.

Jung, Carl G. 1951. "Fundamental Questions of Psychotherapy." In *The Collected Work of C.G. Jung*, Vol. 16, edited by Herbert Read, Michael Fordham, Gerhard Adler, and William McGuire, 116–25. Translated by R.F.C. Hull. Princeton: Princeton University Press.

Premawardhana, Devaka. 2018. *Faith in Flux: Pentecostalism and Mobility in Rural Mozambique*. Pennsylvania: University of Pennsylvania Press.

Prince, Raymond. 1977. "Foreword." In *Case Studies in Spirit Possession*, edited by Vincent Crapanzano and Vivian Garrison, 17. New York: John Wiley.

Seeman, Don. 2004. "Otherwise than Meaning: On the Generosity of Ritual." *Social Analysis* 48, no. 2: 55–71. https://doi.org/10.3167/015597704782352500.

Silva, Sónia. 2011. *Along an African Border: Angola Refugees and Their Divination Baskets*. Pennsylvania: University of Pennsylvania Press.

–. 2018. "Taking Divination Seriously: From Mumbo Jumbo to Worldviews and Ways of Life." *Religions* 9, no. 12: 1–9. https://doi.org/10.3390/rel9120394.

–. 2021. "Touch and Other Senses: Feeling the Truth in Basket Divination." In *Religion and Touch*, edited by Christina Welch and Amy Whitehead, 175–92. Sheffield, UK: Equinox.

Tucker, Leona S. 1940. "The Divining Basket of the Ovimbundu." *Journal of the Royal Anthropological Institute of Great Britain and Ireland* 70, no. 2: 171–202. https://doi.org/10.2307/2844369.

Turner, Victor. (1957) 1972. *Schism and Continuity in an African Society: A Study of Ndembu Village Life*. Manchester: Manchester University Press.

–. 1967."Betwixt and Between: The Liminal Period in Rites of Passage." In *The Forest of Symbols: Aspects of Ndembu Ritual*, 93–111. Ithaca: Cornell University Press.

–. 1975. "Chihamba the White Spirit: A Ritual Drama of the Ndembu." In *Revelation and Divination in Ndembu Ritual*, edited by Victor Turner, 37–203. Ithaca: Cornell University Press.

–. 1982. *From Ritual to Theater: The Human Seriousness of Play*. New York: PAJ.

Van Gennep, Arnold.1960. *The Rites de passage*. Chicago: University of Chicago Press.

Wrathall, Mark A. 2014. "Introduction: Hubert Dreyfus and the Phenomenology of Human Intelligence." In *Skillful Coping: Essays on the Phenomenology of Everyday Perception and Action*, edited by Hubert Dreyfus and Mark A Wrathall. Oxford: Oxford University Press.

10 Sartre's Jews and Jackson's Witches: What (Who) Is Real in Existential Anthropology?

DON SEEMAN

How burdensome and pervasive is the search for truth – to connect the dots, identify a cause, place blame, deliver a judgement, or arrive at an explanation ... What I seek is not a philosophy of the absurd but a way around philosophy, morality, nationality, and all the other systematizing forms we deploy to mask the complexity and chaos of existence ... not only because I doubt the possibility of certainty but because of the liberating effect of living in uncertainty by contrast with the bondage of living in belief.

– Michael Jackson (2019, 54)

Shortly after the liberation of Paris (but before the liberation of Auschwitz), in the autumn of 1944, Jean-Paul Sartre turned his attention to the existential contours of European antisemitism and to the dilemma of Jews who might return to France after the war.[1] He could not have known that of seventy-six thousand individuals deported, only some twenty-five hundred (around 3 per cent) would return alive (Marrus and Paxton 2019). In his *Réflexions sur la question juive* (which he describes as "hastily written"), Sartre portrays French Jews as caught in an impossible predicament between the claims of the particular and the universal, represented politically by antisemites and by liberal democrats, respectively. "The former wishes to destroy [the Jew] as a man and leave nothing in him but the Jew, the pariah, the untouchable; the latter wishes to destroy him as a Jew and leave nothing in him but the man, the abstract and universal subject of the rights of man and the rights of the citizen ... Between his enemy and his defender, the Jew is in a difficult situation ... Is the solution of the problem to be found in the extermination of all the Israelites or in their total assimilation? Or is there some other solution?" (Sartre 1948, 57–8).

Sartre's "other solution" was of course an existential one. Jews facing antisemitism or genocide have the capacity (like all people) to live or die "authentically" by unflinchingly acknowledging, and then unapologetically inhabiting, the specific predicament into which they have been cast against their will. To do so, to the extent possible, on one's own terms, is what Sartre calls "freedom" (1969, 45), and it is invoked as such in Sartre's name by anthropologist Michael Jackson on the very first page of his *Existential Anthropology: Events, Exigencies and Affects* (2005, 1): "our capacity to *make ourselves* out of what we are made."[2] Together with Hannah Arendt's (2018) "natality," (which Jackson describes as "the generative or initiatory aspect of human activity ... this capacity for rebirth" [2018]), Sartre's understanding of freedom is central to almost every one of Jackson's many ethnographies and may be described as a fulcrum of his whole project in existential anthropology.

Sartre himself made use of this idea in a wide variety of different contexts, including essays on the poetry of Black solidarity or Negritude (Sartre 1964). "Insulted, enslaved," Sartre writes, the poet "redresses himself; he accepts the word 'negro' which is hurled at him as an epithet, and revindicates himself, in pride, as black in the face of the white" (Irele 1964, 11). If I begin with Sartre's reflections on Jewishness and antisemitism rather than these other contexts, it is because these reflections touch in a very personal way on the themes and affordances of my own anthropological vocation (Seeman 2008, 2009, 2021; Seeman and Stern, forthcoming). It also represents one of the clearest and earliest expressions of Sartre's view that existential "authenticity" represents a solution to the conundrum of universals and particulars that has helped to shape both anthropology and the academic study of religion since their inception as disciplines.

I will have a bit more to say about the trajectory of religious studies in this regard – and its subsequent reception of existential anthropology – towards the end of the chapter. On the anthropological side, it can be said that phenomenological-existential approaches like the one associated with Michael Jackson represent an "other solution" to the problems raised by claims of incommensurable cultural particularity on the one hand and the lowest common denominator of universal "human nature" (sometimes inflected by racial or biological theories), on the other (see Lambek 2015). Both Sartre and Jackson have sometimes been understood as making universalist claims (Desjarlais and Throop 2011, 91), but this may only be a part of the story. Sartre probably owes more to the radical individual "decisionism" of Kierkegaard than to the grand categorical imperatives of Kant (Glendinning 2007; Flynn 2018), and so it seems to be with existential anthropology. For one thing, Jackson doesn't deny the importance of culture, just its deterministic power over human affairs – its seeming occlusion of freedom (in the Sartrean sense) and its power to distract our attention from the human predicament that all members of the species share but which every *human person* must navigate for themselves. The "epistemological posture" of existential anthropology, writes Laurent Denizeau (2015, 214), "may be characterized by a withdrawal from the level of cultural representation in anthropological understanding and an engagement with the relation of a human being to the world, which is fundamentally equivocal." Existence comes before essence, predicament before culture, life before thought.

There is also a more specific reason for starting this chapter with Sartre. One of Michael Jackson's most characteristic analytic moves requires the juxtaposition of seemingly disparate human phenomena in such a way that a shared existential *ground*, prior to culture, may emerge (see Seeman 2018). "Despite cultural variations," Jackson (1998, 13) writes in one exemplary passage, "the connotations of *mana* in Polynesian, *dumba* in Sewa, *miran* in Kuranko and honour in circum-Mediterranean societies suggest that similarly embodied sensations of amplitude – 'substantiality' (cf. Laing 1965, 41–2), 'weight' (cf. Riesman 1977, 185), 'standing' (Strauss 1966, 143), 'voice' (Keane 1997, 202–3), 'containedness' (Jackson 1982, 22; Reisman 1977, 226) and charismatic forcefulness – *everywhere* constitute our sense of existence and autonomy." I will argue that Jackson's essays on African witchcraft and Sartre's writings on antisemitism do some of the same intellectual work for each author. They are each primary cases for thinking through the human capacity to bear up and assume one's condition despite violence or dispossession. Jackson's writings on witchcraft, moreover, may be said to presage, for both better and worse, his whole existential account of religious life. My appeal to Sartre, a figure frequently invoked by Michael Jackson as a formative intellectual presence and ancestor, therefore aims to clarify the moral, political, *and* analytic stakes of the binary between particulars and universals that both writers sought to overcome, and to consider what it might mean to succeed – or to fail to succeed – at overcoming it.

1. Are Jews Real?

It would have been obvious to many of those reading Sartre's *Réflexions sur la question juive* that the choice between a narrow particularism culminating in murder and a universal ideal premised on more-or-less forced assimilation was just one version of a long-standing dialectic in which "the Jewish question" had already been framed since as early as the French National Assembly's famous emancipatory bargain of 1789. "The Jews should be denied everything as a nation," the Assembly declared, "but granted everything [i.e., access to citizenship and protection under the law] as individuals" (Mendes-Flohr and Reinhartz 1980, 114; Judaken 2006, 10). Sartre claims to have known very few Jews and to have read not even a single book about Judaism or Jewish history before writing the *Réflexions*, but he intuitively grasped that one implication of this demand was a desire to "separate the Jew from his religion, from his family, from his ethnic community, in order to plunge him into the democratic crucible whence he will emerge naked and alone, an individual and solitary particle like all the other particles" (Sartre 1948, 57). This, he immediately adds, is what is called in the United States "the policy of assimilation," to which I will return. It presumes that religious, historical, or kinship solidarities are less real than (or should be nullified in favour of) loyalty to the state, which is itself an embodiment of the universal liberal order and guarantor of "The Rights of Man."

Sarah Hammerschlag (2010, 3) describes the paradoxical outcome of this approach, in which the most prominent advocates for emancipation of the Jews in eighteenth century France simultaneously "described the Jew as a tribal remnant of an outmoded culture ... a figure attached to backward customs and superstition" (compare Jackson's account of state tropes about Aboriginal peoples in this volume).[3] "The Jew was a symbol of particularism," Hammerschlag notes trenchantly, "which the Revolution was meant to *overcome*." A century later, however, "when the Catholic Right wanted to communicate its resistance to the Third Republic, its vocal leaders identified the *cosmopolitan Jew* as the secret victor of the 1789 revolution." Portrayed as lacking "a relationship to French soil and, thus, to the natural world more generally ... [and] aligned with abstract reason rather than tradition," this *cosmopolitan* Jew was now understood to be "uprooted and in danger of corrupting the heritage of the true France."

The protean capacity of antisemitism to assume whatever contradictory shapes the ideology of the moment requires has helped to define a characteristic modern Jewish condition. Jews may be reviled as capitalists or as communists, depending on who is doing the reviling; as insufficiently white or as beneficiaries of *extreme* white privilege; for lack of a state or for having one (Levy 2017). Thus, "if for [the French writer] Barrès the Jews represent universalism, abstraction, and rootlessness," concludes Hammerschlag (2010, 65), "for Péguy, on the contrary, they are the instantiation of particularism – not because they have *terroir* [soil], but because they are a *race*, because they are riveted to their roots by the

What (Who) Is Real in Existential Anthropology? 221

blood in their veins." This was the charged literary context into which Jean-Paul Sartre dropped his little book on Jews and antisemitism. On the one hand, he seems to side with those French writers like Barrès, who accuse the Jews of "universalism, abstraction, and rootlessness," except that for Sartre these were not marks of shame, but of honour. If Sartre seemed to "be the first French intellectual to valorize Jewish root-lessness," writes Hammerschlag (2010, 17), it was "because he calls into question the [existential] *value of [all] roots*."[4] For Sartre, that is to say, the Jewish predicament was "an intensification of the human situation [as such], and thus ... a window into the stakes of existentialism." This was not just another case to which existentialist principles might be applied, but a significant context for *thinking existentialism through,* just as African witchcraft would later become for Michael Jackson.

Jonathan Judaken (2006) has shown that Sartre returned to the Jewish question at important junctures throughout his intellectual career – it was, for example, a major part of his last published interview in 1980 (Sartre and Levy 1987). Judaken (2006, 42–3) notes that Roquentin, the protagonist of Sartre's 1938 novel, *Nausea,* already invokes the image of the Jew at the moment of his breakthrough to authentic existential consciousness. Roquentin has been writing in a café while his favourite song, "Some of These Days," plays in the background. He asks for the song to be replayed while he reflects upon the Black woman singer he imagines "suffering in rhythm," and the "clean-shaven Jew with black eyebrows" he imagines to have written the words. This is the reverie that finally brings home to Roquentin that like the Black singer and the Jewish songwriter he, too, must transcend the predicament into which he has been thrown. The singer "is an elegiac figure," writes Judaken, "who redeems because she responds to her suffering creatively" – this is a nice summary of Sartre's whole existentialist paradigm – while "'the Jew' is the figure that writes the song of salvation ... a mirror to the human condition, a martyr-witness to the human experience" (Judaken 2006, 43). Jews and Blacks frequently recur in Sartre as paired exemplars of suffering and the possibility of its creative existential reclamation.

The scene, however, is complicated. Aren't the Black woman whose "suffering in rhythm" becomes a source of aesthetic pleasure for Roquentin and the beardless (rootless? assimilated?) Jew who alone knows how to "pour her suffering into words" themselves stereotyp-ical representations? Perhaps, but it is also possible that Sartre knew full when he wrote *Nausea,* as Judaken (2006, 144) suggests, that "Some of These Days" was actually written by a Black man named Shelton Brooks and prominently sung by Sophie Tucker (Sofiya Kalish), a

222   Don Seeman

Russian-born Jewish immigrant to the United States. In her autobiographical prologue to a September 1927 recording, Tucker even calls attention to both her gender and Jewishness when she describes the "*Yiddische* hunch" (i.e., Jewish intuition) that helped her avoid being taken advantage of by male producers.[5] If Sartre did know the true identities of the writer and singer, wouldn't that make this scene into an ironic mockery of all such stereotyping and an example of Sartre's "extreme anti-foundationalism?" asks Judaken (144).

I like the term anti-foundationalism even better than anti-racism with respect to Sartre because it emphasizes his distrust of all foundational accounts of human life and institutions, including the very idea of a relatively stable "human nature" below the surface of our individual choices. This is a significant part of the existentialist ethos that Sartre fostered, in which nothing about our lives is fixed and everything stands, at any given moment, to be decided. One potential difficulty with this approach, which is meant to be existentially liberating, is its potential for systemic erasure of shared identities, mores, and ways of being-in-the-world that some communities or individuals might actually experience as sources of inherent or foundational value. Sartre did not deny the plausibility of Jewishness as a racial category, "though perhaps," he says wryly, with an eye towards Ashkenazim and Sefardim, "we had better say, Jewish *races*" (Sartre 1948, 60). But these dilations on biological race are peripheral to his larger, still unsettled (and for many readers unsettling) inquiry into the existential grounds of Jewishness and antisemitism. "Does the Jew exist?" Sartre asks. "And if he exists, what is he?" (1948, 58). In some ways Sartre was merely reformulating the old conundrum of European liberalism confronting the demand for Jewish citizenship and civil rights: "Is he first a Jew [a concrete embodiment of the particular] or first a man [an instantiation of the universal]?" (1948, 58). We will see that Sartre's answer remained equivocal, and that this equivocation is related to problems of representation that continue to perplex anthropologists who would like to think about the representation of different groups in existential terms.

2. Existentialism and Anthropological Anti-racism

Sartre's early existentialist response to racism and antisemitism may be better understood by contrast with that of formative figures in American cultural anthropology such as Franz Boas. Rather than call upon stigmatized groups to embrace or even double down on what the sociologist Erving Goffman (1963) later termed "spoiled identities," as Sartre seems to do, cultural anthropologists tended to argue that since racial inferiority was an illusion, the best antidote was to promote a colour-blind liberal individualism, in which all *significant* difference was put down to culture. Increasingly, this stance has been subject to critiques like that of Mark Anderson (2019), who argues in *From Boas to Black Power* that the political individualism and cultural relativism of Boasian anthropology worked to elide the unshakeable salience of race to the American context. "Their project *was* anti-racist," Anderson (2019, 21) admits. But by too heavily analogizing anti-Black racism with the debilitations of racial and religious discrimination suffered by many (non-Black) European immigrants, cultural anthropology also "deferred a full confrontation with white supremacy and the colour line, disavowed the possibility that racism was a constitutive feature of the US social order, and reproduced a foundational presupposition of the republic that equated 'America' with whiteness." Some writers (Appiah 2020; Glazier 2020; Lewis, forthcoming) have responded that Boasian anti-racism was both more effective politically and had more in common with positions adopted by contemporary African American thinkers than Anderson permits, but I won't attempt to adjudicate closely on that question here. Previous observers (Stocking 1986; Seeman 2005) have already called attention to some of the ways in which culture theory (and especially cultural determinism) unintentionally replicated certain effects of the racist worldview they were intended to repudiate.

There is however at least one alternative to thinking that Boas either underestimated the persistence of American racism or misconstrued it because of his focus on the problems of non-Black immigrants. A different but no less stunning conclusion might be that the reticence of Boas and some other anthropologists (including those of Jewish descent) to directly address antisemitism before, during, or after the Holocaust may be related to the very *same* liberal conditioning that defined their approach, for better and worse, to both antisemitism and anti-Black racism. This may, for instance, be the context in which to read Boas's 1921 essay, "The Problem of the American Negro," which Anderson critiques. Because he was "a devoted liberal," as Anderson (2019, 71) notes, "Boas held that only when people treat people as individuals – and not as members of a social category – could equality of condition and opportunity emerge." But that does not mean he was optimistic about achieving this outcome. On the contrary, his pessimism about white society's ability to overcome racial antagonism led him to remark gloomily that "man being what he is, the Negro problem will not disappear in America until the Negro blood has been so much diluted that it will no longer be recognized *just as anti-Semitism will not disappear until the last vestige of the Jew as a Jew has disappeared"* (Anderson 2019, 72). The "just as" in this last sentence can hardly be treated as incidental coming from a German Jewish immigrant like Boas, whose own reticence about Jewishness helped to inform the shape of early cultural anthropology (Seeman and Stern, forthcoming). The successes and inadequacies of Boas's approach to racism and antisemitism are harder to disentangle than some critics might allow.

It is worth noting that Sartre's critique of liberal European responses to antisemitism also foreshadows some of the current critique of early cultural anthropology's approach to anti-Black racism and of "colour-blind" approaches to discrimination more generally. Like Boas, Sartre flirted with the possibility that racial, ethnic, and religious distinctions would eventually vanish (probably through the revolution of the proletariat), but unlike Boas he was constitutionally opposed to the active *erasure* of such distinctions, even consensually, while persecution was ongoing. This had both a practical and an ideological or philosophical dimension. In practice, Sartre noted that the liberal democratic celebration of the universal at the expense of the particular did not put an end to the persecution of people identified with "the particular" (i.e., Jews), but only rendered it invisible to those not directly affected by it (this is close to contemporary critiques of colour-blind policies in the United States). On a philosophical level, however, Sartre also thought that an individual's attempt to accommodate the dominant society under these circumstances was tantamount to a bad faith or inauthentic refusal "to be what one already is." This is all the more remarkable given that Sartre was not willing to acknowledge that Jewishness really *is* anything.

In one of the most controversial passages in his whole essay on antisemitism, Sartre (1948, 91) opines that "the Jews have neither community of interests nor community of beliefs. They do not have the same fatherland; they have no history" – for revision of this latter claim one must look to his final interview with Benny Levy (Sartre and Levy 1987). *"The sole tie that binds them,"* he insists, *is the disdain and hostility of the societies which surround them."* Even so, he uses the apparently pejorative term "inauthentic Jew" to describe a person "whom other men *take* for Jews" but has "decided to run away from this insupportable situation." The result, he says, "is that they display various types of behaviour, not all of which are present at the same time in the same person but each of which may be characterized as *an* [inauthentic] *avenue of flight"* (Sartre and Levy, 93). Even those who may find his moralistic language off-putting may however acknowledge that Sartre's anti-foundationalism frees him to offer compelling vignettes of the sheer facticity – or predicament – of Western European Jewry, like a photographer who achieves clarity in the foreground of an image precisely by allowing its background to be made obscure.

To choose just one example from among many, Sartre praises those Jewish fighters in the Resistance who "formed the principal cadres [against German forces] before the Communists went into action (Sartre 1948, 96)." Yet he also suggests that many French Jews hesitated to join the Resistance because they feared that its aims might accord *too well* with the interests of their own specific group. "They wanted to be sure," Sartre says, "that they resisted *as Frenchmen and not as Jews*." Sartre does not provide any documentation for this claim, but I think it passes the test of verisimilitude – which is to say that it rings true – as a recurrent theme of the modern Jewish experience, for which one scans the impoverished anthropological literature on Jews and Judaism to this day almost in vain (see Dominguez 1993; Seeman and Stern, forthcoming). It is only his sensitivity to the *existential* (as opposed to cultural or theological) condition of Jews that allows Sartre to make these sorts of observations, but his existentialist and Marxist leanings also come with their own characteristic blind spots.

Sartre found it hard to believe, for example, that there was any antisemitism among the proletariat (Sartre 1948, 35–6), and his critique of liberalism falls more than a little flat given his own flirtations with "revolutionary" – and sometimes anti-Jewish – violence on the totalitarian left (see Sartre and Levy 1987). More significant to my own ethnographic project, he seems unable or unwilling to acknowledge that "communities of interest, belief or history" – to these I would add covenant, ritual, kinship, and more – certainly *do* bind many Jews, and they arguably stand somewhere in the near background for many others who do *not* feel themselves so bound, or even resist such binding (Seeman 2009, 2017; Seeman and Stern, forthcoming). This may be a function of the sorts of Jewish individuals Sartre encountered in Paris before and during the war (Misrahi and Marks 1999), but I am arguing that it also represents a form of *existentialist reductionism* pulling in the opposite direction to the racial and cultural reductions against which he rightly rebelled. Sartre's question "does the Jew exist?" to which I have already alluded needs to be understood against this frame. It seems to have been only his later engagement with individuals who became invested in distinctive forms of Jewishness – like his Egyptian-born, Maoist-turned-Talmudist disciple Benny Levy, his adopted Algerian-Jewish daughter Arlette **Elkaïm**-Sartre, and the Lithuanian Jewish phenomenologist Emmanuel Levinas – that helped him to understand the significance of this aporia (see Sartre and Levy 1987; Friedlander

226   Don Seeman

1990). Given Sartre's example, existential anthropologists and scholars of religion ought to be mindful of the potential for unwarranted reduction, whether they are navigating "the Jewish question," the question of anti-Black racism and other drivers of social suffering, or even, like Michael Jackson, the problem of why some Kuranko women seem so willing to confess that they are witches.

3. On the Authenticity of Witches

In his 1989 monograph, *Paths toward a Clearing*: *Radical Empiricism and Ethnographic Inquiry*, Michael Jackson recounts thirteen different cases of witchcraft confession by Kuranko women in Sierra Leone. "When a small boy died suddenly," he recounts (1989, 91) with almost brutal concision, "a diviner was consulted; witchcraft was diagnosed as the cause of death. The witch [in this case, the sister of the boy's father] was cursed. Ten days later [the "witch"] fell ill and confessed to having killed the child because her brother refused to give her rice." And then, with chilling matter-of-factness: "the woman was buried alive" (Jackson 1989, 91). In another case (1989, 95), a woman grows ill after she too has been accused of bewitching her brother's child (for the sake of concision I am omitting Jackson's extended analysis). She admits not only to taking the child's life in payment of a debt to her "witches' coven," but also of having once transformed herself into an elephant in an attempt to murder her husband in the bush. The husband survived but the confessed witch "was taken out into the backyard," notes Jackson laconically, "and left to die" (1989, 95).

This was neither the first nor the last time Jackson would work through these episodes, which appear repeatedly and at crucial junctures in his voluminous published corpus (Jackson 1975; 1998, 89–91; 2004, 38–9; 2005, 167–75; 2011, 138–40; 2015a, 168–9), almost always returning to the deadly opposition between persons and categories ("witch," "refugee," "outsider") to which persons or groups of persons may be subjected. The categories themselves are falsely ontologized and cruelly misapplied, almost exactly as Sartre had described the racist or antisemitic fixation on a form of hyper-particularity ("racial characteristics") that elides the fundamental indeterminacy of human being. Jackson likens witchcraft accusation to the taxonomic power of the state bureaucratic apparatus over refugees and migrants, who are themselves likened to accused witches for their vulnerability to organized and capricious violence. Occasionally, he also makes other comparisons. "If the paradigmatic scapegoats of Europe have been the gypsy and the jew," Jackson (2005, 45) writes in *Existential Anthropology* –

What (Who) Is Real in Existential Anthropology? 227

I assume the lower case nominal is a nod to Derrida (cf. Gaon 2014) – then "the scapegoat in West Africa has been the witch. As a neighbor, wife or mother, she is one of us. But in other ways she has never ceased to be a stranger." Then, in terms entirely reminiscent of Sartre: "Scapegoating does *not ... assume an a priori ontological difference between self and other*; rather it is a strategy in which some distinctive trait in the other's appearance, situation or behaviour is foregrounded and stigmatized – as bestial, antisocial or inhuman – while everything that makes the other resemble us is backgrounded, eclipsed and denied." Like Sartre's antisemitism, witchcraft according to Jackson is an assertion of absolute, exaggerated particularity that occludes the shared contingency of human conditions.

Many of the witchcraft accusations Jackson describes are based on old reports or oral histories (some going back to 1944, the same year Sartre wrote his *Réflexions*), but one more recent episode seems to have been most formative. In February 1970, Jackson and his research assistant Noah were conducting fieldwork in the Sierra Leonean village of Kamadugu Sukurela. They left for a few weeks during an outbreak of deadly insect-born encephalitis. Upon their return they were told by Morowa, a friend of Noah's, about a man from the village who had died during their absence. During his illness a *Gbangbane* or "witchhunter" had been summoned. The Gbangbane discerned that the man had been attacked by witchcraft and explained to village elders that if he died, the killer would also grow ill. Sure enough, he did die, and eight days later his sister became sick. The Gbangbane was recalled to the village, where the now gravely ill woman confessed not only to killing her brother but to "hunting him for a year" and trying to kill him on several occasions because he had once denied her some rice.

Jackson does not dwell too much on the grisly details of what happened next. The Gbangane ordered that the witch be buried immediately. "Men bound her by her hands and feet and dragged her to the outskirts of the village. There they dug a shallow grave and buried her alive. Banana leaves and stones were thrown in on top of her. During the entire episode, all the women of the village remained indoors." Morowa is astonished by Jackson's outrage and by his accusation that Morowa himself was now an accessory to murder. Didn't the anthropologist understand what was at stake? Morowa and his wife had previously lost children to witchcraft. "If it had been my choice," Morowa fumes indignantly, "*I* would have had her thrown her into the bush *without* burial ... A witch deserves no respect. *A witch is not a person.*" Many other anthropologists had written about African witchcraft accusations and their violent consequences, but Jackson's account stands out because he claims that while *accusations* were relatively rare among the Kuranko, *confessions* by accused witches were much more common than elsewhere. This is the aspect of Kuranko life that both troubled and fascinated him. Why would a woman confess to a crime she could not possibly have committed?

In his early essay, "Structure and Event: Witchcraft Confession among the Kuranko," Jackson (1975) was still writing in a conventional anthropological mode about "patterns of beliefs," even though his existential concerns had already started coming to the fore. He entertains the possibility that women who confess to witchcraft might be suffering some kind of psychopathology – otherwise, why put themselves so needlessly in harm's way? – but quickly pivots to themes that would increasingly come to define a unique ethnographic perspective. "[T]he alleged disorder or abnormal state [i.e., witchcraft confession]" he writes, "is *both* an existential reality for the individual concerned [i.e., the accused witch] *and* an objective, collectively defined symbol for others [such as bystanders and accusers]" (Jackson 1975, 388). Implicit here is the observation I have made elsewhere (Seeman 2004, 2008) in a critique of Geertz's famous "Religion as Culture System" (1973), that too myopic a focus on culture tends to put anthropologists in the position of seeing the world from the vantage point of the accuser rather than the accused. Remember that for Geertz, religion is defined as a kind of social theodicy that defends cultural meaning from collapse in confrontation with suffering (Seeman 2004, 2008). "The problem of suffering from a religious point of view," Geertz (1973, 104) declares, "is not how to end suffering but … how to make suffering *sufferable*." The anthropologist as an interpreter of culture inevitably spends her time focused on order rather than disorder, stability rather than change, and semiotic "webs" rather than the people who might be caught struggling in their sticky strands (Seeman 2015).

By the time Jackson (1989) returned to these witchcraft accounts in *Paths Toward a Clearing*, he had decisively rejected the idea that witchcraft confession could be analysed through the lens of psychopathology and was instead contemplating "the *pathology of conventional Kuranko thought* [i.e., culture], which denies personhood to a woman who, in extreme distress, confesses herself a 'witch,' [and] *buries* the experience of the individual subject in the categories of totalizing explanation" (Jackson 1989, 89). In this rhetorical elaboration, Jackson insists that lived experience is being "buried" by certain kinds of social scientific theorizing just as surely as women who are accused of witchcraft are being buried alive by Kuranko men, and this recognition brings to a head something of philosophical import that had been building in Jackson ever since his earliest ethnography. "[B]y relegating the subjective view of the patient to the category of *delusion* and defining the objectively defined (i.e., the collective) category the status of *real*," Jackson insisted already back in 1975, "we [anthropologists] often tend to forget that *all definitions of order and disorder* are relative and arbitrary" (Jackson 1975, 388). Jackson's impatience with all kinds of cultural metaphysics, religious languages, and "totalizing" social theory that he has continued to articulate until today is already apparent in this early formulation. Indeed, I would argue that there is a direct line between Jackson's response to witchcraft confession and his later fateful statement (at least for religious studies) in *Palm at the Edge of the Mind* (2009, 99–100) that "we need to approach religiosity without a theological vocabulary, repudiate the notion of religion as a sui generis phenomenon, and distance ourselves from the assumption of a necessary relationship between espoused belief and subjective experience."

Jackson (1989, 101) purports to have "no sympathy with those anthropologists and philosophers who debate endlessly over the rationality or irrationality of witchcraft beliefs." Investigating "how beliefs *correspond* to some allegedly 'objective' reality or how they *cohere* as a so-called 'system' seems to me far less edifying," he writes, "than trying to see what people do with beliefs in *coping* with the exigencies of life."[6] This appeal to exigency (see Silva, this volume) at the expense of relatively fixed cultures and beliefs is at the heart of Jackson's existential anthropology (Jackson 2005, 2012a) and may be its most important potential contribution to the academic study of religion (Seeman 2015; Nabhan-Warren 2011). It is also nevertheless a site for potential confusion, because despite Jackson's claim to be unconcerned with the empirical reality of Kuranko witchcraft, he is also too honest an ethnographer to retreat into the familiar anthropological conceit that the "suspension of disbelief" is sufficient to free anthropologists from the need to grapple with what is really real in the settings they study. "What existentialism and realism share," notes sociologist Margaret Archer (2000, 185), "is the understanding of life as a *predicament*," and this forces some hard descriptive choices. Underlying all of Jackson's analytic turmoil around witchcraft confession, for example, is his search for a way to simultaneously avoid both the solipsism of cultural relativism and the epistemological hubris of positivism. It seems improper to describe women who confess to witchcraft as mere dupes of culture, Jackson seems to say, yet this *cannot mean that witches and witchcraft are real.*

This is where Sartre's "other solution" to racism and antisemitism, which I described above, comes to seem so appealing. Jackson (1989, 101) cites Sartre's (1963) biography of Jean Genet, an orphan who was

230   Don Seeman

falsely accused of theft and later chose "to become what crime had made of me," (which is to say, an actual thief). "Since he cannot escape fatality," Sartre glosses, "he will *be* his own fatality; since they have made life unliveable for him, he will live this impossibility ... He decided to be what he was ... *It was a constraint; he makes of it his mission.*" And so it is, Jackson, suggests, with witchcraft. "Certainly, the advice of a diviner, the carping of a husband or senior co-wife ... and the terrifying sound of *Gbangbane* moving about in the night all work to erode a woman's confidence." But confession, precipitated in more than half the cases he describes by serious illness, "is also a desperate stratagem for reclaiming autonomy in a hopeless situation ... Confession to witchcraft exemplifies what [Holocaust survivor and psychotherapist] Victor Frankl ([1946] 2006) calls 'the last freedom' – that which remains to us when external circumstances rob us of the power to act: *the choice of determining how we will construe our plight, the freedom to live it as if it were our will.*"

This is a compelling interpretation of witchcraft confession. What I have always found troubling ever since I read this passage as a graduate student, however, is that none of the accused witches could or did represent *themselves* in this way to the anthropologist at all. Determining "how she will play out the role which circumstance has thrust upon her," Jackson asserts, "she dies deciding her own identity, sealing her own fate." This may well constitute the kind of startling intuitive insight I have already ascribed to both Jackson and Sartre at their best, but should an ethnographer really take the same interpretive liberties with their materials as a philosopher or a writer of fiction might be justified in doing? I perceive a basic decency in Jackson's impulse to grant executed women the dignity of agency and of voice within his ethnography. Yet there is also a trap here, for it seems that voice can only be heard in the concepts and language of a few existentialist philosophers, particularly Sartre. On some level, I wonder whether silence and acknowledgment of what is opaque to our understanding of these women's horrifying deaths (Willen and Seeman 2012) might have spoken louder.

Jackson is an evocative and accomplished writer who has returned again and again over the course of a long career to certain key themes or insights, almost like the composer of a musical score whose refrain grows in emphasis and sophistication at each repetition. I smiled when I came across a more subtle and, to my mind, more compelling account of Sartre's significance for ethnography in Jackson's (2014) essay, "Ajala's Head: Reflections on Anthropology and Philosophy in a West African Setting":

It was Sartre's *Search for a Method* that helped me articulate the inchoate understandings I reached in the course of my first fieldwork among the Kuranko. While Sartre's observations resonated with the West African views I have described, it was ironically his remoteness from the subject of my ethnographic work that helped me write about it. It wasn't that Sartre's existentialism "explained" Kuranko social processes and lived experiences. Rather in *juxtaposing* his concepts with my Kuranko materials I began to find a way of writing about those materials.

We do not need to portray Kuranko women as channelling Sartrean existentialism in order to believe that reading Sartre in this *juxtapositional* way might make us more reflective interpreters of the human conditions we witness and participate in as ethnographers. Juxtaposition comes at the beginning of a project of thinking things through, not the end of it.

Perhaps this is also one reason that Jackson indeed moves away from conventional strategies in ethnographic writing over time to embrace the relative freedom offered by fiction (Jackson 2013b, 2015b; see Stoller this volume), literary memoir (Jackson 2012c, 2013b, 2019), and the use of ethnography as a platform for reflection on broad existential themes like want (2011), the relationship between self and other (2012b), mobility (2013c), storytelling (2013a), temporal experience (2018), and, with some initial ambivalence, religiosity and art (2009, 2016b). It may be ironic, given his allergy to theological language, that Jackson's professional career took him to Harvard Divinity School and to the training of many students whose initial orientation was to the academic study of religion or even theology. Could this be part of the reason that Jackson's more recent work, including *As Wide as the World is Wise* (Jackson 2016a), takes the more modest but also more defensible position that awareness of order and disorder are *both* deeply imbricated into the human perceptual apparatus, so that both forms of attention should be given their due as endemic to human experience? Without abandoning the crucial scepticism it provides – for we *are* more than we can ever say or think – might this reformulation of Jackson's earlier position provide an opening for existential anthropology to reengage with conceptual orders (Brandel and Motta 2021; Jackson 2021), everyday language (Roberts, this volume), and possibly even the more specialized languages of religion and theology (Seeman 2018) that some existential writers seem to eschew? This is a question with significant repercussions (Premawardhana, this volume) for the ultimate reception of existential anthropology within religious studies.

4. Existential Anthropology and Religious Studies

"Painting runs in my family," Michael Jackson (2016b, xiii) writes in the introduction to his *The Work of Art*, "but not religion." It is interesting therefore that most of the book that follows, subtitled *Rethinking the Elementary Forms of Religious Life*, is devoted to breaking down the apparent dichotomy with which it began. "Art and religion [both] provide conduits between our individual lives and the life of the world," Jackson writes, "enabling us to be reborn into an artificial realm that precedes and outlasts us – ultimate reality, the brotherhood of man, the kingdom of God, the Dreaming, tradition, or nature" (Jackson 2016b, 54). This is the kind of startling juxtaposition of concepts that Jackson is famous for. "[T]here is a family resemblance," he continues, "between Christian notions of being-reborn-in Christ (John 3:7) and Walpiri notions of regeneration through ritual. On both worldviews, initiation is a kind of death – the painful price one must pay for exchanging one form of life for another that is potentially more bountiful and fulfilling" (Jackson 2016b, 54).

The idea of family resemblance is by design somewhat vague. Yet note how seamlessly and almost breathlessly Jackson has argued that a list of seemingly incommensurate beliefs, cultures, and practices from around the globe are all rooted in an avowedly more fundamental set of universal human concerns. For the reader who is used to narrow accounts of cultural and religious particularity the effect is breathtaking. *Art is religion is the Dreaming is the brotherhood of man is regeneration through ritual is being reborn in Christ is ... initiation into a more bountiful and fulfilling form of life.* Anthropologists have been slow to acknowledge the significance of what George Pattison and Kate Kirkpatrick (2018) call "the mystical sources of existentialist thought," but I suspect that for many religion scholars these mystical genealogies lie somewhat closer to the surface. For religion scholars, the commitment to an idea of underlying unity within difference may also recall the perennialism-constructivism debates that have roiled their discipline for at least half a century. Anthropologists who wish to write persuasively for religious studies audiences need to understand what this implies.

Both anthropology and the academic study of religion have been shaped and consumed by tensions between particularism and universalism that mirror those I have described in the crisis of modernity, race, and antisemitism. But they have not done so on the same schedule, and here disciplinary trajectories matter. It is striking, for example, that precisely when Boas and other early cultural anthropologists were levying their vision of human plasticity and malleable "cultures" against a vicious politics of racial determinism, some scholars in religious studies were also struggling against racial determinism in a very different way, by emphasizing what they considered to be universal qualities of religion, and especially mystical experience. Consider for example the groundbreaking scholar of Islam Louis Massignon, a French convert to Catholicism who published *Essay on the Origins of the Technical Language of Islamic Mysticism* in 1922. Although his topic required great expertise in philology and the history of ideas, Massignon insisted that underlying all this seeming particularity was "a human phenomenon on the level of the spirit," which is to say mystical experience, that no "boundaries could contain" (Massignon [1922] 1977, 46). He was refuting what he called "the overly popular theory of pro-Aryans like Gobineau and anti-Semites like Friedrich Delitszch," who held that "the Semitic peoples [i.e., Jews and Arabs] are unfit for the arts and sciences in general," and incapable of mysticism in particular. On the racialized view, Sufi Islamic mysticism must have derived almost entirely from Persian (i.e., "Aryan") rather than Arab sources. It is against *this* view that Massignon ([1922] 1977, 46) rails: "it is impossible for mysticism to be the exclusive privilege of one language, race, or religion." It is hard to imagine a scholar more different in temperament to the radical French atheist Jean-Paul Sartre, yet both men identified undue *particularism* – on both moral and analytic grounds – with the politics of racial and antisemitic exclusion.

To set the stage in religious studies very briefly, *Philosophia perennis et universalis* or "perennial wisdom" was originally a Renaissance term associated with the Platonic idea of an underlying unity and origin of all things (Schmidt-Biggeman 2004). It was applied approvingly by Aldous Huxley in 1945 to the search for "highest common factor" in all religions, both "primitive" and "modern" – focused on finding "man's final end in ... knowledge of the immanent and transcendent Ground of all being." Such universalizing claims – locating a certain kind of mystical experience at the ostensible heart of universal religion – were popular among comparative scholars of mysticism (James [1902] 1982; Otto 1917; Paper 2004; Smith 1967, 1979; Stace 1960; Underhill [1911] 1990), as well as some public figures like Mahatma Gandhi, who believed that all religions should be viewed as varied paths to the same unwavering spiritual goals (Smith 1967, 1979). William James's membership in this list is not entirely uncontested (see Bruner 2004; Proudfoot 2004; Rorty 2004), but he is often included among the perennialists for some of the same reasons that his work was so heavily invoked by Michael Jackson: his refusal to delimit religious life by institutions or theologies, his appeal to an underlying stream of human experience,

234   Don Seeman

and his assertion of a penumbral dimension he sometimes refers to as "the more" all found their place in Jackson's existential anthropology. Some perennialists sought to demonstrate the universalism of specifically Christian truths but others took more ecumenical positions (Eliade 1971; Neumann [1948] 1968; van der Leeuw 1938). The academic "comparative religion" paradigm tended to skew perennialist as well, inasmuch as different religious traditions were said to have roughly analogous features (like "mysticism" or the "myth of eternal return") that could be compared without too much concern for the historical genealogies and stability of these categories. Crucially, perennial features of religion were sometimes treated not just as reflections of the shared religion-making habits of human societies but of transcendent realities irreducible to any human language or culture.

It was not until the 1970s and 1980s that this paradigm came increasingly under attack by scholars who emphasized the historically contingent "social construction" of religious discourse, practice, and ideas. Not surprisingly, mysticism was again central to this rethinking. "Mystical reports do not merely indicate the *postexperiential description of an unreportable experience*," writes Steven T. Katz (1992, 5; also see Katz 1978, 1983) in an influential constructivist essay. "Rather, the experiences themselves are inescapably shaped by prior linguistic influences such that the *lived experience conforms to a preexistent pattern that has been learned, then intended, and then actualized* in the experiential reality of the mystic." To the same degree that perennialism was characterized by a persistent language-scepticism, and informed by the idea of *ineffable* religious experience, constructivism sometimes implied that historically determinate traditions of language and practice are *all that really exist* (or at least all that researchers can study), and sometimes even claimed that whole categories like "mysticism," "religion," or "religious experience" were incoherent because they were applied to such widely differing local phenomena. Though it has proven difficult to do without catchall terms like "religion," constructivist accounts have generally come to dominate many religious studies departments and major fields like the history of religion, while perennialist arguments have been shunted aside to subfields like contemplative or mindfulness studies (Forman 1990; Miller 2005; Paper 2004), the burgeoning cross-disciplinary literature on "spirituality" (see Bender 2010; Herman 2014; Seeman et. al. 2016), or certain corners of neuroscience and philosophy (Steinbock 2009). The debate has not really been settled (how could it be?) so much as it has sputtered into an increasingly sterile stalemate in which few scholars on either side feel the need to engage with or debate one another.

An exception that may prove the rule is contemporary Buddhist studies, where a variety of historians, anthropologists, and textual scholars (Dunne 2011; Dunne and Harrington 2011; Kirmayer 2015; McMahan 2008; Seeman and Karlin 2019; Sharf 1995, 2015) have been actively working to problematize what they see as the perennialist tendency of "mindfulness" literature to unmoor certain kinds of contemplative practice from their native ritual and cosmological contexts or to universalize the ontological claims of particular Buddhist schools. Some of the strongest critiques of "experience" as an analytic category in religious studies (Sharf 1998, 2000, 2012) have emerged from historians of Buddhism opposed to perennializing trends in their own field. There is a danger that unless it learns better to engage with specific, historically, and culturally situated dimensions of religious life, including their particularistic theological languages and textual traditions, existential anthropology will find itself marginalized as a new form of perennialism. This would be unfortunate.

Existential anthropology emerged in the last decades of the twentieth century as part of a broader revolt against cultural determinism among a small but influential group of scholars, all of whom sought an "other solution" to the dichotomy between theories of "human nature" (such as sociobiology or evolutionary psychology) on the one hand, and the arbitrary relativism of "cultures" on the other (see Desjarlais and Throop 2011; Willen and Seeman 2012). Though eager to explain the significance of economic and social forces on local settings, they have also tended to avoid strictly materialist approaches to the analysis of human affairs, preferring to leave room for subjectivity, the unfinished struggle for meaning, and the strategies that people employ to make the best of things. Around the same time that Michael Jackson published *Paths Toward a Clearing* (1989), Arthur Kleinman (1988; Kleinman and Kleinman 1991) was publishing his early, groundbreaking studies on the relationship between suffering, illness, and moral experience; Uni Wikan (1990) was showing how ethnographic focus on the grief and loss of an individual Balinese girl could upend anthropological assumptions about the cultural determination of emotional life; and Byron Good (1994) delivered the Lewis Henry Morgan lectures on "Medicine, Rationality and Experience." These new "experience-near" ethnographies and others like them drew on varied philosophical roots going back to William James's "radical empiricism," the "life-world" of continental phenomenology, the "predicament" of existentialist thought or – in Michael Jackson's extraordinary case – all three simultaneously (see Jackson 1989, 1996, 2005).

Religion scholars and anthropologists who would like to speak effectively across disciplinary lines may need to show more awareness of how these divergent histories have shaped their fields. Experience-oriented anthropologist Arthur Kleinman (2014, 130) tellingly describes what it was like to teach William James's *Varieties of Religious Experience* to a mixed audience of medical and theology students at Harvard. For the medical students in the class," he writes, "James's understanding of religion as based in [universal] psychological processes was convincing." For the Divinity School students, by contrast, James's approach was deemed entirely inadequate. For them, James's "smooth dismissal of theology, religious institutions, and the work of religionists rendered the Jamesian perspective deeply suspect." In terms that should already be somewhat familiar to readers of this chapter, furthermore, "James's universalist orientation also came in for their criticism, because, as Talal Asad (1993) argues, these students recognized partisan commitments as central to what makes most religions *religious*."

Kleinman's account is well taken, but it says more about the current intellectual climate in different academic fields than it says about the intrinsic particularism of theology or religious studies. As we have seen, academic religious studies were once deeply committed to perennialism, which was after all the climate in which James was writing. Those same views today run afoul not just of social constructivism but are sometimes represented as moral or political failures to recognize alterity and celebrate difference (at least certain *kinds* of difference) for its own sake. James might have gotten off easier on both counts if he had simply titled his book *The Varieties of Christian Experience* instead of *The Varieties of Religious Experience*. Personally, I remain sympathetic to both James *and* his critics, because I think both universalizing and particularizing tendencies capture something important about the phenomena they are describing, just as both have been invoked in different contexts to oppose bigotry or racism in scholarship. One thing it might be wise to learn from existential anthropology is the recognition that since life does indeed exceed our ability to *think about life*, it may be more important to avoid entrapment by any singular theoretical construct than it is to consistently choose whatever theoretical approach is currently touted as morally correct.

While existential anthropology may sometimes seem to slip into perennialist modes, it seems to me that its commitment to focusing on concrete human predicaments will ultimately frustrate universalist theoretical models as much as culturally deterministic ones. "Rather than identify religion with belief and liturgy," writes Jackson (2016b, xv), "I prefer to focus on the existential situations in which divinities and spiritual entities as well as ideas about ultimate reality, fate, and natural justice come into play as *potential* means whereby human beings gain some purchase on shattering experiences and regain some measure of comprehension and control over their lives." I agree with this assessment (Seeman 2015, 2018), except that I think "belief and liturgy" are frequently more important to the everyday worlds we are trying to describe than Jackson admits.

Here, indeed, is the rub. Part of the gambit of good existentialist writing (in both its philosophical and anthropological varieties) is that it tends to provoke a kind of shocking inner recognition of some fundamental *stance* defining our way of inhabiting the world, whether that be "nausea" or "freedom" (Sartre), or "fear and trembling" (Kierkegaard). The contributors to this volume have all pushed back with great energy against cultural reductionism by calling attention to the imponderables of everyday life and the human conditions within which they unfold. My contrapuntal intervention here at the close is to warn of the *existentialist reduction* that can result from translating witchcraft confessions or religious confessions into Sartrean or Heideggerian manifestos. Is there not a way of breaking through the stifling particularities of culture without falling prey to an existentialist mono-linguicism? Perhaps this is where the academic study of religion might also contribute something to existential anthropology. It isn't that we need to avoid reading ethnographic materials in light of great existentialist thinkers (though the more we learn about some, like Heidegger, the less there is to like), but rather that we need to be more open about inhabiting the aporias that emerge when juxtaposing the insights of philosophers with those of professed witches, religious believers, or survivors of racism and genocide. Rather than approaching religiosity "without a theological vocabulary," as Jackson (2009, 99–100) suggests, we ought to expand our own vocabularies to include "vernacular theologies" (Seeman 2018) that may contribute to better conceptual vocabularies for describing the things that have existential import to the people who populate our ethnographies.

5. Coda

I wrote to Michael Jackson during the pandemic lockdowns of 2020 to discuss our plans for this volume and to ask whether he thought there was any merit to the comparison I had been trying to draw between his account of Kuranko witchcraft and Sartre's essay on antisemitism. Certainly, Sartre had been important to his thinking, he wrote in response, with specific reference to *The Family Idiot* (Sartre 1987), *Search for a Method* (Sartre 1968), and in a general way to Sartre's essays on Negritude. "Rightly or wrongly," Michael told me, "I regarded the act of confessing to a crime one had not committed and *could not possibly have committed* [killing through witchcraft], as a way of magically escaping a persecutor's power to decide one's identity and determine one's fate." With characteristic candour, he also told me that he did not remember ever having read Sartre's *Réflexions sur la question juive*, but suggested reasonably enough that it would make sense to read that essay alongside Arendt's contemporary work,"The Jew as Pariah" (Arendt 1944), which Jackson (2013a) had already invoked to such good effect in his *Politics of Storytelling*.

Then Michael said something that stopped me in my tracks – and still does. "I shudder to think," he wrote, "that this argument [his own argument about the unreality of witches] might apply to the victims of the Shoah [the Holocaust], which makes me question the use I made of it in understanding witchcraft confession among the Kuranko. Was this the unconscious reason I avoided Sartre's essay on the Jew?" Having always admired his intellectual generosity, I admit that I was still unprepared for that stark, unapologetic willingness to reconsider, to reflect on consequences, and when necessary to seek another path towards a different clearing. Is it possible that the intuitive juxtaposition Jackson has modelled for us so frequently *always* has this potential to cut both ways? An argument that feels like a defence of the humanity of women accused of witchcraft in one setting may turn out to feel like an erasure of people subject to genocide in another, and I am willing to concede that *both* feelings might be justified. These waters remain roiled, and I remain uneasy, uncertain how to proceed. Perhaps there really is no safe haven in anthropological representation, no final resting place; just a need to constantly reassess the effects of life on thought, and of thought on life.

NOTES

1 I have adopted the current spelling "antisemitism," rather than the older "anti-Semitism" which appears in some of the sources cited. Despite the potential confusion of having a word spelled more than one way in the same chapter, the newer non-hyphenated spelling is supported by scholars in the field (Lipstadt 2019) and by a growing consensus among groups such as the Anti-Defamation League, the New York Times, the Associated Press, and others. The hyphenated spelling was based on the debunked notion of a distinctive semitic race which one could "be anti." This in turn was

What (Who) Is Real in Existential Anthropology? 239

sometimes used to render specific forms of bias against Jews effectively invisible, so long as all "Semites" were not equally targeted.

2 Emphasis added. Unless otherwise noted, all italics for emphasis in this chapter are my own addition.

3 Jonathan Boyarin (1992, 9–31; 2009) has offered a more sustained argument for this analogy, "The Jew as Europe's Indian."

4 Devaka Premawardhana's (2018) probing ethnography of religious mobility in contemporary Mozambique draws implicitly on this same Sartrean theme.

5 https://www.youtube.com/watch?v=3heCSPJrO70. Accessed 18 July 2021.

6 Emphases in the original.

WORKS CITED

Anderson, Mark. 2019. *From Boas to Black Power: Racism, Liberalism and American Anthropology*. Stanford: Stanford University Press.

Appiah, Kwame Anthony. 2020. "The Defender of Differences: On Franz Boas and His Critics." *New York Review* 28 May 2020. https://www.nybooks.com/articles/2020/05/28/franz-boas-anthropologist-defender-differences/.

Archer, Margaret. 2000. *Being Human: The Problem of Agency*. Cambridge: Cambridge University Press.

Arendt, Hannah. 1944. "The Jew as Pariah: A Hidden Tradition." *Jewish Social Studies* 6, no. 2: 99–122.

–. 2018. *The Human Condition*. 2nd ed. Chicago: University of Chicago Press.

Asad, Talal 1993. *Genealogies of Religion: Discipline and Reasons of Power in Islam and Christianity*. Baltimore: Johns Hopkins University Press.

Bender, Courtney. 2010. *The New Metaphysicals: Spirituality and the American Religious Imagination*. Chicago: University of Chicago Press.

Boyarin, Jonathan. 1992. *Storm from Paradise*. Minneapolis: University of Minnesota Press.

–. 2009. *The Unconverted Self: Jews, Indians and the Identity of Christian Europe*. Chicago: University of Chicago Press.

Brandel, Andrew, and Marco Motta. 2021. *Living with Concepts: Anthropology in the Grip of Reality*. New York: Fordham University Press.

Bruner, Jerome. 2004. "James's *Varieties* and the New Constructivism." In *William James and a Science of Religions,* edited by Wayne Proudfoot, 73–85. New York: Columbia University Press.

Denizeau, Laurent. 2015. "Considering Human Existence: An Existential Reading of Michael Jackson and Albert Piette." In *What is Existential Anthropology?*, edited by Michael Jackson and Albert Piette, 214–36. New York: Berghahn Books.

Desjarlais, Robert, and Jason C. Throop. 2011. "Phenomenological Approaches in Anthropology." *Annual Reviews in Anthropology* 40 (October): 87–112. https://doi.org/10.1146/annurev-anthro-092010-153345.

Dominguez, Virginia R. 1993. "Questioning Jews." *American Ethnologist* 20, no. 3 (August): 618–24. https://doi.org/10.1525/ae.1993.20.3.02a00090.

Dunne, John. 2011. "Toward an Understanding of Non-dual Mindfulness." *Contemporary Buddhism* 12, no. 1: 71–88. https://doi.org/10.1080/14639947 .2011.564820.

Dunne, John, and Anne Harrington. 2015. "When Mindfulness Is Therapy: Ethical Qualms, Historical Perspectives." *American Psychologist* 70, no. 7: 621–31. https://doi.org/10.1037/a0039460.

Eliade, Mircea. 1971. *The Myth of Eternal Return: Cosmos and History*. Princeton: Princeton University Press.

Flynn, Thomas R. 2018. "The Later Sartre: From Phenomenology to Hermeneutics to Dialectic and Back." In *The Oxford Handbook of the History of Phenomenology*, edited by Dan Zahavi, 302–19. Oxford: Oxford University Press.

Forman, Robert K.C. 1990. *The Problem of Pure Consciousness: Mysticism and Philosophy*. Oxford: Oxford University Press.

Frankl, Victor E. (1946) 2006. *Man's Search for Meaning*. Boston: Beacon.

Friedlander, Judith. 1990. *Vilna on the Seine: Jewish Intellectuals in France*. New Haven: Yale University Press.

Gaon, Stella. 2014. "'As if' There Were a 'Jew': The (Non)Existence of Deconstructive Responsibility." *Derrida Today* 7, no. 1: 44–58. https://doi .org/10.3366/drt.2014.0076.

Geertz, Clifford. 1973. *The Interpretation of Cultures*. New York: Basic Books.

Glazier, Jack. 2020. "Review of *From Boas to Black Power* by Mark Anderson." *American Ethnologist* 47, no. 1: 90–1. https://doi.org/10.1111/amet.12871.

Glendinning, Simon. 2007. *In the Name of Phenomenology*. London: Routledge.

Good, Byron. 1994. *Medicine, Rationality and Experience*. Cambridge: Cambridge University Press.

Hammerschlag, Sarah. 2010. *The Figural Jew: Politics and Identity in Postwar French Thought*. Chicago: University of Chicago Press.

Herman, Jonathan R. 2014. "The Spiritual Illusion: Constructive Steps toward Rectification and Redescription." *Method and Theory in the Study of Religion* 26, no. 2: 159–82. https://doi.org/10.1163/15700682-12341264.

Huxley, Aldous. 1945. *The Perennial Philosophy*. New York: Harper.

Irele, Abiola. 1964. "A Defense of Negritude," *Transition*, no. 13 (March–April): 9–11. https://doi.org/10.2307/2934416.

Jackson, Michael. 1975. "Structure and Event: Witchcraft Confession among the Kuranko." *Man* 10, no. 3 (September): 387–403. https://doi.org /10.2307/2799809.

What (Who) Is Real in Existential Anthropology?　241

–. 1982. *Allegories of the Wilderness: Ethics and Ambiguity in Kuranko Narratives*. Bloomington: Indiana University Press.

–. 1989. *Paths toward a Clearing: Radical Empiricism and Ethnographic Inquiry*. Bloomington: Indiana University Press.

–. 1996. *Things as They Are: New Directions in Phenomenological Anthropology*. Bloomington: Indiana University Press.

–. 1998. *Minima Ethnographica: Intersubjectivity and the Anthropological Project*. Chicago: University of Chicago Press.

–. 2004. *In Sierra Leone*. Durham: Duke University Press.

–. 2005. *Existential Anthropology: Events, Exigencies and Effects*. New York: Berghahn Books.

–. 2009. *The Palm at the Edge of the Mind: Relatedness, Religiosity and the Real*. Durham: Duke University Press.

–. 2011. *Life within Limits: Well-Being in a World of Want*. Durham: Duke University Press.

–. 2012a. *Lifeworlds: Essays in Existential Anthropology*. Chicago: University of Chicago Press.

–. 2012b. *Between One and Another*. Berkeley: University of California Press.

–. 2012c. *Road Markings: An Anthropologist in the Antipodes*. New Zealand: Rosa Mira Books.

–. 2013a. *The Politics of Storytelling: Variations on a Theme by Hannah Arendt*. Copenhagen: Museum Tusculanum Press.

–. 2013b. *The Other Shore: Essays on Writers and Writing*. Berkeley: University of California Press.

–. 2013c. *The Wherewithal of Life: Ethics, Migration and the Question of Well-Being*. Berkeley: University of California Press.

–. 2014. "Ajàlá's Heads: Reflections on Anthropology and Philosophy in a West African Setting." In *The Ground Between: Anthropologists Engage Philosophy*, edited by Veena Das, Michael Jackson, Arthur Kleinman and Bhirubati Singh, 27–49. Durham: Duke University Press.

–. 2015a. "Existential Aporias and the Precariousness of Being." In *What Is Existential Anthropology?*, edited by Michael Jackson and Albert Piette, 155–77. New York: Berghahn Books.

–. 2015b. *Harmattan: A Philosophical Fiction*. New York: Columbia University Press.

–. 2016a. *As Wide as the World Is Wise*. New York: Columbia University Press.

–. 2016b. *The Work of Art: Rethinking the Elementary Forms of Religious Life*. New York: Columbia University Press.

–. 2018. *The Varieties of Temporal Experience: Travels in Philosophical, Historical and Ethnographic Time*. New York: Columbia University Press.

–. 2019. *The Paper Nautilus: A Trilogy*. New Zealand: Otago University Press.

242 Don Seeman

–. 2021. *Coincidences: Synchronicity, Verisimilitude, and Storytelling*. Berkeley: University of California Press.

James, William. (1902) 1982. *The Varieties of Religious Experience: A Study in Human Nature*. New York: Penguin Classics.

Judaken, Jonathan. 2006. *Jean-Paul Sartre and the Jewish Question*. Lincoln: Nebraska University Press.

Katz, Steven T. 1978. "Language, Epistemology and Mysticism." In *Mysticism and Philosophical Analysis*, edited by Steven T. Katz, 22–74. New York: Oxford University Press.

–. 1983. "The Conservative Character of 'Mystical' Experience." In *Mysticism and Religious Traditions*, edited by Steven T. Katz, 3–60. New York: Oxford University Press.

–. 1992. "Mystical Speech and Mystical Meaning." In *Mysticism and Language*, edited by Steven T. Katz, 1–41. Oxford: Oxford University Press.

Keane, Webb. 1997. *Signs of Recognition: Powers and Hazards of Representation in an Indonesian Society*. Berkeley: University of California Press.

Kirmayer, Lawrence J. 2015. "Mindfulness in Cultural Context." *Transcultural Psychiatry* 52, no. 4: 447–69. https://doi.org/10.1177/1363461515598949.

Kleinman, Arthur. 1988. *The Illness Narratives*. Boston: Basic Books.

–. 2014. "The Search for Wisdom: Why William James Still Matters." In *The Ground Between: Anthropologists Engage Philosophy*, edited by Veena Das, Michael Jackson, Arthur Kleinman, and Bhirubati Singh, 119–37. Durham: Duke University Press.

Kleinman, Arthur, and Joan Kleinman. 1991. "Suffering and Its Professional Transformation: Toward an Ethnography of Interpersonal Experience." *Culture, Medicine and Psychiatry* 15: 275–301. https://doi.org/10.1007/BF00046540.

Laing, R.D. 1965. *The Divided Self: An Existential Study in Sanity and Madness*. Harmondsworth: Penguin.

Lambek, Michael. 2015. "Both/And." In *What Is Existential Anthropology?*, edited by Michael Jackson and Albert Piette, 58–83. New York: Berghahn Books.

Lewis, Herbert S. Forthcoming. "Review of: Mark Anderson, *From Boas to Black Power*." *American Historical Review*. https://www.academia.edu/50755307/Review_of_Mark_Anderson_From_Boas_to_Black_Power.

Levy, Bernard-Henri. 2017. "The New Guise of the Oldest Form of Hate." In *The Genius of Judaism*, 3–23. New York: Random House..

Lipstadt, Deborah. 2019. *Antisemitism: Here and Now*. New York: Schocken Books.

Marrus, Michael R., and Robert O. Paxton. 2019. *Vichy France and the Jews*. 2nd ed. Stanford: Stanford University Press.

What (Who) Is Real in Existential Anthropology? 243

Massignon, Louis. (1922) 1997. *Essay on the Origins of the Technical Language of Islamic Mysticism*. Translated by Benjamin Clark. Notre Dame: Notre Dame Press.

McMahan, David L. 2008. *The Making of Modern Buddhism*. Oxford: Oxford University Press.

Mendes-Flohr, Paul, and Judah Reinhartz. 1980. *The Jew in the Modern World: A Documentary History*. Oxford: Oxford University Press.

Miller, John P. 2005. *Educating for Wisdom and Compassion: Creating Conditions for Timeless Learning*. New York: Corwin.

Misrahi, Robert, and Carol Marks. 1999. "Sartre and the Jews: A Felicitous Misunderstanding." *October* 87 (Winter): 63–72. https://www.jstor.org/stable/779169.

Nabhan-Warren, Kristy. 2011. "Embodied Research and Writing: A Case for Phenomenologically Oriented Religious Studies Ethnographies." *Journal of the American Academy of Religion* 79, no. 2: 378–407. https://doi.org/10.1093/jaarel/lfq079.

Neumann, Erich. (1948) 1968. "Mystical Man." In *The Mystic Vision: Papers from the Eranos Yearbooks*. Translated by Ralph Manheim. New York: Bollingen Books.

Otto, Rudolf. 1917. *The Idea of the Holy: An Inquiry into the Non-rational Factor in the Idea of the Divine and Its Relation to the Rational*. Translated by J.W. Harvey. New York: Penguin Books.

Paper, Jordan. 2004. *The Mystic Experience: A Descriptive and Comparative Analysis*. Albany: State University of New York Press.

Pattison, George, and Kate Kirkpatrick. 2018. *The Mystical Sources of Existentialist Thought*. Abingdon: Routledge.

Premawardhana, Devaka. 2018. *Faith in Flux: Pentecostalism and Mobility in Rural Mozambique*. Philadelphia: University of Pennsylvania Press.

Proudfoot, Wayne. 2004. "Pragmatism and an 'Unseen Order' in James's *Varieties*." In *William James and a Science of Religions,* edited by Wayne Proudfoot, 31–47. New York: Columbia University Press.

Riesman, Paul. 1977. *Freedom in Fulani Social Life: An Introspective Ethnography*. Chicago: University of Chicago Press.

Rorty, Richard. 2004. "Some Inconsistencies in James's *Varieties,*" In *William James and a Science of Religions,* edited by Wayne Proudfoot, 86–97. New York: Columbia University Press.

Sartre, Jean-Paul. 1948. *Anti-Semite and Jew: An Exploration of the Etiology of Hate*. Translated by George J. Becker. New York: Schocken Press.

–. 1956. *Being and Nothingness*. Translated by Hazel E. Barnes. New York: Philosophical Library.

–. 1963. *Saint Genet*. Translated by Bernard Frechtman. New York: George Braziller.

–. 1964. "Black Orpheus." Translated by John Macombie. *The Massachusetts Review* 6, no. 1 (Autumn–Winter): 13–52. https://www.jstor.org/stable/25087216.

–. 1968. *Search for a Method*. Translated by Hazel Barnes. New York: Vintage Press.

–. 1969. "Itinerary of a Thought." *New Left Review*, no. 58 (November–December): 44–66. https://newleftreview.org/issues/i58/articles/jean-paul-sartre-itinerary-of-a-thought.

–. 1987. *The Family Idiot: Gustave Flaubert 1821–1857*, Vol. 2. Translated by Carol Cosman. Chicago: University of Chicago Press.

Sartre, Jean-Paul, and Benny Levy. 1987. *Hope Now: The 1980 Interviews*. Translated by Adrian van den Hoven. Chicago: University of Chicago Press.

Schmidt-Biggeman, Wilhelm. 2004. *Philosophia Perennis: Historical Outlines of Western Spirituality in Ancient, Medieval and Early Modern Thought*. Dordrecht: Springer.

Seeman, Don. 2004. "Otherwise than Meaning: On the Generosity of Ritual," *Social Analysis* 48, no. 2: 55–71. https://doi.org/10.3167/015597704782352500.

–. 2005. "Ritual and its Discontents." In *A Companion to Psychological Anthropology: Modernity and Social Change*, edited by Connerly Casey and Robert Edgerton, 339–54. London: Blackwell.

–. 2008. "Ritual Efficacy, Hasidic Mysticism and 'Useless Suffering' in the Warsaw Ghetto." *Harvard Theological Review* 101, no. 3/4: 465–505. http://www.jstor.org/stable/40211979.

–. 2009. *One People, One Blood: Ethiopian-Israelis and the Return to Judaism*. New Brunswick: Rutgers University Press.

–. 2015. "Coffee and the Moral Order: Ethiopian Jews and Pentecostals against Culture." *American Ethnologist* 42, no. 4: 734–48. https://doi.org/10.1111/amet.12167.

–. 2017. "Kinship as Ethical Relation: A Critique of the Spiritual Kinship Paradigm." In *New Directions in Spiritual Kinship: Sacred Ties Across the Abrahamic Religions,* edited by Rose Wellman, Asiya Malik, and Todne Chipumuro, 85–108. New York: Palgrave-Macmillan.

–. 2018. "Divinity Inhabits the Social: Ethnography in a Phenomenological Key." In *Theologically Engaged Anthropology*, edited by Derrick Lemons, 336–54. Oxford: Oxford University Press.

–. 2021. "Pain and Words: On Suffering, Hasidic Modernism, and the Phenomenological Turn." In *Hasidism, Suffering, and Renewal*, edited by Don Seeman, Daniel Reiser and Ariel Evan Mayse, 333–60. Albany: State University of New York Press.

Seeman, Don, and Michael Karlin. 2019. "Mindfulness and Hasidic Modernism: Towards a Contemplative Ethnography." *Religion and Society: Advances in Research* 10, no. 1: 44–62. https://doi.org/10.3167/arrs.2019.100105.

Seeman, Don, Iman Roushdy-Hammady, Annie Hardison-Moody, Laurie M. Gaydos, Winnifred Thompson, and Carol G. Hogue. 2016. "Blessing Unintended Pregnancy: Religion and the Discourse of Women's Agency in Public Health." *Medicine Anthropology Theory* 3, no. 1: 29–54. https://doi.org/10.17157/mat.3.1.168.

Seeman, Don, and Nehemia A. Stern. Forthcoming. "Anthropology, Judaism and Jews: The Anthropology of Jewish Life." In *Blackwell Wiley Companion to the Anthropology of Religion*, edited by Simon Coleman and Joel Robbins. London: Blackwell.

Sharf, Robert. H. 1995. "Buddhist Modernism and the Rhetoric of Meditative Experience." *Numen* 42, no. 3: 228–83. https://doi.org/10.1163/1568527952598549.

–. 1998. "Experience." In *Critical Terms for Religious Studies*, edited by Mark Taylor, 94–116. Chicago: University of Chicago Press.

–. 2000. "The Rhetoric of Experience and the Study of Religion." *Journal of Consciousness Studies* 7, no. 11–12: 267–87. https://www.researchgate.net/publication/262970390_The_rhetoric_of_experience_and_the_study_of_religion.

–. 2012. *Religious Experience*. New York: Routledge.

–. 2015. "Is Mindfulness Buddhist? (and Why It Matters)." *Transcultural Psychiatry* 52, no. 4: 270–84. https://doi.org/10.1177/1363461514557561.

Smith, William Cantwell. 1967. *Questions of Religious Truth*. New York: Charles Scribner's Sons.

–. 1979. *Faith and Belief*. Princeton: Princeton University Press.

Stace, W.T. 1960. *Mysticism and Philosophy*. New York: Macmillan.

Steinbock, Anthony. 2009. *Phenomenology and Mysticism: The Verticality of Religious Experience*. Bloomington: Indiana University Press.

Stocking, G.W., Jr. 1986. "Introduction." In *Malinowski, Rivers, Benedict, and Others*, edited by G.W. Stocking, Jr., 3–12. Madison: University of Wisconsin Press.

Strauss, Erwin. 1966. *Phenomenological Psychology*. New York: Basic Books.

Underhill, Evelyn. (1911) 1990. *Mysticism*. New York: Doubleday.

Van der Leeuw, Gerardus. 1938. *Religion in Essence and Manifestation: A Study in Phenomenology*. Translated by J.E. Turner. London: George Allen & Unwin.

Wikan, Uni. 1990. *Managing Turbulent Hearts: A Balinese Formula for Living*. Chicago: University of Chicago Press.

Willen, Sarah S., and Don Seeman. 2012. "Introduction: Experience and Inquietude." *Ethos: Journal of the Society for Psychological Anthropology* 40, no. 1 (March): 1–23. https://doi.org/10.1111/j.1548-1352.2011.01228.x.

Afterword:
"Not Ethnology but Ethnosophy!"[1]

MICHAEL LAMBEK

In the beginning was the word, but what comes after word? What might come after the words in all these chapters? Perhaps the body, perhaps images, perhaps silence. I am fond of the remark attributed to painter Mark Rothko (who is also mentioned in Jackson's chapter) that "silence is so accurate." However, an afterword is simply more words, less accurate.[2]

This volume does three things. First the chapters cumulatively make the case, whether by telling or showing, for an existentially focused anthropology. Second, they think about the relationship between existential or phenomenological anthropology and the field of religious studies. And third, insofar as the contributors are, with one notable exception,[3] what Kristy Nabhan-Warren calls Jacksonians, they follow paths opened up by Michael Jackson.

Jackson's presence inevitably looms large given his expansive body of work traversing the borders between philosophy and anthropology. He has been one of the earliest and strongest voices advocating and exemplifying phenomenological and existential approaches to and through ethnography. Jackson is also an exceptionally generous and nurturing interlocutor; at least so he has been to me. Hence this afterword is something of a debt of honour and a sign of my deep respect for both the man and his body of work.

In Jackson's hands, existential anthropology exemplifies a deliberate attentiveness to the world and to the people the ethnographer meets in it. These are fellow humans (not informants), each on their own journey, with their own struggles to act, respond, create, and make their way in the world. Existential anthropology does not fool itself with romantic notions about going native, but rather reveals the thinness of the boundaries between others and ourselves. There are no informants because existential anthropologists are not primarily concerned with

248   Michael Lambek

some discrete object that the people they encounter could inform them about; existential anthropology is interested less in institutions, structure, or some reified abstraction we could call culture, religion, or even theory than in the intersubjective experiences of life as it is lived, pondered, and created anew. As Don Seeman once remarked, one reads Jackson's ethnographically rich essays not so much for their theoretical bottom line but in order to walk away a changed reader.

What anthropologists do, wrote Clifford Geertz, is write. The quality of writing, both its faithfulness to the experience of the author and her subjects and its openness to readerly reception, is of central concern for existential anthropologists no less than for existential philosophers. Sartre wrote novels and plays. Kierkegaard experimented (playfully, seriously) with multiple genres. So too do existential anthropologists like Jackson and Paul Stoller. Whatever the genre, in existential anthropology, the ethnographic and the autobiographical, the encounters with people and the encounters with texts, are continuous, and the abstractions drawn from them are fully integrated with the circumstantial. We might say, with Franz Steiner, that the object is less ethnology than ethnosophy.[4]

Jackson's strengths are on display in his beautiful chapter here. He deftly shows the centrality for Warlpiri of bringing life into being and sustaining it and then suggests that the accidental destruction of an ancestral site exemplified "the existential loss people had suffered in having their voices ignored, their land trampled on, their views unrecognised, and their pleas dismissed." One facet of this loss is the increasing abstraction of Aboriginal religiosity from everyday practice to an etherealization and inwardness, characteristic of both Christianity and secularization. In trying to "bracket out the vocabulary of transcendence, spirituality, mysticism, divinity, and sacrality with which we sustain the illusion of religion's sui generis character," Jackson challenges the very kind of phenomenology that, as Devaka Premawardhana shows in the volume's introduction, once characterized religious studies.

Where I depart from Jackson is his depiction of religion in the second part of this essay "not as a systematic theology or metaphysics of existence, but as a practical coping skill." This is hardly what the Aboriginal incident illustrates. We can agree that it is an illusion to consider that forms of being correspond to forms of thought (though here again Aboriginal life may offer a counter-example) and that people's attention and commitments shift, but between religion conceived as systematic theology or metaphysics and as a practical means of coping, isn't there still a lot to say? There are, for example, the ways that religion (for want

Afterword 249

of a better word) artfully shapes the environment that needs coping with, and the ways that practice is ethically formed no less than it is instrumentally formed. Jackson himself transcends his point, turning to limit situations and the movement beyond concepts. Stoller's chapter further illustrates how Jackson goes far beyond "coping" in his discussions of art and of alternately engaging and disengaging with the world. The deep insight from Jackson is the "indeterminate relationship between life and thought," and hence that "human thought and action are never entirely reducible to the terms with which we classify, categorize and conceptualize them."

Each of the other contributors pulls on a thread of Michael's work, whether drawing on his ideas, following his mode of honest exposition, or courteously challenging or developing one of his points. Rather than review the chapters systematically I will offer short personal responses to each.

Working with Angolan basket diviners, Sónia Silva evokes a set of ideas and practices widespread among Bantu-speakers in equatorial and southern Africa in which ancestors protect their descendants but also sometimes impose illness or misfortune in order to activate the living to take up curative and divinatory practices. Undergoing cure from the ancestrally imposed illness is simultaneously an initiation into a given practice. This is territory well covered by authors such as Victor Turner and John Janzen, among others, and has provided concepts such as that of the wounded healer and the cult of affliction that have been more widely applied. Silva gives voice to two senior and successful diviners, pointing out that they each cope with affliction from two distinct sources – ancestral intransigence and external political and economic turmoil. Silva rightly points to the fact that the work of a diviner is understood equally as liminal or sacred and as a mundane means to livelihood. The diviners suffer in their role, one they cannot escape, but simultaneously they become rich and esteemed members of their community. Their suffering is one of the indexes of their truthfulness as diviners, but so is their own success and well-being. Wounded healers exemplify the ordinary condition that Jackson describes of simultaneously acting and being acted upon.

Silva's portrait prompts me to ask whether the trope of the wounded healer might apply to ethnographers? *Might we think of the wounded ethnographer*? Is ethnography simultaneously a wounding and enriching calling? Might the existential condition of the ethnographer, at once acting and being acted upon, influence how we see the human situation more generally? Is the ethnographer perhaps exemplary of the human – or would it be our professional blind spot to think so?

250   Michael Lambek

Mattijs van de Port's beautiful chapter is perhaps closest to Jackson in style. But where Jackson moves between his experiences in Australia and Sierra Leone, one could be forgiven for suspecting that Brazil has been van de Port's only field site. As readers of his superb and troubling monograph on Serbia (van de Port 1998) will know, that is not the case. They will also know that the ethnographer might have been wounded by the Serbian experience and turned to candomblé in search of something more joyful. Serbia appears permanently closed off. In Bahia, van de Port is told, one needs to be closed to be safe, yet the pleasures of life require a body that is "wide open." Paradoxically, the body needs to be closed in order to open to receive an orixá. In a delightful existential twist, it turns out that it is less that practices of closure make you invulnerable than that they make you more daring. I wonder whether the opening and closing of van de Port's camera lens and the images it shapes might be a way to develop (pun intended) what is at hand in Bahia.

Ethnographers of religion may study life but they compose texts. These texts are not always as readable as some would like. Paul Stoller offers valuable lessons in evocative writing and how we might better depict what he wonderfully calls "the sensory splendour of the world." Following the comparison between religious studies and anthropology in this volume, it might be interesting to reflect on the respective styles of ethnographers working from lived experience and scholars of religion who draw on texts. Stoller's Songhai mentors advise patience and, in a sense, Stoller proposes a kind of "slow anthropology" manifesto. And incidentally he highlights one of my favourite fictional characters, Easy Rawlins. Easy Rawlins! One of the things I love about Walter Mosley's depiction of the African American detective is that "Easy" does not simply describe a character trait but is a short form of Ezekiel.

Of course, the most readable texts are not necessarily the most insightful. And much of what goes into the composition of a given monograph lies beneath the surface. A possible implication of Stoller's encouragement to draw on writers of fiction is to turn as well to literary criticism and hence to think about such things as the alternative forms that ethnography can take, for example, its employment as comedy, tragedy, romance, satire, or some combination.[5]

Kristy Nabhan-Warren vividly evokes the overwhelming sensations of working in a slaughterhouse. The experience is so different from what I have observed in a Muslim village in Mayotte where the killing of each animal is acknowledged seriously, much as the subsequent consumption of meat is a joyous affair. Each killing is a sacrifice; it begins with an invocation over the animal, who is fed a last sip of water,

Afterword   251

followed by a quick and powerful slicing of the neck. There is a surge of masculine excitement among all the youths and boys present as the animal is butchered, falling from a crescendo to the methodical cutting, parcelling, and delivery of the meat; all in all, a communal event but one in which gendered difference is highly marked. Both the owner of the animal and the person who cared for it are singled out with specific cuts of meat. By contrast, the slaughterhouse offers an impersonal, anonymous, industrial mass killing performed by alienated workers, provoking quite different visceral reactions. Nabhan-Warren offers us ethnography as embodied and ethical responsivity, from which one might need either therapy or religion to recover, though she also tells us, with remarkable honesty, that "the plant was a wondrous place" and that she "felt alive on the kill floor."[6]

I cannot avoid a small personal digression. Nabhan-Warren's exposition evoked for me an urban mass circumcision I once attended in northwest Madagascar. Large numbers of families took the opportunity for the free service, sponsored by a political candidate, in a public building. The operations were conducted by trained medical personal using topical anaesthesia and presumably sterile instruments, but following Malagasy practice, they were carried out in the middle of the night.[7] As musicians and dancers performed frenetically on an outdoor stage, a long line of boys, each accompanied by a parent, snaked down the street. I was there with my friend Nazir and his young son. As we approached the building, screams could be heard, provoking unrest in those at the head of the line. Nothing prepared me for the scene inside. Under glaring lights, some twenty boys of varying ages were splayed over bed frames and tables, their legs held wide apart. Personnel rushed to and fro, jostling each other with anaesthetic needles, scalpels, ointments, and bandages. I feared for surgical mishaps in the pandemonium. Nazir and his son kept their cool. Nazir held his son tightly on his lap as a nurse approached with a needle. But to my consternation I felt faint and feared collapsing in the pools of blood and urine that sloshed on the floor.[8] Shamefully, I rushed to the exit, surprised at my fully embodied response to an experience I came to think of as a vision of hell.

From religious studies, Tyler Roberts provides a deeply thoughtful comparison between Jackson's concern for "the life of ordinary people" and the Wittgensteinian ordinary as found in the work of Stanley Cavell and of Veena Das. Both parties reject the abstract language of metaphysics, but Jackson makes a sharper division between the conceptual and the experiential and sees in the "remembering of the non-conceptual" the source of productive change, whereas Das and Cavell explore

252   Michael Lambek

"a movement deeper into the words and concepts that matter." Jackson, Roberts says, "is suspicious of ordinary language" and tends to reject its conventionalism in favour of "pure experience." This is a very insightful discussion, one that implicitly raises larger questions concerning the relationship between Continental (phenomenological, existential) and analytic (ordinary language) philosophy. It is a tragedy that Roberts died young and before this book reached its final stage.

It is for Jackson to respond, not me, but I do not think Jackson invests as much in extreme experience or is quite as suspicious of ordinary language as Roberts suggests. Jackson learns by means of conversation that he provides the reader, and he writes mostly about ordinary life, albeit life full of troubling circumstances like witchcraft accusations, warfare, and migration. There is considerable overlap with the Wittgensteinians (including Das et al 2014, Brandel and Motta 2021), and the comparison is worth pursuing. Jackson is certainly more eclectic in the thinkers he draws upon.

Samuli Schielke offers a lively discussion of destiny. Despite all the care we take, the unexpected can happen. One way in which people rationalize that things are ultimately out of their hands (notably the time and manner of their deaths) is to claim that events are preordained or orchestrated by powerful meta-humans. Where Schielke emphasizes destiny as a relationship, I would note that it is often considered blind and impersonal. Schielke usefully reviews debates internal to Islam, but in East Africa, the spread of Islam has been accompanied by an astrological corpus, written originally in Arabic but not specifically Muslim and likely predating Islam itself. Among the Muslims I lived with in Mayotte, a text-supported model of impersonal, astrologically based destiny existed alongside the concept of God's will (Lambek 1993). Practically, this meant consulting a diviner who could make astrological calculations. The critical relationship was with the diviner himself[9] since he could pass on the wrong information, whether by miscalculating or out of maliciousness. People developed relationships with diviners they could trust, yet they often discreetly sought second opinions. Impersonal destiny offered a partial answer to the question of theodicy; in effect, it absolved God of direct responsibility for the bad things that happened to good and pious people. Often people would say they trusted in God or threw up their hands, saying, God alone knows. God was understood as a benign, if unknowable protector and benefactor, as reflected in the common phrase *Masha 'Allah* (by the grace of God ...). As Schielke importantly observes, no single theory is likely to be fully satisfactory to meet human existential concerns and therefore any society is likely to offer incommensurable models. And as he rightly says, "Few

Afterword   253

people try to consistently think about the link between [predestination and responsibility], however, because to do so is seldom helpful and potentially unsettling." Schielke's discussion of destiny also illustrates Jackson's general point that humans struggle to find the right balance between acting and being acted upon (action and passion, agency and patiency).

Kim Knibbe asks how the spread of transnational religion, in this case, a Nigerian-originated Christian Pentecostal church, may be viewed through a phenomenological and existentialist lens. She emphasizes the novelty, natality, or world creative aspects (what she calls worlding) of the implantation of the church in new venues. It is striking that congregants refuse the ascription of marginality, claiming to have arrived in the Netherlands not as tenants but as landlords and not as premodern but as post-secular. Hence the critical point is how the church "brings into being a world in which people are existentially oriented in ways that contribute to their flourishing rather than block and diminish them." As this church has been spectacularly successful it would be of interest to consider her argument with respect to the multitude of churches that have not.[10] This chapter connects nicely with Schielke's discussion of destiny as well as with Seeman's discussion on appropriating labels. The contribution supplements existential anthropology's concern with individuals by turning to an institution, the church itself, as actor.

Aditya Malik describes the work of interpreters and the layers of interpretation at a remote mountain fortress in India and the ways in which dreams and poetry create and support historical accounts. Following the work of the great religious studies scholar David Shulman, dreams in South Asian thought are not subjective but real, hence "the poem is real because it has been dreamt … Dream world and real world are conjoined like a Mobius strip that has a single contiguous surface." This speaks to Jackson's interest in the spaces between what can and cannot be fully grasped as we come up against the limits of language. Malik argues that if experience is always immediate, past experiences can come to us only as mediated, whether by dreams or texts, but also, as his first image shows, by landscape and architecture. Moreover, what we experience in the present can be passed on to others who are not immediately with us only by means of words or images. Whether history – as the study or recounting of the past – thereby promotes "alienation and detachment from what is" is the unsettling question with which this line of thinking leaves us.

Don Seeman's chapter is provocative and deeply interesting, comparing how we think of Jews and witches and how those so-named

254 Michael Lambek

think (or are to think) of themselves. Seeman quotes Sartre's question, "Is the Jew first a Jew or first a man?" Doesn't Geertz (1973) solve this, and for everyone? We are human by being each a culturally particular kind of person – Kuranko, Pakeha (New Zealander of European descent), or French Jew – and also, of course, by being singular, oneself. But these are forms of life (existence), fluid and overlapping, not fixed categories (essence). In any case, as Seeman says (citing Sarah Hammerschlag), "For Sartre … the Jewish predicament was 'an intensification of the human situation [as such], and thus … a window into the stakes of existentialism.' This was not just another case to which existentialist principles might be applied, but a significant context for *thinking existentialism through.*" The question is whether existentialism takes cultural and religious particularity sufficiently into attention. Sartre's liberal option, which, in a distinctively French manner, implicitly equates being universal with being "French," appears to prefigure recent events in France concerning Muslims.

With respect to Kuranko witchcraft, Jackson shows "the deadly opposition between persons and categories … to which persons or groups of persons may be subjected." Nevertheless, people appear to acquiesce to the label when it is pinned on them. If I understand him, Seeman uses the weakness of Jackson's argument concerning why someone identified as a witch would accept the label (as a claim of autonomy) to point to the weakness of Sartre's argument, and the converse. There is a whole history of sociological labelling theory to be disinterred here but the comparison is good to think with.[11]

While I cannot know why a Kuranko woman accused of witchcraft confesses, I suspect such confessions are largely stories that Kuranko tell each other (rather than actual confessions) in order to validate confession in principle and to intimidate women. It is when men die that women are (said to be) killed as witches. The key point in Seeman's summary is the quotation from Jackson that "during the entire episode, all the women of the village remained indoors."

In the later section of his chapter Seeman argues that experience-near ethnography pushes back against what he calls cultural reductionism. Agreed, but not all cultural accounts are reductionist. Indeed, it was Geertz who invoked the term experience-near, and I take for granted that existentialist and culturalist expositions work together. As all these chapters show, existential quandaries are mediated by culture, just as culture is never sufficient to encompass or resolve them. As Seeman puts it, the existential contribution is to see how things are mediated through some actual individual predicament.[12]

Seeman's concluding discussion of trends in religious studies is taken up with a different inflection in Devaka Premawardhana's essay concerning the shifting relationship between religious studies and anthropology. This is a lucid and comprehensive account, and I will make only a few remarks. Premawardhana opens with the important point that an existential approach bridges anthropology with the humanities and refocuses on the human. He suggests that existential anthropology is renewing religious studies and, conversely, that religious studies has much to offer anthropology. He very usefully distinguishes an older, and largely discredited phenomenology of religion that characterized religious studies – what Jackson calls a "sui generis modality of existence" with respect to religion – from the newer phenomenology that avoids reified abstractions like society, culture, or religion itself[13] and turns to actual experience.

Many anthropologists now find positions in departments of religious studies, as Jackson has in a divinity school, and it will be interesting to follow the impact this has on the respective disciplines. Inevitably, historians of religion study texts, much as ethnographers of religion study life. One is not necessarily better than the other, and they are not mutually exclusive. Indeed, there is a whole intermediate field that explores the way people receive and interpret texts. One of the ways they do so is by composing further texts. Acts of reading, writing, and interpretation are part of lived religion (as of studying it). Conversely, anthropologists could be less naïve about the content of religious texts; that has been a gap in my understanding of Muslim life in Mayotte, and I admire those anthropologists of Islam who are literate in the texts. Anthropologists have also worked in societies without written texts, and here we have faced bias, whether tacit or explicit, from the textual orientation in religious studies (not to mention the missionizing tendency of theology). This is distinct from but parallel to the matter of ignoring lived religion.

Premawardhana focuses on four features of phenomenological anthropology, namely embodiment, experience, epistemic openness, and intellectual humility. These are all critical points and well stated. Premawardhana nicely describes Jackson's move to existential anthropology as a "commitment to the irreducibility of lived experience," and notes his cognisance of the ways people's attention and perspectives are constantly shifting. If life is "irreducible to the terms with which we seek to grasp it," the "we" here must refer not only to scholars of religion but equally to our subjects. They too have terms by which they seek to grasp life and, as Premawardhana observes, part of our work as anthropologists includes understanding those terms and those attempts.

256   Michael Lambek

I have two minor points of disagreement with Premawardhana. First, I have a more positive view of constructivism, which needn't be reductionist and is critical in many ways, for example, in understanding how there are witches with which Kuranko have to contend in the first place.[14] Second, I find it questionable that conversion is indispensable for understanding. To the contrary, as a concept it is intrinsically linked to monotheism and as a self-attribution it is easily self-deceptive and produces naïve anthropology. I favour a hermeneutic approach.

Indeed, both Premawardhana and Seeman support Jackson's critique of identity thinking. Perhaps in lieu of anthropologies *of* Christianity or *of* Islam we might speak of anthropology *with* Christianity or Islam? This would not only reduce the objectification implicit in the labels, but also signal that anthropologists interact with these traditions as much as their subjects live alongside them.

No one is going to discover the "best" way to conceptualize or describe, let alone explain religion. There is a forceful argument in this book concerning a route through embodied experience. One of its signal contributions, as Premawardhana notes, is to do so without hypostatizing forms or objects of experience, as in the older phenomenology of religion of thinkers like Rudolf Otto, Mircea Eliade, or Gerardus van der Leeuw. Moreover, to avoid hypostatizing experience itself, it needs to be set in relation, whether to ritual or belief, structure, action, representation, or simply ordinary life.

Just as lived experience is "irreducible" to culture, religion, etc., so too neither culture nor religion is reducible to experience. Don Seeman puts this well: "the contributors to this volume have all pushed back with great energy against cultural reductionism by calling attention to the imponderables of everyday life and the human conditions within which they unfold. But is it not possible that there is also the risk of an *existentialist reduction* … in translating divine presence or witchcraft confession into manifestos of being …? Is there not a way of breaking through the stifling particularities of culture without falling prey to an existentialist mono-linguicism?"

I would add to Seeman's concern that, as used here, "experience" itself is not an experience-near concept. The arguments for attending to lived experience draw authority from philosophy: for example, the rephrasing of Hubert Dreyfus by Jackson that "an existential perspective avoids the illusion of thinking that forms of being correspond to forms of thought." You cannot say this except by means of abstract thought.

As a concept, "experience" itself remains somewhat underthought. Citing Robert Desjarlais, Premawardhana rightly speaks to the "contingency of the category of experience itself, its romantic associations with inwardness, introspection, and individualism." There is also an unspoken ambiguity between what German distinguishes as *Erlebnis* and *Erfahrung*, that is, between experience as a singular event, possibly a life-altering one, and experience as cumulative, leading to some kind of maturation or wisdom, coming to terms with the world.[15] Experience (presumably in the first sense) may be "more than" – but if so, how can we possibly claim to describe it?

Existential anthropology is pulled between attention to the ethnographer's experience (in either the first or the second sense) and attention to that of the ethnographer's subjects. As Tyler Roberts notes, "in many respects, Jackson himself is as much the object of his philosophical and ethnographical work as the people he studies." In lesser writers it can become problematic when these perspectives are confused.

I want to ask: can a particular existential account be challenged, and if so, on what grounds?

As Premawardhana argues, and as these essays show, the study of religion is perfectly capable of encompassing both existential or phenomenological and, let's say, structural, hermeneutic, ordinary language, or political economic perspectives. Theoretical approaches are not necessarily mutually exclusive and anthropologists should not be stuck with tight-fitting labels. Likewise, the multiplication of anthropologies (*the* anthropology *of* Christianity, *of* Thailand, *of* religion, etc.) objectifies a fluid and holistic field, thereby serving particular interests at the expense of existential recognition itself. This is not to deny, however, that people seek the security of labels for themselves.

In sum, the question is not whether the study of religion should be specifically or exclusively existential or phenomenological. Rather, in lucidly demonstrating the affordances and contributions of these perspectives, the question that this lively collection provokes us to consider is whether the study of religion can do without them.

NOTES

1 Franz Steiner, in Adler and Fardon (2022, 70). By ethnosophy I do *not* mean ethno-philosophy.
2 My thanks to Devaka and Don for the invitation and for very helpful comments on the first draft.
3 I.e., Jackson himself.
4 Steiner did little fieldwork and wrote little ethnography, but he too brought philosophical questions and poetic insight into conjunction with anthropology. Among his many genres was the aphorism.

258   Michael Lambek

5 These are ideal types, taken from Hayden White (1973) as borrowed in turn from Northrop Frye (1957). Strangely, despite the "writing culture" movement, anthropology has yet to produce its Erich Auerbach (1953) or Hayden White to discern alternative forms of mimesis or composition.
6 For a cooler look at a slaughterhouse, see the photographs by Jacqueline Solway as displayed in Livingston (2019).
7 Circumcision is practised over most of Madagascar. The boys here came from both Muslim and non-Muslim families. For a strong interpretation of circumcision among non-Muslims in a different region of the island, see Bloch (1986).
8 One reviewer remarked that this reads like hyperbole; it isn't.
9 Most diviners were male.
10 Compare Daswani (2015).
11 Limitations to the comparison appear twofold. First, there is much substantively positive in proudly accepting the identity of Jew or Black but none in accepting the identity of witch (among Kuranko). And second, while accepting the former identities generates whole ways of living, accepting the latter leads only to immediate and violent death.
12 A great deal of cultural anthropology does precisely that. Consider contributions to person-centred, psychological, or psychoanalytically informed anthropology like those of Vincent Crapanzano (1980) and Gananath Obeyesekere (1981), or work in medical anthropology by Andrew Irving (2017), Cheryl Mattingly (2014), or Tine Gammeltoft (2014), to name only a few. The latter addresses the sharp existential questions with which agent orange and ultrasound technology confront Vietnamese women.
13 Deity itself may be another such abstraction. See Lambek (2008, 2021).
14 A founding – and dialectical – constructivist text is Berger and Luckmann (1966). Think also of Ian Hacking's *Historical Ontology* (2002), among other works.
15 As in the related German concept of *Bildung*. On *Erlebnis* and *Erfahrung* see Jay (2005).

WORKS CITED

Adler, Jeremy, and Richard Fardon. 2022. *Franz Baermann Steiner: A Stranger in the World*. New York: Berghahn.
Auerbach, Erich. 1953. *Mimesis: The Representation of Reality in Western Literature*. Princeton, NJ: Princeton University Press.
Berger, Peter, and Thomas Luckmann. 1966. *The Social Construction of Reality*. Garden City, NY: Doubleday.
Bloch, Maurice. 1986. *From Blessing to Violence: History and Ideology in the Circumcision Ritual of the Merina*. Cambridge: Cambridge University Press.

Brandel, Andrew, and Marco Motta, eds. 2021. *Living with Concepts: Anthropology in the Grip of Reality*. New York: Fordham University Press.

Crapanzano, Vincent. 1980. *Tuhami: Portrait of a Moroccan*. Chicago: University of Chicago Press.

Das, Veena, Michael Jackson, Arthur Kleinman, and Bhrigupati Singh, eds. 2014. *The Ground Between: Anthropologists Engage Philosophy*. Durham, NC: Duke University Press.

Daswani, Girish. 2015. *Looking Back, Moving Forward: Transformation and Ethical Practice in the Ghanaian Church of Pentecost*. Toronto: University of Toronto Press.

Frye, Northrop. 1957. *Anatomy of Criticism*. Princeton, NJ: Princeton University Press.

Gammeltoft, Tine. 2014. *Haunting Images: A Cultural Account of Selective Reproduction in Vietnam*. Berkeley: University of California Press.

Geertz, Clifford. 1973, "The Impact of the Concept of Culture on the Concept of Man." In *The Interpretation of Cultures*, 33–54. New York: Basic Books.

Hacking, Ian. 2002. *Historical Ontology*. Cambridge, MA: Harvard University Press.

Irving, Andrew. 2017. *The Art of Life and Death: Radical Aesthetics and Ethnographic Practice*. Chicago: University of Chicago Press.

Jay, Martin. 2005. *Songs of Experience: Modern American and European Variations on a Universal Theme*. Berkeley: University of California Press.

Lambek, Michael. 1993. *Knowledge and Practice in Mayotte: Local Discourses of Islam, Sorcery, and Spirit Possession*. Toronto: University of Toronto Press.

–. 2008. "Provincializing God? Provocations from an Anthropology of Religion." In *Religion: Beyond a Concept*, edited by Hent de Vries, 120–38. New York: Fordham University Press.

–. 2021. *Concepts and Persons*. Toronto: University of Toronto Press.

Livingston, Julie. 2019. *Self-Devouring Growth*. Durham, NC: Duke University Press.

Mattingly, Cheryl. 2014. *Moral Laboratories: Family Peril and the Struggle for a Good Life*. Berkeley: University of California Press.

Obeyesekere, Gananath. 1981. *Medusa's Hair: An Essay on Personal Symbols and Religious Experience*. Chicago: University of Chicago Press.

van de Port, Mattijs. 1998. *Gypsies, Wars and Other Instances of the Wild: Civilization and its Discontents in a Serbian Town*. Amsterdam: Amsterdam University Press.

White, Hayden. 1973. *Metahistory: The Historical Imagination in Nineteenth-Century Europe*. Baltimore, MD: Johns Hopkins University Press.

Contributors

Michael Jackson is a senior research fellow in World Religions at Harvard Divinity School. He is the author of numerous books of anthropology, including the prize-winning *Paths Toward a Clearing* (1989) and *At Home in the World* (1995), and has also published seven works of fiction, a memoir, and nine volumes of poetry. His most recent books are *Coincidences: Synchronicity, Verisimilitude, and Storytelling* (2021), *The Genealogical Imagination: Two Studies of Life over Time* (2021), *Critique of Identity Thinking* (2019), *The Work of Art: Rethinking the Elementary Forms of Religious Life* (2016), and *The Wherewithal of Life: Ethics, Migration and the Question of Well-Being* (2013).

Kim E. Knibbe is an anthropologist who researches various forms of religion and spirituality in the Netherlands and Europe. She has recently completed the project "Sexuality, Religion and Secularism" at the University of Groningen.

Michael Lambek is a professor and Canada Research Chair emeritus at the University of Toronto. He has carried out extensive ethnographic research in the Western Indian Ocean. Recent books include *The Weight of the Past: Living with History in Mahajanga, Madagascar* (2002); *The Ethical Condition: Essays on Action, Person and Value* (2015); *Island in the Stream: An Ethnographic History of Mayotte* (2018); *Concepts and Persons* (2021); and *Behind the Glass: The Villa Tugendhat and Its Family* (2022).

Aditya Malik is a founding professor in humanities and social sciences at Plaksha University. He has a doctorate and habilitation in South Asian religions and modern Indian studies from the University of Heidelberg. Aditya has done extensive ethnographic fieldwork in rural areas of western and northern India, and has taught

262   Contributors

anthropology, religious studies, history, and South Asian studies at the universities of Heidelberg (Germany), Nalanda (India), and Canterbury (New Zealand). He has been a fellow of the Max Weber Centre for Advanced Social and Cultural Studies (Erfurt) and visiting professor at the Israel Institute for Advanced Studies (Jerusalem). Aditya's publications include *Nectar Gaze and Poison Breath: An Analysis and Translation of the Rajasthani Oral Narrative of Devnarayan* (2005), *Tales of Justice and Rituals of Divine Embodiment: Oral Narratives from the Central Himalayas* (2018), *Hinduism: Modern and Contemporary Movements* (2016), and *Hammira: Chapters in Imagination, Time, History* (2021) as well as *Realizing Justice? Normative Orders and the Realities of Justice in India* (forthcoming).

Kristy Nabhan-Warren is a professor and the inaugural V.O. and Elizabeth Kahl Figge Chair of Catholic Studies at the University of Iowa in the departments of religious studies and gender, women's and sexuality studies. She is associate vice president of research and development for the arts, humanities, and social sciences at the University of Iowa. Kristy's books focus on U.S. Latinx Catholics in the United States and include *The Virgin of El Barrio: Marian Apparitions, Catholic Evangelizing, and Mexican-American Activism*; *Cursillos in America: Catholics, Protestants, and Fourth-Day Spirituality*; *Américan Woman: The Virgin of Guadalupe, Latinos/as and Accompaniment*; and *Meatpacking America: How Migration, Work and Faith Unite and Divide the Heartland*. She is editor of *The Oxford Handbook of Latinx Christianities in the United States* and creator and series editor for the UNC Press book series Where Religion Lives.

Devaka Premawardhana is Winship Distinguished Research Associate Professor of Religion at Emory University. He has been conducting ethnographic fieldwork in south-east Africa for over a decade and focuses on issues of religious change and religious multiplicity. He is author of the prize-winning *Faith in Flux: Pentecostalism and Mobility in Rural Mozambique* (2018). His other publications related to existential anthropology include "Faith and the Existential" in *The Routledge International Handbook of Existential Human Science*, and "In Praise of Ambiguity: Everyday Christianity through the Lens of Existential Anthropology" in the *Journal of World Christianity*.

Tyler Roberts was a professor of religious studies at Grinnell College in Iowa, where he taught courses in religions of the Western world, modern religious thought, theory and method in the study of religion, and religion and politics. He is the author of *Contesting Spirit:*

Nietzsche, Affirmation, Religion (1998) and *Encountering Religion: Responsibility and Criticism after Secularism* (2013). His passing in 2021 was a terrible loss.

Samuli Schielke is a senior research fellow at Leibniz-Zentrum Moderner Orient in Berlin, Germany. He is the author of *Shared Margins* (with Mukhtar Shehata, 2021), *Migrant Dreams* (2020), *Egypt in the Future Tense* (2015), and *The Perils of Joy* (2012).

Don Seeman is an associate professor in the Department of Religion and the Tam Institute for Jewish Studies at Emory University. He is the author of *One People, One Blood: Ethiopian-Israelis and the Return to Judaism* (2009), and co-editor of *Hasidism, Suffering and Renewal* (2021), as well as the book series on *Contemporary Anthropology of Religion* at Palgrave-Macmillan. Works in progress are *An Ethiopian Jew Goes to Uman: Existential Anthropology of the Jews* and *How the World Becomes Real: Nullification, Mysticism, and Everyday Experience in Habad Hasidism.*

Sónia Silva is an associate professor of anthropology at Skidmore College. She is the author of *Along an African Border: Angolan Refugees and Their Divination Baskets* (2011).

Paul Stoller is a professor of anthropology at West Chester University and permanent fellow at the Center for Advanced Research in the Humanities and Social Sciences at Friedrich Alexander University/ Erlangen-Nuremberg. He has been conducting ethnographic research for more than thirty years and is the author of sixteen books including ethnographies, memoirs, a biography, and three novels. He is the recipient of a Guggenheim Fellowship, the Robert B. Textor Family Prize for Anticipatory Anthropology and the American Anthropological Association Anthropology in Media Award. In 2013 the King of Sweden awarded him the Anders Retzius Gold Medal for his contributions to anthropology.

Mattijs van de Port is an associate professor in visual anthropology at the University of Amsterdam and is full professor at the Vrije Universiteit Amsterdam, where he holds the chair of Popular Religiosity. His publications include *Gypsies, Wars, and Other Instances of the Wild* (1998) and *Ecstatic Encounters: Bahian Candomblé and the Quest for the Really Real* (2011). The last film of his Bahian trilogy, *The Body Won't Close* (2021), won the Basil Wright Film Prize and the Excellence in Visual Anthropology Award.

Index

Aboriginal societies, 35–40, 59, 220, 248
Adler, Jeremy, 257
Adogame, Afe, 155, 162
Adorno, Theodore, 97–9, 110
Agee, James, 62
agency, 12, 151, 253; and dignity, 230; fallacy of agency exclusively against tradition, 23; and freedom, 101, 137–9; in Islam, 137–9; and Pentecostalism, 155, 159, 167–72; and subjectivity, 14–17
Ahmed, Sara, 119
Al-Ash'ari, 'Ali ibn Isma'il Abu al-Hasan, 139–42
Al-Azm, Sadiq Jalal, 148–9
Al-Tanukhi, Al-Qadi Abu Ali al-Muhassan ibn Ali, 148
Amsterdam, 123, 157–70
Anderson, Mark, 223–4, 239–40
Angola, 209–10, 249
animals, 73–92, 189–90, 250–1
antisemitism. *See* Judaism
Appadurai, Arjun, 156
Appiah, Kwame Anthony, 35, 47, 52, 223
anthropology, comparative, 135; cultural, 3, 5, 222–4, 258; phenomenological, 1–28, 79,

155–8, 218, 247–8, 255, 257; philosophical, 4, 95–7
Archer, Margaret, 229
Arendt, Hannah, 51–2, 101, 213, 218, 238
art, 5, 50–1, 55–71, 85, 95, 114, 125, 231–2, 249
Asad, Talal, 27, 45, 236
Auerbach, Erich, 258
Australia, 35, 40, 58, 60, 158, 250
authenticity, 48, 218, 226; inauthenticity, 224

Bacchiddu, Giovanna, 27
Badkhen, Anna, 62, 67
Bakunin, Mikhail, 146
Balkenhol, Markus, 169
Bandyopádhyáya, Brajanátha, 180–1
Barnosky, Anthony, 149
Barrett, Justin, 47
Bartelink, Brenda, 169
Bear, Laura, 166–7
Behar, Ruth, 64–6
being-in-the-world, 21–2, 26, 55, 60, 76, 79, 90, 187–8, 222
Bell, Catherine, 201–2
Bender, Courtney, 234
Benson, Susan, 119
Berger, John, 86

266 Index

Berger, Peter, 258
Berry, Thomas, 80, 90
Bharati, Agehananda, 45–8
Bible, 134, 209
Blanchette, Alex, 82, 91
Blaser, Mario, 157–9
Bloch, Maurice, 258
Boas, Franz, 81, 222–4, 232
body, 6–7, 56, 247, 250; and coping,
    207–12; disavowal of, 50;
    embodiment, 3–10, 17, 20–6, 55,
    60, 73–80, 84, 90–3, 137, 159–60,
    171–2, 208, 219–22, 251, 255–6; and
    fieldwork, 74–88, 114–31, 133; and
    health, 133; in religion, 40–1, 181,
    185; in religious narrative, 181, 185
Bourdieu, Pierre, 210
Boyarin, Jonathan, 239
Bracke, Sarah, 169
Brandel, Andrew, 231, 252
Bray, Karen, 81
Brooks, Shelton, 221
Bruner, Jerome, 70, 233
Buddhism, 15, 17, 149–50, 235

Candomblé, 10, 113–31, 250
capitalism, 19, 40, 161–3
Carrette, Jeremy, 24, 26
Cavell, Stanley, 96, 100–10, 251
Chabon, Michael, 67
Charbonnier, Georges, 56
Chaves, Mark, 18
Chidester, David, 27
Christianity, 18, 248; anthropology
    of, 18; 25, 27, 256–7; Catholicism,
    8, 15–17, 74, 80, 108, 116, 133, 220,
    244; and European expansion,
    41; Pentecostalism, 17, 45, 155–72,
    253; Protestantism, 8, 40, 80;
    theological ideas, 213, 232–6; and
    theories of destiny, 133–6, 144, 149
Clooney, Francis, 10

Coleman, Simon, 162–3
colonialism, 146, 160–2, 170;
    postcolonialism, 27, 160–2, 170
Comaroff, Jean, 161
communitas, 106
comparison, 18, 97, 226, 237, 250–4, 258
comparative religion. *See* religion,
    comparative
constructivism, 3, 9, 232–6, 256, 258
conversion, 10–11, 45, 77, 109, 256
Crapanzano, Vincent, 258
Csordas, Thomas, 6–7, 22

D'Angelo, Lorenzo, 145
Das, Veena, 99–106, 109, 251–2
Daswani, Girish, 258
Debevec, Liza, 17, 22
de Certeau, Michel, 46
DeConinck, Kate, 17, 19
Denizeau, Laurent, 12, 27, 219
Derrida, Jacques, 45, 53, 58–9, 227
description, 6–8, 11, 41, 61–9, 131,
    210, 229, 234, 237
Desjarlais, Robert, 6, 15, 21–2, 26–8,
    218, 235, 256
destiny, 13–17, 133–51, 252–3
de Vries, Hent, 48, 53
Dewey, John, 26, 48, 53
diviners, 144, 197–213, 226, 230, 249,
    252, 258
Dominguez, Virginia, 225
dreams, 12, 16, 35–45, 81, 103,
    179–95, 232, 253
Dreyfus, Hubert, 11, 20, 45, 198–9,
    207–8, 212, 256
Dunn, Mary, 9–10, 26
Dunne, John, 235
Durkheim, Emile, 49, 59
Duyvendak, Jan Willem, 169

Egypt, 135–51
Eliade, Mircea, 4, 202, 256

Elliot, Alice, 144
Ellis, Stephen, 161
emotion, 19, 24, 36, 40–52, 63–4, 75–8, 86, 90, 117, 145, 209, 235; affect, 75, 81
empiricism, 15, 20–6, 41, 46, 95, 229; radical, 2–3, 9–10, 24, 26, 52, 97, 235
enlightenment, 55, 185
Enwerem, Iheanyi, 161,162
epistemology, 5, 7–12, 21, 25, 27, 40, 81, 90, 105, 158, 219, 229, 255
Essakouti, Asmaa, 149
ethics, 51–2, 97–105, 134–6, 249, 251; anthropology of, 18, 25, 145; and dilemmas, 44, 46, 166; and responsibility, 90; and value, 37
ethnography, 6–10, 21–5, 47, 51, 210, 247–57; as art, 55–71; experience-near, 235–7; and Michael Jackson, 16, 96–100, 105–8, 228–31; and study of religion, 1–3, 78–9, 90
Eurocentrism, 23, 168–72
evil eye, 115–24
exigency, 42, 229
existentialism, 11–12, 15, 20, 26, 89, 134, 208, 217–25, 229–31, 248, 254
experience, religious, 8–10, 15–16, 24, 27, 40, 47–50, 53, 234

Fardon, Richard, 257
Fassin, Didier, 100–1
Fesenmyer, Leslie, 27
film, 61, 69–71, 114, 118–19, 123–5, 128, 130, 139
Fitzgerald, Timothy, 4
Fleischmann, Fenella, 169
Flynn, Thomas, 218
Forman, Robert, 234
Fox, Michael, 77
France, 50, 217, 220, 254
Francis, Philip, 26

Frankl, Victor, 230
Freston, Paul, 156, 171
Friedlander, Judith, 225
friendship, 41, 50, 70–1, 113, 145, 195
Frye, Northrop, 258

Gaibazzi, Paolo, 137, 145
Gammeltoft, Tine, 258
Gaon, Stella, 227
Geertz, Clifford, 7, 63, 136, 228, 248, 254
Gell, Alfred, 47
Gellner, David, 18
George, Kenneth, 50–1
Geschiere, Peter, 161
Glazier, Jack, 223
Glendinning, Simon, 218
González, George, 19, 27
Good, Byron, 235
Gordon, Lewis, 23
Gottschall, Jonathan, 70
Grandin, Temple, 85–6
Graw, Kent, 27
Griffel, Frank, 140
Grosfoguel, Ramón, 171
Guinness, Daniel, 144, 147

Haberman, David, 80, 92
Hacking, Ian, 258
Hadot, Pierre, 27
Hammer, Joshua, 64–5
Hammerschlag, Sarah, 220–1, 254
Harrington, Anne, 235
Hausner, Sondra, 18
healing, 7, 17, 68, 117, 124, 169, 197–202, 205, 211, 249
Heidegger, Martin, 11, 101, 237
Herman, Jonathan, 234
Hinduism, 102–3, 181–2, 209, 213
history, 51, 179–95, 253, 255; as category, 5, 12–13, 21; change over time, 28; and destiny, 144–9;

268 Index

historicization, 9; and Judaism, 220, 224–5; Nigerian, 161; and Pentecostalism, 168–73; of religion, 234–5; social, 107; and theory, 139
Homola, Stéphanie, 144–7
Houston, Christopher, 26
Hsu, Hsin-Ping, 145
Husserl, Edmund, 5, 11
Huxley, Aldous, 233
Hwang, Kwang-Kuo, 145

imagination, 17, 42, 51, 58–60, 83, 107, 158, 184–6, 193–5
India, 47, 103, 180, 186, 191–3, 253
Indonesia, 50
intersubjectivity. *See* subjectivity
Irele, Abiola, 218
Irving, Andrew, 258
Islam, 17–19, 43–4, 50–1, 102–3, 133–43, 148–9, 151, 167, 169, 181–2, 233, 250, 252, 254–6

Jackson, Michael, 1–3, 20–7, 81, 145, 184, 188, 217–21, 247–57; and art, 55, 58–60; and ethnography, 70, 75–6, 79; and existential anthropology, 11–20, 89–91, 130, 133–5, 151, 198, 212–14; and migrants, 158–9, 163; and phenomenological anthropology, 4–7, 9–10, 83, 155; and philosophical anthropology, 95–110; and religion, 172; on witchcraft, 226–38
James, William, 2–3, 9, 24, 26, 28, 45, 48, 52–3, 97, 99, 233, 235–6
Janzen, John, 200–1, 249
Jaspers, Karl, 45–6, 53, 198, 199, 212–15
Jay, Martin, 258
Jeffrey, Craig, 146

Jesus, 80, 116, 123, 144, 155, 161–2, 167–8, 232
Judaism, 17–18, 209, 217–26, 233, 238; antisemitism (*see* racism)
Judaken, Jonathan, 220–2
Jung, Carl, 201
juxtaposition, 219, 231–2, 237–8

Kalmanson, Leah, 23
Kant, Immanuel, 98, 218
Katz, Steven, 234
Keane, Webb, 219
Khan, Naveeda, 51
kinship, 37, 41, 51, 70, 80, 181, 220, 225
Kirkpatrick, Kate, 232
Kirmayer, Laurence, 235
Kleinman, Arthur, 235–6
Knibbe, Kim, 5–6, 9, 16, 26–7, 155, 157–8, 160, 163, 165–8, 170–1, 253
Koning, Danielle, 160, 171
Kuranko, 16, 44, 47, 95–9, 106, 219, 226–31, 237–8, 254, 256, 258

Laidlaw, James, 101, 151
Laing, R.D., 219
Lambek, Michael, 12, 19–20, 27, 100–1, 103, 145, 218, 252, 258
Lamberth, David, 24, 26
language, 100, 104, 107, 231, 234
law, 35–8, 56, 220
Lemons, Derrick, 28
Levinas, Emmanuel, 98, 225
Levi-Strauss, Claude, 95
Levitt, Peggy, 157
Levy, Benny, 220, 224, 225
Lewis, Herbert, 223
Lienhardt, Godfrey, 20–1, 27
lifeworld (*Lebenswelt*), 5, 13, 16, 19, 23–4, 90, 157–8, 235
Lingis, Alphonso, 131
Lipstadt, Deborah, 238
Livingston, Julie, 258

Loustau, Marc, 16–17
Lucht, Hans, 17
Luckmann, Thomas, 258
Luhrmann, T.M., 27

Mahmood, Saba, 23, 146
Maier, Katrin, 163
Malik, Aditya, 16, 20, 253
Malinowski, Bronisław, 60
Marcuse, Herbert, 52
Marks, Carol, 225,
Marrus, Michael, 217
Marshall, Ruth, 161
Massey, Doreen, 163
Massignon, Louis, 233
Masuzawa, Tomoko, 27
Mattingly, Cheryl, 258
Maxwell, David, 162
McCutcheon, Russell, 4
McGuire, Meredith, 8, 18–19
McMahan, David, 235
meaning, 6–9, 13, 22, 79–80, 83, 101,
    107–8, 183, 186–9, 228
memory, 43, 61, 80, 125, 185–94
Mendes-Flohr, Paul, 220
Menin, Laura, 144
Mepschen, Paul, 169
Merleau-Ponty, Maurice, 5, 11, 55–7,
    70, 83, 97
methodology, 8, 10, 18, 21, 35, 51–2,
    60, 78, 210
Meyer, Birgit, 27, 160–2
Mignolo, Walter, 171
migration, 49, 159–60, 222–4, 226,
    252; labour, 78, 80, 84, 89, 91;
    Nigerian, 156, 163–72; Sierra
    Leonean, 42–3, 99, 106
Miller, John, 234
Misrahi, Robert, 225
modernization, 157, 161, 167–73
monotheism, 17, 50, 134, 143–5,
    150, 256

Moore, Henrietta, 161
Moore, Stephen, 81
moral categories, 96–105, 138–9,
    145–7, 219, 235–6
Mosely, Walter, 64–5, 250
Motta, Marco, 231, 252
myth, 1, 35, 40, 50, 90, 191, 201–2,
    213, 234

Nabhan-Warren, Kristy, 6, 8, 76, 79,
    90, 229, 247, 250, 251
Narayana Rao, Velcheru, 191
Ndlovu-Gatsheni, Sabelo, 171
Neumann, Erich, 234
Nevola, Luca, 136, 144, 147
Nietzsche, Friedrich, 27, 56–8
Nigeria, 155–73
Nirvana (band), 89
Nolfi, George, 148

Obeyesekere, Gananath, 258
Olkes, Cheryl, 61
ordinary, the, 5, 12, 14–15, 46, 95–110,
    206, 249–52, 256–7; and everyday
    religion, 17, 27; ordinary language,
    101–7, 110, 252, 257
Orsi, Robert, 1–2, 10, 15, 18–19, 21–2,
    35, 41, 78, 108–9, 135, 145
Otto, Rudolf, 4, 233, 256

Pachirat, Timothy, 82, 84
Pandian, Anand, 2
Paper, Jordan, 233–4
particularism, 20, 26–7, 98–9, 105,
    218–20, 226–7, 232–7, 254, 256
Patel, Roshni, 20
Pattison, George, 232
Patton, Kimberley, 80, 92
Paxton, Robert, 217
perennialism, 232–6
Peterson, Jennifer, 27
Phalet, Karen, 169

270   Index

phenomenology, 4–5, 11–12, 20–2, 26, 55, 83, 96, 105–6, 208, 225, 235, 252, 255–6
Piette, Albert, 1, 11–22, 26–7, 130, 198
Polcari, Stephen, 53
positivism, 11, 56, 229
possession, 10, 17, 41, 62–3, 117, 199
postcolonialism. *See* colonialism
prayer, 43–4, 86, 103, 116–17, 123, 125, 136–7, 165, 171, 209
Premawardhana, Devaka, 45, 48, 156, 214, 239, 248, 255–7
Prince, Raymond, 199
Proudfoot, Wayne, 233
psychoanalysis, 119, 258
psychology, 24–5, 28, 45, 47, 201, 228, 236, 258

Quaas, Anna, 160
Qur'an, 103, 134, 136, 139, 148, 151
Qutb, Sayyid, 146

race, 25, 218, 220–6, 232–3, 238
racism, 41, 74, 121, 172, 222–6, 229, 236–8; anti-racism, 222–3; antisemitism, 217–39
Ram, Kalpana, 26
reality, 46–9, 96–100, 142, 155–8, 179, 217–38; experiences of, 5, 8–9, 106, 184–8; inner, 56; lived, 12, 59
reductionism, 5, 9, 12–13, 19–20, 23–4, 41, 157, 214, 225–6, 237, 254–6
Reinhartz, Judah, 220
religion, academic study of, 1–27, 41–52, 218, 228–37, 247–57; and the body, 78–80, 90; comparative, 233–4; and coping, 130–1, 198–201, 208–11; lived, 35, 108–9; transnational, 155–6
revolution, 138–42, 146, 220, 224–5
Riesman, Paul, 219

ritual, 7, 27, 53, 82, 95, 103, 136, 190, 225, 232, 235; action and practices, 8, 16–17, 37, 40–1; and belief, 47, 256; and the body, 114, 119, 128; *communitas*, 106; healing, 197–214; and religious studies, 90, 232; ritualization, 100; slaughter, 86–7
Robbins, Joel, 21
Roberts, Tyler, 5, 10, 13, 26, 231, 251–2, 257
Rodman, Selden, 53
Rorty, Richard, 26, 233

Said, Edward, 49
Sanders, Todd, 161
Sartre, Jean-Paul, 11–12, 14–15, 134, 217–40, 248, 254
scapegoat, 226–7
Schaefer, Donovan, 80–1
Schaeublin, Emanuel, 151
Schielke, Samuli, 16–19, 22, 27, 135–6, 141, 150–1, 252–3
Schilbrack, Kevin, 7
Schiller, Nina Glick, 157
Schmidt-Biggeman, Wilhelm, 233
science, 9–11, 26, 28, 40–1, 48, 52, 56–7, 70, 85, 143, 146, 158, 234; social sciences, 1, 7, 10, 14, 61, 97, 151, 194, 228
Seeman, Don, 8, 18, 23, 27, 92, 214, 248, 253–6
senses, 5–6, 56, 61–3, 67, 70, 78–9, 83, 185, 187, 250
shamans, 201–2
shapeshifting, 16, 52
Sharf, Robert, 235
shrines, 8, 45, 50, 103, 113, 181–2, 190, 195, 199
Shulman, David, 185–6, 191, 253
Silva, Sónia, 16–17, 208, 212, 214, 229, 249
Smit, Regien, 160

Smith, Daniel Jordan, 162
Smith, James K.A., 24–5
Smith, Jonathan Z., 53
Smith, Wilfred Cantwell, 20–1, 45, 52, 233
Smiths, The, 89
Soyinka, Wole, 161
Stace, W.T., 233
Stacey, Jackie, 119
Steinbock, Anthony, 234
Stern, Nehemia, 218, 224–5
Stevens, Wallace, 46, 110, 193–4
Stocking, G.W., 223
Stoller, Paul, 2, 6, 7, 55, 61, 78, 83, 231, 248, 250
Strauss, Erwin, 219
subjectivity, 12, 23, 40, 109, 186, 228–9, 235; and agency, 14–18; intersubjectivity, 6, 11, 22, 27, 186, 214, 248; intersubjectivity beyond the human, 37, 75, 79–80, 84, 88–92; liberal, 23; and reality, 48–9
Subrahmanyam, Sanjay, 191
suffering, 37, 40, 74, 89, 106, 197–214, 221, 226, 228, 235, 249

Tarusarira, Joram, 170–1
tattoos, 114, 119–25, 128, 131
Taves, Ann, 47–8, 53
Taylor, Charles, 115
Ter Haar, Gerrie, 161
theology, 9–10, 23–5, 27–8, 44–9, 96, 108, 130, 134–51, 231, 235–7, 248, 255; comparative, 10
Throop, Jason, 26–8, 218, 235
Tonkens, Evelien, 169
tragedy, 19, 50, 57, 135, 147–9, 250
transcendence, 41, 96, 99, 102–10, 233–4, 248
translation, 97, 145, 157, 209, 214, 237, 256

transnationalism, 16, 155–73, 253
Tucker, Leona, 209
Tucker, Sophie, 221–2
Turner, Victor, 198–201, 208–14, 249

Ukah, Asonzeh, 155, 160, 162, 171
Underhill, Evelyn, 233
United States, 42, 77–82, 220, 222, 224
universalism, 6, 14, 48, 99, 122, 186, 213, 217–24, 232–6

Van de Port, Mattijs, 10, 19, 62, 113–15, 127, 130, 250
Van der Leeuw, Gerardus, 234, 256
Van der Meulen, Marten, 163
Van Gennep, Arnold, 211–12
Van Houtert, Els, 5–6, 26
Vasquez, Manuel, 7
violence, 17, 80, 101, 103, 118–19, 125–6, 130–1, 149, 162, 219, 225–7
Vonnegut, Kurt, 143, 147

Waldau, Paul, 80, 92
Wardle, Huon, 12, 21
Weber, Max, 28, 210
White, Hayden, 186, 188, 258
Wiering, Jelle, 169
Wikan, Unni, 8, 235
Willen, Sarah, 21, 230, 235
Winnicott, D.W., 49
witchcraft, 161–2, 217–21, 226–30, 237–8, 252–6, 258
Wittgenstein, Ludwig, 101, 251
worlding, 156–63, 166–7, 170–1, 253
Wrathall, Mark, 11, 45, 207

Zambia, 197–213
Zigon, Jarrett, 22

Printed and bound by CPI Group (UK) Ltd, Croydon, CR0 4YY
31/08/2025

14727214-0001